TOWARD REUNION IN PHILOSOPHY

Other Books by Morton White

The Origin of Dewey's Instrumentalism
Social Thought in America: The Revolt Against Formalism
The Age of Analysis

Toward

REUNION IN

PHILOSOPHY

Morton White

Professor of Philosophy, Harvard University

HARVARD UNIVERSITY PRESS • CAMBRIDGE • 1956

Distributed in Great Britain by
GEOFFREY CUMBERLEGE, OXFORD UNIVERSITY PRESS, LONDON

Library of Congress Catalog Card Number 56-6527

PRINTED IN THE UNITED STATES OF AMERICA

To

Nelson Goodman and W. V. Quine

Preface

The collapse of absolute idealism at the turn of the twentieth century coincided with a series of fresh philosophical starts in England and America. Pragmatists and realists were the first to attack the drowsy giants of post-kantianism, preparing the way for the philosophical analysts, the logical positivists, and the linguistic therapists of the second quarter of the century. First came the Anglo-American quartet: William James, John Dewey, Bertrand Russell, and G. E. Moore, and then the Austro-German team of Ludwig Wittgenstein, Moritz Schlick, Rudolf Carnap, and Hans Reichenbach, who followed the lead of Russell and their own Ernst Mach and Gottlob Frege. Some of the dissidents, like Dewey and Charles Peirce before him, adopted the manner and gait of their idealistic opponents, alternately mauling and hugging them in a kind of philosophical wrestling match, while James, Russell, and Moore were more like Lilliputians, using the slings, the arrows, and cutting ropes of logic, short sentences, and colloquial English. Some of them, like James and Dewey, called upon psychology for aid; some of them, like Russell and Frege, came from mathematics; others were as widely separated as Mach and Moore, one a physicist and the other a passionate devotee of common sense with an extraordinary ear for ordinary language. The result was an uneasy alliance against a common enemy, strained by internal tensions and differences that would lead to sectarian squabbles and illuminating controversy.

It is now a half-century since the appearance of Russell's *Principles of Mathematics* (1903) and almost as long a time since his great collaboration with Whitehead resulted in *Principia Mathematica* (1910–1913); it is a half-century since the appearance of G. E. Moore's *Principia Ethica* and Dewey's *Studies in Logical*

Theory in 1903 and almost that since the publication of James's *Pragmatism* in 1907. A generation has passed since Wittgenstein added his positivistic *Tractatus Logico-Philosophicus* (1921) to the deflationary books of the twenties. Now Wittgenstein and Dewey are dead, while Russell and Moore are octogenarians who have lived to see the triumph of analytic philosophy in England. The course catalogues of American colleges have registered the branches of philosophy most closely associated with the spirit of analysis and pragmatism in a way that signalizes respectability. The philosophy of science, once a philosophical pariah, is now an important discipline, and symbolic logic, that natural child of mathematics and philosophy, has become the ward of a distinguished journal and the full-time concern of distinguished scholars. A good deal has happened since the days when it was worth a graduate student's academic life to be caught turning the pages of Carnap and Reichenbach unless he was scrawling nasty remarks in the margins, for Carnap now is, and Reichenbach before his death was, a leader of a new orthodoxy; they have taught and their disciples teach their doctrines in a way that reminds us that the radicals have entered the parliament and, indeed, the cabinet of philosophers. A whole generation of philosophers has grown up in an atmosphere clouded by the smog of pragmatic controversy and dazed by the glare of positivistic manifestoes. The problems of analytic philosophy, logical positivism, pragmatism, and linguistic analysis have become staples of philosophic training and the substance of philosophic teaching at many centers in England and America. Indeed, the wheel has come full circle when, as is true at the writing of this sentence, Oxford, that ancient haven of idealism and piety, is a philosophical boom town where linguistic analysis is all the rage.

In this book I hope to deal with some of the fundamental questions that emerge out of the intermingling of these tendencies in the first half of the twentieth century. I shall examine three fundamental concepts: existence, a priori knowledge, and value, concepts which have been recurrent concerns of western philosophy and which also serve to reveal important similarities and differences between the movements from which I take my departure. Considering these concepts as a trinity is justified by the fact that they underlie the disciplines of metaphysics, logic, and ethics re-

spectively, and also because simultaneous and connected treatment
of all three will contribute to a better understanding of each. Moreover, each concept may be identified as a primary concern of the
movements examined—existence with the metaphysically oriented
analytic platonism of the early Russell and Moore, the a priori
with the epistemology of logical positivism, and value with the
pragmatism of Peirce, James, and Dewey.

Despite the fact that the analytic, the positivistic, and the pragmatic movements arose out of a decisive rejection of absolute
idealism, they began with very different positive views on the
fundamental questions of philosophy. And therefore while a great
and genial figure like William James gave comfort to both the
realists and pragmatists among his admirers, this hardly established
a happy coalition between, say, Bertrand Russell and John Dewey.
Nor did Charles Peirce's interest in logic tempered with darwinism
and transcendentalism serve to heal the breach between the logically oriented metaphysics of the English realists and the more
practical and psychological views of American instrumentalists.
But today these originally diverging streams of post-idealistic philosophy show signs of converging through the efforts of those who
are seriously occupied with the living problems of philosophy, and
in spite of the scholastics in all camps who are bound by formula
and prejudice. I have in mind the increased use of pragmatic language by some of our positivistically trained logicians, as well as
the increased use of the words 'role', 'function', and 'job' that
emanates from England under the influence of the later Wittgenstein and others; I have in mind the abandonment of platonism
and cartesianism on all sides. And while I do not wish to underestimate the differences between these converging tendencies, it
would be unwise to disregard the points of community and to be
misled by silly talk about American preoccupation with mathematical logic, calculating machines, and the hydrogen bomb, or
by equally silly talk about Oxford's concern with genteel usage.
I do not fix on these signs of *rapprochement* out of any ambassa-
dorial interest in cozy philosophical collaboration—for good as
that might be, it would be worthless without mutual understanding—but in the hope that convergence is indicative of and conducive to philosophical progress.

In planning this work I came to feel that the reader—even the professional philosopher—would best understand its concerns and its point of view if he were provided with some insight into the different movements and ideas that form its background. And so my first thought was to provide an elaborate historical introduction, replete with inverted commas and cross references. But I swiftly realized that such a project was hardly feasible within the space at my disposal, and that it might very well smother my inclination to express my own views. And so a compromise resulted. Instead of offering many full-fledged historical chapters cluttered with *ipsissima verba,* no matter how profound and interesting, I have occasionally offered a somewhat streamlined account of certain phases of twentieth-century philosophy in an attempt to depict their distinctive qualities. Perhaps the phrase of Max Weber—'ideal type'—is appropriate here, in which case some of my accounts of these different tendencies in twentieth-century philosophy are ideal types of intellectual movements. However, because of an incurable concern for real historical fact, I have often resorted to notes and quotes as a way of showing the connection between my constructions and the words of the actual philosophers upon which the constructions are based. Although the views which I expound and criticize are not always totally contained in the writings of an actual philosopher, they come sufficiently close on many occasions to name names. Unless explicitly indicated, any similarity between the ideal type and the real thinker should be regarded as purely coincidental! It is hoped that the expository parts of this work will have intrinsic interest for students of the development of ideas in the twentieth century, in addition to providing the background and ambience of this study. But the *main* purpose of the book is philosophical rather than historical. In it I hope not only to expound and interpret but to indicate some of the virtues and shortcomings of the views epitomized, and to deal with the topics of existence, the a priori, and value, in a positive and illuminating manner.

In the course of the argument it will be necessary to show that some of the most influential concepts and distinctions of twentieth-century philosophy have outlived their usefulness through excessive rigidity: that what was once liberating and exciting, and for that reason to be admired, has become constraining. I have in mind the traditional trichotomy of fact, necessity, and value as perpetuated in the more recent classification of statements as synthetic, analytic, and ethical; the different senses of 'existence' to which so many recent philosophers have appealed; the universals of neoplatonists; the meanings, both cognitive and emotive, of neopositivists; the simple, nonnatural qualities of certain ethical theorists. In their place I offer a philosophy that does justice to differences without exaggerating them, and that sees reflective thinking as a process in which we cannot distinguish radically between different methods of discovering what is, what must be, and what should be. In coming to this view I have been forced to criticize the views of philosophers from whom I have learned an enormous amount, but if we begin—as we all do—by sitting on the shoulders of giants, we cannot help pinching them a bit when we start to stand.

It is difficult to set down the names of all those who have helped me with this book, but some deserve very special mention. First I wish to thank Nelson Goodman and W. V. Quine, who have provided me with more philosophical stimulation and instruction than I could possibly absorb, and whose interest in systematic philosophy has served to revive my own when it would have been far easier to devote myself to less taxing, warmer, and more popular subjects. My dedication cannot express, nor can my references and footnotes fully record, their exciting effect on my philosophical thinking. They have both read my manuscript and have saved me from error and awkwardness of expression. Next I wish to thank my former students, Stanley L. Cavell and Burton S. Dreben, who were at different times assistants in the course of lectures out of which this book grew, and who have read the manuscript with exceedingly generous care and mature insight. In many places I have revised my text to meet their helpful criticism. I am very grateful to my former student, Marshall Cohen, for helping me with the index and the proofs. I owe a special word of thanks to J. L. Austin of Oxford who was kind enough to read a number of chapters in the spring of 1955 while he was at Harvard. I have derived invaluable help from his views on the notion of a performatory utterance as treated in his published writing and regret that this manuscript was completed before I was familiar with his more extended development of the subject in his William James Lectures. Finally, I want to acknowledge my perpetual debt to my wife, Lucia Perry White, who has given me indispensable help on matters of style and who has encouraged me enormously, as she has with every book I have written.

I also want to express my deep appreciation to a number of teachers, colleagues, friends, and students who have not had any direct connection with the manuscript but who have contributed to my philosophical education. My friend and colleague Henry David Aiken has done more than anyone to make me see the general significance of ethical problems. My teacher and friend Ernest Nagel introduced me to many of the problems that concern me in this book, taught me the value of careful criticism in philosophy, and made me aware of the harmonies and the dissonances within the analytic, positivistic, and pragmatic movements. I have been helped by logical discussions on existence and necessity with Alfred Tarski a long time ago and more recently with Hao Wang. My former student, Thompson M. Clarke, has taught me much about the problem of a priori knowledge.

I wish to acknowledge gratefully a fellowship from the John Simon Guggenheim Memorial Foundation which allowed me to begin active work on this book in 1950–51, and I wish to thank the Clark Fund of Harvard University for grants which helped defray the costs of secretarial assistance. I am grateful to Harvard University for leaves of absence during the academic years 1950–51 and 1953–54. And finally I should like to thank the Institute for Advanced Study in Princeton, New Jersey, and its brilliant and humane director, Robert Oppenheimer, for having provided me with a year of peace and quiet in 1953–54 when the main draft of this book was completed. It was one of the most profitable and pleasant years of my scholarly life, and had I stayed at the Institute just a little longer, I might even have been converted to platonism by Harold Cherniss—a radical conversion indeed, as the reader of the following pages will swiftly discover.

MORTON WHITE
Cambridge, Massachusetts
December 24, 1954

Contents

PART IV

WHAT IS, WHAT MUST BE, WHAT SHOULD BE

PART I

WHAT IS

CHAPTER I

From Existence to Decision

1. *The argument*

'Are there any such things?' 'How do you know?' and 'Why should I do that?' are three of the most important questions that a man can ask when he is confronted with the statements or proposals of others. They have been the fundamental questions of philosophy, and they form the basis of this study. According to tradition they distinguish three philosophical disciplines, since metaphysics usually deals with existence, epistemology with knowledge, and ethics with the justification of conscious action and decision. And yet I believe that these questions are so intimately connected with each other that we can achieve more insight by treating them together than by approaching them separately. The demonstration of this claim is, I hope, the book itself, but its stimulus may be more clearly seen by looking at certain philosophical tendencies in the histories of these subjects. In doing so we will also discover the basic terminology and concepts used in some of the most important discussions of existence, knowledge, and ethics in the twentieth century. In this introductory chapter I do little more than describe or indicate philosophical usage governing these basic terms. I do not explain these terms as clearly as one might expect, simply because they are not always, in my opinion, susceptible of the kind of clarification that justifies using them with confidence. In fact, a great part of this book will be devoted to showing this in detail.

In each of the main parts of the book I shall deal critically with the views of three types of philosophers: first with the views of those who adopt what I shall call analytic platonism, as illustrated in the writings of the young Bertrand Russell and the young G. E. Moore, then with the views of what I shall call orthodox logical positivism,

and finally with certain pragmatic doctrines that have been offered
in an attempt to solve the same problems. But while criticizing
them I shall also offer certain positive suggestions that seem to me
more satisfactory, and these suggestions will then be collected and
developed in the last part of the book where I offer a philosophical
outlook that goes beyond analytic platonism, logical positivism,
and pragmatism.

2. *The age of meanings*

The problems of existence are among the oldest and most
actively debated in philosophy. Generally speaking they may be
divided into two different kinds. The first kind of problem is relatively specific and substantive. In this vein the traditional metaphysician asks, 'Do universals, or properties which are common to
different things, exist?' 'Do minds exist?' and even 'Do bodies
exist?' But because of certain difficulties that arise in connection
with these questions, another kind of question must then be asked.
Relatively early in the history of the subject it was seen that some
philosophical statements of existence do not meet with general or
immediate acceptance. The statement that universals exist is the
most striking example. And because of the difficulty in gaining
outright assent to this assertion, some philosophers took to saying
that the word 'exists' is ambiguous, that the sense in which universals exist is different from the sense in which physical objects
exist. The chief consideration in all of this was the fact that universals as conceived by some followers of Plato and by some scholastics do not exist in space and time, whereas physical objects do.
Universals or properties cannot be seen, touched, heard, tasted, or
smelled; nevertheless they were thought to be "objective", and a
special sense of the word 'exists' was provided for them that would
be wholly suitable to their transcendental nature.

In this way metaphysicians came to discuss not only what exists,
but also the allegedly different meanings of the word 'exists', the
second kind of problem already mentioned. By turning to this
second kind of question they took a path that brought them into
close contact with theorists of knowledge. Having said that the
word 'exists' is ambiguous, a word that shifts its meaning from
sentence to sentence, depending on the kind or category of thing

whose existence is asserted, metaphysicians were then called upon to distinguish between the mental activity by which we come to know about physical objects—sensation—and that by which we come in contact with universals—understanding. In this way the metaphysical problem of existence merged with one of the central problems of modern epistemology in the seventeenth century, the relation between sensation and understanding. But sometimes the order was reversed. Sometimes the epistemologist came to the metaphysician for help rather than the other way around. The traditional epistemologist had often asked what we do when we understand a word, and had come to the conclusion that we grasp a meaning that is neither a physical object nor a word. For the epistemologist, therefore, the existence of meanings illuminated a datum or fact of epistemology, whereas for the metaphysician in search of an extrasensory method of establishing contact with universals the epistemologist's concept of understanding was a godsend. The trip that began in epistemology and concluded in metaphysics was the more common one in twentieth-century philosophy, but the street obviously allowed two-way traffic. The epistemologist began with an act for which he needed an object; the metaphysician began with an object for which he needed a corresponding act; they met, and a deal was made.

The situation may be made more concrete by comparing the way in which attributes were introduced into philosophical discussion with the way in which meanings were introduced, and then seeing how they met. At one point the argument for attributes reached a statement like 'This typewriter has something in common with that typewriter'. Clearly, the argument continued, that which they have in common is distinct from both typewriters—it is not a typewriter at all—and it is in fact nothing other than the attribute of being a typewriter, *typewriterhood, typewriterishness,* or whatever it is that you want to call it. It is not a physical object and therefore, according to some philosophers, it must be said to exist in a sense different from that in which a typewriter is said to exist. But neither is it a construct of the mind according to platonists or realists, and therefore they had to describe the epistemological relation between human beings and the universal, *typewriterhood.* One answer was that we grasp it in some way vaguely analogous to physical grasping; therefore from this point of view, I suppose, we should speak of the mind's hand as well as the mind's eye.

Coming the other way were epistemologists who began by saying that they understood the general term 'typewriter' and who then asked what is involved in understanding a general term. Their conclusion was that there must be something nonlinguistic which we grasp and which they called the meaning, intension, or connotation of the word. Therefore, they said, there must be meanings of general terms else there could be no such thing as understanding.

The possibility of exchange is now obvious. The attribute is just the sort of thing that can be a meaning, and the meaning of a general term may be an attribute. The understanding grasped the attribute and thereby a contract was made between the platonic metaphysician and the rationalistic epistemologist.

The relationship was made even more secure when the platonic rationalist came to consider a priori knowledge. A priori knowledge was defined as knowledge which we gain without recourse to experience. According to philosophical tradition it is illustrated chiefly in mathematics and logic. And if only one could show that universals—meanings now—are the sole subject matter of mathematics and logic, the agreement between platonic metaphysics and rationalistic epistemology might be extended even further. The understanding might then be regarded not only as the faculty (the mind's hand) whereby we grasp the meanings of the terms which make up mathematical statements, but also as the faculty (the mind's eye) whereby we see the connections between these meanings. There might be debate over whether all of the connections are like those involved in 'Every black cat is a cat', where the meaning expressed by the subject term is said to contain the meaning of the predicate term, and hence where the statement is said to be "analytic". But this did not destroy essential agreement among platonists on the fact that meanings or universals alone constitute the subject matter (in a sense we shall examine later) of so-called a priori statements. Even some who followed Kant, in asserting that some a priori statements like '$7 + 5 = 12$' are not analytic but rather synthetic, continued to be platonists in regarding the subject matter of a priori statements as timeless universals; they differed only about the connections or relations between those universals. By providing a priori knowledge with a special subject matter, all disputants believed that they had gone a long way in showing how a priori knowledge was possible.

So far, then, we have at least two senses of 'exist'—one for physical objects and one for universals; we have two corresponding senses of 'grasp'—one for physical objects and the other for meanings; we have two senses of 'see'—the ordinary seeing of physical objects that we do with our own eyes and the extraordinary seeing that we do with our mind's eye. In short, the primary distinction of senses for the word 'exists' provided as effective a sealing off of physical objects from universals as could be desired. In a special sense of 'there are' (as in Plato's heaven) there are mirror images of physical things and sensory activities (or perhaps it should be put the other way, in view of Plato's tendency to think of the physical object as image and the universal as original). The result was a distinction between "categories" of entities which are not regarded as entities in the same sense. 'Physical object' and 'universal' came to be distinguished as categorial terms and it was said that there is no all-embracing sense of 'exists'.

This somewhat stylized outline is, of course, a fairly old one in the history of western philosophy. Part of it was well formed by the seventeenth century and anticipations of it may be found in antiquity, but it received its most striking clarification and filling in at the beginning of the twentieth century by the young Bertrand Russell while he was in his so-called platonic or realistic phase. For this reason his version of the doctrine will receive careful and critical treatment in each main part of this book: the part on existence, the part on a priori knowledge, and the part on value. I have already outlined something of the viewpoint as far as metaphysics and epistemology are concerned, and now I will add something on the ethical views of Moore, for they round out the picture of what has been called analytic platonism.

Moore distinguished between those universals which were expressed by the general terms of natural science and those expressed in ethics. He came to the conclusion that 'good' is a nonnatural predicate, a predicate which is used in the process of evaluation and therefore radically different from those used in the process of description. In the case of both description and evaluation we ascribe properties or attributes, according to Moore, but when we evaluate something we ascribe a "nonnatural" property or attribute to it which cannot be identified with any property expressed by natural science. In this way Moore completed one aspect of the metaphysics of pre-positivistic, analytic platonism, which begins with the epistemological or linguistic facts of understanding, description, and evaluation and then seeks to explain them or illuminate them by reference to universals as meanings, universals as natural qualities, and universals as nonnatural qualities. In answering the question 'What exists?' therefore, the early analysts were exceedingly liberal. They thought that physical objects exist, that universals exist, that there are nonnatural attributes as well as natural ones, simple attributes as well as complex ones, intrinsic properties as well as nonintrinsic. These distinctions, as we shall see later, were related to the early analysts' distinction between scientific and ethical predicates, and also connected with the tendency of Moore and Russell to say that while some attributes could be subjected to analysis, others were unanalyzable. Philosophical analysis was conceived as the analysis of the universals or meanings we grasp in the process of understanding. For this reason the period in which this view dominated analytic philosophy may be called the age of meanings or the age of existence, the first when we wish to stress the fact that objective, platonic meanings formed the subject matter of analysis for the early Moore and the early Russell, and the second when we wish to emphasize that their existence was asserted in what was later regarded by positivists as excessively metaphysical and even meaningless language.

It should be said at once that my own views on the problems of existence, the a priori, and ethics are very much opposed to those of this tradition. I should like to explain and illuminate the problem of existence without resorting to what I call 'multivocalism'—the view that 'exists' must have many different senses in philosophical discourse—without postulating platonic meanings or universals in clarifying the notions of understanding and a priori knowledge, without appealing to nonnatural qualities in ethics, without regarding undefined predicates as those which express or connote metaphysically simple properties. To this extent my views coincide with those of many so-called logical positivists, but, as the reader will see, our common rejection of the platonism of the early Moore and Russell leaves room for a great deal of disagreement between positivists and myself on how to deal with the problems of existence, the a priori, and ethical judgment. Logical positivism is in many respects an advance on analytic platonism, but it leaves much to be desired for any philosopher who wishes to clarify or illuminate the questions 'What exists?' 'How do I know?' and 'Why should I do that?' as these are understood by the ordinary man or the scientist who turns to philosophy.

3. *The age of words*

The historical relationship between logical positivism and the philosophies of the early Moore and Russell is partially explained by the fact that Moore and Russell did not break as thoroughly with the philosophical tradition as positivists would have liked. Moore and Russell were in revolt against the absolute idealism of Hegel and his British followers, F. H. Bradley and J. E. McTaggart, but the positive doctrines put forth by the two young rebels were often the result of their attachment to pre-hegelian philosophy, notably to Plato and Kant. The young Moore and the young Russell were interested in the problem of universals, in the nature of ethical judgments, in the problem of a priori knowledge, in the problem of induction, and in the problem of the external world— to mention only a few of their traditional concerns. And the answers they gave (although often inconsistent with each other because Moore and Russell were very different philosophers from the beginning) form a philosophical jetty which was severely pounded by the first waves of logical positivism. The views on these questions which most aroused the opposition of positivists were those which Moore or Russell had derived from Plato or Kant.

I have in mind first of all what I have called the platonic theory of universals defended by the early Moore and Russell. (The small 'p' is used in order to avoid debate as to whether Plato with a capital 'P' really believed this doctrine in the same form, but it is important to recall that Russell in his *Problems of Philosophy* supposed that he was advancing a view like Plato's on universals.) I also have in mind Moore's belief in nonnatural ethical qualities.

And turning from metaphysics, where the influence of Plato pre-dominated, to the theory of knowledge, we find that Kant continued to exercise great influence on Russell's theory of a priori knowledge and the external world. For example, Russell held in his *Problems* that Kant was right in supposing that there are synthetic a priori judgments: Russell held that arithmetical statements, certain ethical judgments, and the so-called principle of induction were all synthetic a priori. Quite early in the century Moore maintained that there is a kind of necessity which is neither causal, nor logical, and he has even said fairly recently that there are synthetic a priori propositions. Moreover, both Moore and Russell thought that the existence of the external world might be debated meaningfully, although their positions on this matter differed. In general, the historical point to be made is this: if one approaches the early texts of Moore and Russell with eyes trained in the thirties and the forties, one sees that some of the characteristic doctrines of logical positivism are aimed less directly at the misty metaphysics of obscure hegelians and more directly at the views of two clear-headed Englishmen who are normally regarded as elder statesmen and intellectual progenitors of positivism.

The most conspicuous and radical contribution of logical positivism in these fields was its prodigious concentration on language. In the earlier, pre-positivistic period, dating roughly from the turn of the century to the First World War, the campaign against subjectivism and idealism led Moore and Russell to their view of philosophical analysis as a process of decomposing extra-linguistic platonic meanings, which was explicitly distinguished from anything like psychology or lexicography. Under the influence of logical positivism, however, philosophers working in the analytic manner became more and more absorbed with language and more and more hostile to platonic ideas and cartesian minds, treating some traditional problems as the products of linguistic confusion and drastically revising the formulation of others so that they became more obviously linguistic in character. This may well be called the age of words.

It was Ludwig Wittgenstein who most effectively emphasized the linguistic aspect of philosophical problems in the twenties. Originally a student of Moore and Russell at Cambridge, he came to have an influence which was powerful enough to make it necessary to distinguish a pre-Wittgensteinian and a post-Wittgensteinian phase of the whole analytic movement. His influence shifted its direction so much that the writings of the earlier Russell and Moore seem traditionally metaphysical by comparison with his, in spite of their own philosophically rebellious youth, in spite of the enormous contrast between *their* views and those of the idealists against whom they argued at the turn of the century. For this reason one might almost think of Wittgenstein as the Marx of a movement which counted Russell and Moore as its St. Simon and Fourier. The views of the early Russell and Moore had made advances but were treated as reactionary by those who insisted with Wittgenstein that the problem of universals, the problem of the external world, and the problem of induction were meaningless. Their views could hardly be accepted by a school of thought that passionately rejected nonnatural qualities; and their belief in the synthetic a priori was enough to banish them to a sort of logical Siberia where they might pore over Plato and Kant (but not Hegel!).

Wittgenstein's *Tractatus Logico-Philosophicus,* in which so many of the early positivisitic slogans were set down, was neither a catechistic handbook nor a conventional treatise, and many of its more literal-minded admirers were made somewhat uneasy by its metaphorical obscurity and its intellectual waywardness. The upshot was a kind of organized housecleaning movement dominated by the shrewd suspicion that clarity should begin at home. The partisans of a positivism without oracles and aphorisms banded themselves into circles and congresses and set themselves the task of advancing a cause with all the literal earnestness of a Newer Model Army. Their central theme, in keeping with many views of the earlier Wittgenstein, was that philosophy isn't just another discipline on a par with the sciences, but that it is rather concerned with the logical analysis of scientific language and method. For the positivists, philosophy became a second-order discipline, and philosophical talk became primarily logical talk *about* the talk of others.[1]

[1] Most of this paragraph comes from a review of R. von Mises' *Positivism* which I contributed to the *Kenyon Review,* vol. 14, no. 1 (winter 1952). I wish to thank the editors for permission to reprint. In the following two paragraphs I have reprinted some sentences from my BBC talk "English Philosophy Today," *Listener,* Oct. 11, 1951.

This preoccupation with the speech and writing of others was at one stage mainly a matter of formulating a so-called criterion of meaning. Since so much was to be prohibited as meaningless by positivistic standards, a criterion had to be devised which would allow a decisive application of the anti-metaphysical statute. And since what was of major interest was something called scientific meaning, it had to be made perfectly clear that much of traditional ethics and metaphysics might evoke images, stimulate action, or evince attitudes and yet be scientifically meaningless. Speculation of the kind illustrated by analytic platonism was the first to feel the strong arm of the criterion of meaning. 'Universals exist' and 'Nonnatural qualities exist' were rejected as nonsensical by empiricist standards and debates over their truth dismissed as futile. But in order to placate those who insisted on calling language meaningful even when it did not satisfy what looked like the clear-cut requirements of the positivistic theory of meaning, a new category was invented, that of emotive meaning, and into it a good deal of poetry, traditional metaphysics, theology, esthetics, and ethics was conveniently shoved and grudgingly dignified as *important* nonsense.

Within the class of scientifically meaningful statements (upon *them* most attention was lavished, for they were preëminently susceptible to logical analysis in the strict sense), another distinction was made between statements of mathematics and logic on the one hand and those of empirical science on the other. Statements of the first kind were said to be true by virtue of the meanings of their terms, and not on the basis of experiment or observation of the world; while statements of the second kind were, ultimately, confirmable by nothing else. This revived distinction between analytic and synthetic statements and the new one between emotive and scientific meaning became the two great principles of positivistic philosophy. 'Is it cognitive or emotive?' was the first question to ask about any grammatically correct sentence, and if it were not purely emotive, one asked, 'Is it analytic or synthetic?'

The dichotomy between cognitive and emotive helped positivists preserve the older distinction between descriptive and normative, although on a very different basis, while the distinction between analytic and synthetic allowed the rationalist and empiricist to lie down as lion and lamb. In this way positivism excluded that unruly kantian hybrid—the synthetic a priori proposition, which was allegedly neither analytic nor empirical. With this revival of the humean compromise, the famous post-kantian debate over the status of arithmetical statements was cut short, for, it was argued, one could no longer say that they were synthetic a priori. Indeed, the success of Russell and Whitehead in *Principia Mathematica* was said to cap the climax of a century-old crusade against Kant's conviction that statements like '$7 + 5 = 12$' were synthetic a priori. Moreover, it was held that the appearance of non-euclidean geometry showed the folly of supposing that Euclid's geometry was inescapable, for what did the construction of the geometries of Bolyai, Riemann, and Lobachevsky show, if not the lack of necessity in Euclid's? A squad of logicians and mathematicians who followed in the footsteps of Frege had driven the last golden spike into the deductive railroad that led from logic to mathematics. From now on, one could only draw the line between logic and mathematics at an arbitrary station or in some dark tunnel in *Principia Mathematica* where it might never be seen; there was to be no great divide between 'Everything is identical with itself' and '$7 + 5 = 12$', since the latter had been deduced from truisms like the former with the assistance of definitions alone. The really great divide, it was held, was between logic-*cum*-mathematics on the one side and empirical science on the other. Mathematics had finally been joined to logic; the kantian no man's land of arithmetic and geometry had been emptied of the last displaced statement. From now on a true statement had to choose between the two sides of the iron curtain: the logico-mathematical analytic a priori or the empirical synthetic a posteriori.

"Ancient Greek philosophy," Kant reminds us, "was divided into three sciences: physics, ethics, and logic," and the logical positivist had neatly ticketed all three. For the positivist physics was cognitively meaning*ful* and a body of synthetic a posteriori propositions; ethics was a body of cognitively meaning*less* statements which had failed to satisfy the verifiability theory of meaning but which could be handled in the emotive meaning section; logic and its sister mathematics were safely analytic. That was the clear-cut picture which had been developed from the dark, mysterious negative of early wittgensteinianism, a picture which still hangs in the studies of many philosophers in England and America.

Having been trained in that phase of the history of analytic philosophy which was dominated by several varieties and offshoots of what I have called orthodox logical positivism, I shall often be concerned with the doctrines of that philosophy. And so in my consideration of the problem of existence, to which I turn first, I shall question the positivistic claim that ontology consists of meaningless statements; in my discussion of a priori knowledge I shall criticize certain versions of the positivistic contention that that problem is solved by attention to the distinction between the analytic and the synthetic; in my treatment of the notion of value I shall express grave reservations about the view that the distinction between emotive and cognitive meaning handles that. Nevertheless, at several places in the book this awareness of positivistic doctrine will receive somewhat muted expression, notably when I treat the problem of the existence of meanings and physical objects as viewed by Moore, Russell, and Frege. I shall try to communicate and criticize their views on these questions with a minimum of attention to the disconcerting charge that this whole debate is meaningless, for the charge itself is best evaluated after the criterion of meaning that impels it has been examined.

4. *The two Russells*

The fact that Russell has led a long and varied philosophical life is responsible for a certain amount of confusion about the relation between his views on existence and those of logical positivists. There is no doubt that positivists reacted sharply against the views set forth in Russell's platonic period, when he not only postulated universals but in the manner of Kant conceived of physical objects as the transcendent causes of our sensations. But there is also another Russell, a Russell who has since inveighed against platonic *ideas,* kantian *things-in-themselves,* aristotelian *substances,* and meinongian *objects,* and it was this second Russell who became a positivistic hero. This was the Russell who was moved to invent the theory of descriptions for which he is justly famous both in the history of logic and the history of philosophy.[2] It is

---

[2] For a lucid exposition of this theory, see Russell, *Introduction to Mathematical Philosophy* (New York: Macmillan, 1919), ch. 16.

important to observe the contrast between the deflationary attitude that dominates Russell's theory of descriptions and the inflationary attitude that is illustrated by Russell's early platonism. While the platonist allegedly discovers a universal, a neglected entity that is involved in understanding, the theorist of descriptions seeks precisely the opposite effect. One adds to our universe and the other subtracts. It is Russell the subtracting theorist of descriptions who dominated the early phases of positivism. It was Frank Ramsey, Wittgenstein's friend and admirer, who called Russell's theory of descriptions a "paradigm of philosophy".

The puzzle which stimulated the theory of descriptions has often been presented by Russell and other mathematical logicians as evidence of the fact that ordinary language enshrines "the metaphysics of the stone age", and so they hold that the theory is a blessing of modern logic which corrects an inference created by myopic attention to the grammar of ordinary language. Many mathematical logicians whose philosophies are influenced by Russell are professionally committed to the belief that ordinary language is a source of confusion and paradox, and frequently maintain that less logical philosophers are deceived by the grammar of ordinary language into outrageously fallacious arguments. For after observing that there is no such thing as Pegasus, some bemused philosophers have asked themselves what the word 'Pegasus' denotes, because they hold the view, dictated by grammatical theory, that every true statement must be about something. But since Pegasus does not exist, it is difficult to say that the statement is about Pegasus. Yet grammar must be appeased, and so something immaterial like *the idea of Pegasus* or *the possibility of Pegasus* or whatnot is conjured up in a frantic effort to produce a denotation for the word. In this way a mysterious entity is invented because of the weaknesses inherent in the grammar of ordinary language.

Just such invention has stimulated a good deal of counter-invention on the part of logicians; in Russell's case it called forth a theory of proper names and the theory of descriptions. In the hands of some logicians it leads to the proposal that we translate a puzzle-producing statement like 'There is no such thing as Pegasus' with the help of mathematical logic, and it is held that once we get it into philosophically disinfected language, we shall no longer be tempted to invent anything as weird as the denotation

of 'Pegasus'. 'Pegasus' is defined as short for 'the winged horse captured by Bellerophon', and 'There is no such thing as Pegasus' is
then translated by Russell's theory as 'It isn't true that Bellerophon
captured one and only one winged horse'. In its new, logically
official formulation the statement does not contain the word 'Pegasus', and so the need for appeasing the grammarian in philosophically absurd ways is removed. The moral of this example is held
to be obvious. We must reformulate the infected parts of our
language (and they are many, it is said); we must build a system
which will be free of these puzzle-producing and entity-breeding
features. In some of his writings Russell has called the principle
underlying this attitude the supreme principle of philosophy, Oc-
cam's Razor, whose purpose is the elimination of all the queer
entities born of the grammatical features of ordinary language
and uncritical science. In this way philosophy does more than
record the linguistic behavior of ordinary men, since it also makes
a suggestion as to how we *should* construe sentences of ordinary
English in a way that will not tempt us into philosophical error.
Pegasus does not exist, and any manner of speaking that leads us
to suppose that he exists or drives us into sophistically invoking
his *unactualized possibility* or *idea* as the denotation of the word
'Pegasus' is one that should be avoided.

In the period when the concept of analyticity and the empiricist criterion of meaning were dominant—the age of words—ontological talk necessarily became suspect in spite of the positivistic
admiration of the theory of descriptions. For it is very difficult to
think of statements like 'There are no unactualized possibles' as
analytic, and the empiricist criterion of meaning is aimed at reducing them to nonsense in an unmistakable way. 'What would
it be like if there *were* unactualized possibles?' 'How do you verify
the statement that there are universals (or its contradictory)?' These
are the most typical rhetorical questions asked by the positivist,
and they have had the effect of silencing many an ontologist. In
spite of this, however, Russell's attack on Meinong was quite acceptable to positivists, and the fact that Russell provided a device
which dispensed with the need for postulating Meinong's queer
entities was happily embraced by positivists. In the same way they
regarded phenomenalistic epistemologies as excellent ways of dis-
pensing with the postulation of both Aristotle's *substances* and

Kant's *things-in-themselves*. But if called upon to say that the unactualized possibles or things-in-themselves which they were saved from postulating by the theory of descriptions or phenomenalism did or did not exist, positivists might lapse into gesture or silence. The criterion of meaning prevented them from answering a question which, if answered, would give a forthright picture of their philosophical motivation. With this in mind, I turn first to the consideration of these ontological questions in a pre-positivistic period, for at that time no positivisitic "criterion of meaning" prevented Moore or Russell from asking and answering the metaphysical questions 'Do universals exist?' 'Do unactualized possibles exist?' 'Are there physical objects?'

In Russell's case, the attempt to show that we can construe a statement like 'Pegasus does not exist' without supposing that it entails the existence of a queer entity is dictated by a metaphysical conviction which Russell thought was subject to rational scrutiny. The point is that before positivism entered its challenge, philosophers were not accustomed to making fundamental distinctions between saying that matter does or does not exist and saying that gorgons do or do not exist, but after the emergence of logical positivism the situation changed in a very radical way. Positivists held that much as we might like to, we cannot come straight out and say (meaningfully) that there are no universals, or there are no substances, or there are no unactualized possibles, or there are no gods, or there are no ghosts in the machine, as blandly as we say that there are no unicorns. Neither can we meaningfully assert their contradictories. Nevertheless, the occamistic tendencies of positivists forced them to propose elaborate logical constructions as ways of avoiding the implication that such things did exist. The task of positivism, therefore, was to convey more antiseptically what others had been saying in poisonous, misleading, and metaphysical language. On the subject of existence the aim of positivism is that of urging us to empty the snakepit without entering it ourselves, and therefore from a positivistic point of view much of their writings lead Russell and Moore into the pit.

5. *The age of decision*

The logical positivist's early desire to avoid the postulation of queer entities, when combined with his acceptance of a rigid criterion of meaning, leads to a pragmatic emphasis in a more recent phase of the movement and in some cases to a *justification* of dubious existential statements. The positivist who is moved to speak in a way that does *not* presuppose the existence of what I should call queer entities is forced to state his thesis in a very guarded way, as the later writings of Carnap indicate.[3] The positivist must not give the impression that he can "find out" in advance whether there are attributes, for example, and then decide to build a system which does or does not presuppose their existence. That is precisely what the criterion of meaning precludes, for that smacks too much of the traditional metaphysical speculation that positivists want to avoid. Instead, Carnap says, the positivist must build a "conceptual framework" in which attributes, let us say, are talked about (later on this will be made more precise by reference to certain notions of Quine), and then he must test its scientific usefulness. This he can then compare with a system that dispenses with attributes.

Without entering the details of Carnap's argument in this preliminary discussion, it is sufficient to say here that he tries to convert a number of questions that would have been asked by the early, analytic platonists as straightforward questions of fact into more complicated questions about the advisability, usefulness, and expediency of certain frameworks constructed with the tools of modern logic. Whereas the earlier analysts did not distinguish radically between scientific questions like 'Are there electrons?' and 'Are there bacteria?' on the one hand, and metaphysical questions like 'Are there universals?' and 'Are there numbers?' on the other, it is absolutely imperative for an anti-metaphysical positivist to make this distinction. The more limited, scientific question of existence concerning electrons or bacteria is treated as an "internal question", a factual question, one that is raised *within* a framework whose "categories" like events, numbers, attributes, or physical objects have already been chosen; but the closest thing to the traditional metaphysical question is a so-called "external question" which is to be answered by reckoning the expediency or use-

[3] See especially Carnap, "Empiricism, Semantics, and Ontology," *Revue internationale de Philosophie*, vol. 4, no. 11 (1950), pp. 20–40; reprinted in L. Linsky, ed., *Semantics and the Philosophy of Language* (Urbana: University of Illinois Press, 1952).

fulness of a framework that adopts numbers, physical objects, and universals as its categories. I say 'the closest thing' advisedly, for Carnap insists that these new pragmatic questions, however similar to the older metaphysical questions, are very different from them, if only because the older questions are scientifically or cognitively meaningless while these are not. Through having been transformed into "pragmatic" questions the older metaphysical questions are given a new respectability, but they continue to be sharply distinguished from the factual "internal questions" that are raised by scientists after the framework has been settled on in a more or less philosophical way.

This shift to pragmatism suggests what I mean when I call the most recent phase of analytic philosophy the age of decision. That age is characterized by an avoidance of the kind of blunt, straightforward nonlinguistic questions of Moore, who asked whether and how certain concepts, attributes, or propositions could be analyzed or logically decomposed, who asked whether there are physical objects, and who tried *to prove* that there are. In place of these questions, the philosopher in the age of decision does not always formulate a question about how we actually *do* use language. He does not simply ask whether words *are* used in a certain way (though there are many contemporary philosophers who would limit him to this). To this extent he does more than engage in descriptive linguistics. He goes on to ask whether they *ought* to be used in a certain way, and it is here that the distinctive thesis of this book becomes directly relevant. It is here that we find a confluence of two currents in twentieth-century philosophy: one that runs from the early analytic platonism of Russell and Moore through the decisional stage of logical positivism, another that runs through the pragmatic philosophizing of Charles Peirce, William James, and John Dewey.

In addition to the problem of existence, the problems of meaning and a priori knowledge are also involved in this revival of pragmatism. In recent years it has become more and more evident that the very "criterion of cognitive meaning" which the positivist uses in his attempt to discredit traditional metaphysics is also the product of a decision to speak in a certain way rather than a factual description of scientific language or a Moore-like "analysis" of the concept of scientific meaning. But if it is a resolution to use the word 'meaningful' in a certain way, we must once again ask how this resolution is justified, or in other words, 'Why should we adopt the empiricist criterion of meaning?' Similarly it has become evident (to some) that the notion of an analytic statement, which is so central to the positivistic treatment of a priori knowledge, is at its clearest intimately connected with the question of definition. It has been said, for example, that an analytic statement is one that is true by virtue of the definitions we make, and that this is the clue to the vexing problem of a priori knowledge. But if we do make the definitions that underlie all so-called a priori statements (this is debatable), we must ask not only what that making consists in but also whether we *should* make them.

All of this suggests that the ethical question 'Why should I do this?' is very closely related to the questions to which metaphysicians, logicians, and epistemologists have been brought by their most recent reflections. And this suggestion, this admission of the importance of what are sometimes called normative questions in these other disciplines, is what stimulates the special concerns of this book. The recent revival of pragmatic language among logicians, as well as the view that much of philosophy consists in proposing linguistic conventions, is a steppingstone to the view that dominates this work—the view that we must go beyond orthodox logical positivism, analytic platonism, *and pragmatism* with the help of what we learn by reflection on ethical reasoning. Once logicians and epistemologists begin to speak about justifying conceptual frameworks by reference to considerations of expediency, as some do, and once others begin to counter by appealing to intuition or conscience, as they do, we can see that we are entering a subject which might well profit from the two thousand years or so of moral philosophy in which very similar questions have been discussed.

A turn to ethics as a clue to the logic of decision in epistemology and metaphysics is almost inevitable after we abandon crude notions of "correspondence" between a statement we accept and abstract extra-linguistic entities like "facts" and "propositions". It resembles what has taken place in two other classic episodes in the history of philosophy: Hume's theory of causal connection and James's theory of truth.

In most of the cases which which we shall be concerned in this book, the typical move of recent philosophy has been that of jumping levels in an effort to get a clearer view. Instead of saying that concepts are identical with each other, we've been urged (and rightly so on many occasions) to speak of verbal expressions or predicates as being related to each other in a certain way. Instead of talking about shadowy *meanings* of sentences, some of our logicians talk about sentences themselves, and the more nominalistic among them refuse to stop until they reach actual inscriptions. Instead of looking with the mind's eye to see whether universals really do exist, we've been importuned to see the value of a "conceptual framework" that postulates them. Instead of construing certain philosophical theses as plain assertions of fact to be tested directly, we've been told that they are really linguistic proposals which are to be evaluated in a very different way. Now Hume, though he didn't advise jumping to the so-called formal mode, to palpable bits of language, suggested something very similar in his views on causal necessity. In effect, he urged that we speak about mental entities like impressions rather than about non-mental entities in discussing causal necessity, so that his recoil from the view that the necessary connection is "out there" between the ostensible cause and the ostensible effect is in one respect similar to the early positivistic abandonment of talk about queer extra-linguistic entities in favor of talk about words. Hume's recommendation begins with his failure to find the power or necessity of which his predecessors spoke (or perhaps with an inability to know how he should go about finding it). His next step, parallel to the early positivistic jump from 'The attribute of being a vixen is identical with the attribute of being a female fox' to 'The predicate 'vixen' is synonymous with the predicate 'female fox' ', consists in speaking of the mind's being determined to move from one idea (or impression) to another. "Necessity is something that exists in the mind, not in objects."[4] Presumably, therefore, a humean who is in doubt as to whether a connection is causal (after he has collected instances of constant conjunction) must ask himself the question '*Is* my mind determined to move from the idea of one to the idea of another?' But it is just at this point that one may ask such a humean: 'Isn't it more than a question of whether your

[4] Hume, *A Treatise of Human Nature*, bk. 1, pt. 3, sec. 14.

mind *is* determined to move in a certain way? Isn't it rather a question of whether your mind *ought* to move in a certain way?', thereby inviting him to speak a language which, if not ethical, is very similar to it.

I do not invite the reader to consider this question because I accept or wish to perpetuate certain distinctions between the ways in which we answer questions of fact and questions of what ought to be done or believed. I invite consideration of it because I think that we cannot escape it once we begin to move in Hume's direction. Later in this book I shall offer an account of so-called normative questions in which I deny that they are meaningless and in which I also deny that they are settled by a mode of argument which is *wholly* different from that which is used in science.

Unlike Hume, William James accepted such an invitation in his dealings with truth. I remind the reader of them not to *condone* everything James said on this count—for an extended treatment of truth is beyond our concern in this book—but rather to show how once we start to jump levels, whether to impressions or to words, we are often forced to enter the field of what I shall call the normative (I call it that with other philosophers but with a feeling of uneasiness which I will try to allay at a later point in this book). James exclaimed characteristically: " 'What would be better for us to believe'! This sounds very like a definition of truth. It comes very near to saying 'what we *ought* to believe': and in *that* definition none of you would find any oddity. Ought we ever not to believe what it is *better for us* to believe? And can we then keep the notion of what is better for us, and what is true for us, permanently apart?"[5] And once James abandoned the view that a true statement is one that corresponds with reality or with "the facts", for reasons very like those which impelled Hume to abandon the view that a valid causal inference was one that corresponded to causal powers "out there", James could not say that a true statement is one that *is* believed. He was driven, therefore, to what ought to be believed and thence to the notion of expediency.

We are concerned neither with praising nor exhuming James, but only with reminding the reader that James came closer than Hume did to the path which more recent thinkers have taken in

[5] *Pragmatism* (New York: Longmans, 1907), p. 77.

their flight from the terrors of hypostasis, even to the point of identifying what we ought to accept with what is good for us to accept and what is good for us to accept with what is accepted expediently. James's thinking illustrates in a striking way the dialectical route from the metaphysical to the normative which has become so typical in recent philosophy, whether we turn to those with more logistically articulated views or to those who speak of philosophical theses as linguistic proposals. With the tendency to convert so many questions into questions about language or to jump to higher linguistic levels, I have no quarrel. It is one of the great insights of our time. But it is wrong to transport difficult questions to another level by saying, for example, that they are matters of value, without considering the problem of value, without considering the process whereby we do or should justify these upper-story proposals and decisions that we make. It is good to be able to say all that we want to say without asserting or implying the existence of things like the *powers* of Hume's predecessors, the *ready-made facts* of James's predecessors, Plato's *ideas,* Aristotle's *substances,* and Descartes' *minds.* But it doesn't help to shout 'Proposal!' 'Decision!' or 'Rule!' and then stop. We must not only be clear about what linguistic proposing is and what rule-making is, but also about the ways in which they are or should be justified. And it is this which brings us to what may be called the morals of philosophical legislation.

In studying this question I have turned to the study of ethical language, that is to say, language that evaluates and guides human conduct in the narrow sense, the language in which we are more likely to forbid lying than the logical fallacy of affirming the consequent. I have done this on the assumption that we may get some light from a discipline which has been so long occupied with a variant of the questions to which our value-minded epistemologists have been driven. But I turn to ethics as a source of clues, not as the donor of a tailor-made solution to the problem of justification in logic or epistemology. It won't do to conclude that validity as applied to inferences, and acceptability as applied to statements, and correctness as applied to definitions are merely identical with or special cases of the notions studied in ethics. This is the view to which James either came or came dangerously close, and it is the error which Dewey has tried to avoid, if I understand him correctly. What we should seek are instructive similarities—similarities that will allow us to say clearly that certain statements of epistemologists and logicians are normative, how they are, and how this helps us—without concluding that we are really doing a chapter of ethics in the narrow sense.

When we come to ethical literature we find, as one might have expected, that all is not well. Indeed, we find that before we can get even a satisfactory clue to the problems which send us there, we must plough through a number of ethical views that presuppose the very views in epistemology that we have abandoned. For example, if we have grave doubts about the platonic theory of universals, and work ourselves into a position where we are willing to regard the problem of universals as that of deciding whether a certain framework or way of speaking is *acceptable,* i.e. *worthy* of acceptance, it won't help to analyze this notion of acceptability as a nonnatural characteristic. Nor will it do to explain it as meaning 'I accept universals; kindly do so'. In the light of the situation in ethical theory it is almost as if we came to a drugstore in search of a medicine, found the druggist down with the same illness, and had to fill the prescription ourselves. All is not well in ethics, but some is all right and upon that we shall rely heavily.

6. *Philosophy as a unified discipline*

If I succeed in doing anything of more general import I hope it will be to redemonstrate the virtue of simultaneous interest in all of the so-called major fields of philosophy, because one of the great mistakes of some contemporary philosophers is their conviction that a man must be either an epistemologist, or a moralist, or a metaphysician in the exclusive sense of 'either-or'. Of all the disciplines associated with philosophy, only mathematical logic can avoid reflection on the questions assigned to philosophy without prejudicing its opportunity to create results of great intellectual importance. Yet once logicians ask these questions, as do those who puzzle over the meaning and value of their "ontological commitments" and who appeal to what they call pragmatic considerations, or those who inquire into the kind of necessity which their conclusions allegedly have and resort to the notion of analyticity and to meanings, they will, I believe, be forced to ask philosophical questions that are a good deal like those that concern students of ethics. The reverse is more commonly recognized. As we shall see, one of the distinctive marks of ethical philosophy in the twentieth century is the extent to which it has concentrated on problems that demand a study of logic, ontology, and epistemology: 'Are there nonnatural qualities? Are there simple qualities? Are there intrinsic properties? What is the difference between emotive and cognitive meaning? Are there forms of inference peculiar to the establishment of ethical conclusions?' What I am urging is a revival of two-way traffic on the roads that join all philosophical disciplines, a revival which will not imitate the traditional trips from platonism to rationalism and back.

In taking my point of departure from the analytic, positivistic, and pragmatic traditions, I start from extremes on many issues, since analytical and positivistic thinkers have persistently emphasized contrasts of the sort that pragmatists have tried to blur. Thus Moore thinks that value predicates express simple, intrinsic, and nonnatural qualities while scientific predicates do not, and the positivists erect a similar barrier between ethics and science in terms of their contrast between the emotive and the cognitive; but on the pragmatic side Dewey and James are ethical naturalists who stress the continuity between science and ethics. And while Moore and Russell have defended a sharp division between the a priori and the a posteriori, and the positivists have invested an enormous amount in the contrast between the analytic and the synthetic, pragmatism as I understand it offers a powerful challenge to both of these dichotomies.

One result of this situation is the tendency of pragmatists to be dispositionally opposed to what they denigrate as "dualism". Continuities and similarities between disciplines, kinds of reasoning, varieties of experience are sought with passion and celebrated by pragmatists, while differences and contrasts tend to be treated—if they are recognized at all—as negligible. The opposite and equally stultifying error is that of latter-day analysts who seek differences to the neglect of serious and important similarities. Under the circumstances I can only feel slightly embarrassed by my own simple conviction that there are differences *and* similarities and that a philosopher can call a spade a spade while he points out that it is not a club. But that is my general attitude in philosophy, in spite of the fact that the present study is mainly concerned with counteracting certain *exaggerations* of the differences between logical, empirical, and ethical statements. What I refuse to do, for reasons that will become clearer, is to defend any extant epistemological "ism". What I seek and try to offer in this book is illumination on the concepts of existence, a priori knowledge, and value without the protective security and obscurity of any misleading banner. "There are in logic no preëminent numbers," said Wittgenstein, "and therefore there is no philosophical monism or dualism, etc."[6] I might add in the same spirit that there is in philosophy no positivism, no pragmatism, no empiricism.

[6] *Tractatus Logico-Philosophicus* (New York: Harcourt, Brace, 1922), p. 87.

CHAPTER II

The Existence of Meanings

1. *The semantics of Mill*

We have already observed that in the days before positivism issued its ringing challenge, statements like 'There are universals' and 'There are physical objects' were regarded as profound and fundamental and to that extent philosophical, and in 1912 philosophers like Russell did not regard them as radically different from the statements of ordinary life and science. If it took effort to show that they were true, that did not distinguish them from theorems in mathematics; and if they were difficult to understand, that was the price of doing philosophy. At no point, however, were such statements shunted off into the limbo of nonsense or thought of as needing psychiatric rather than logical treatment. These were the days of straightforward philosophy when a man was called upon to say what he believed and then to give arguments for it. This was the era in which philosophers thought of themselves not as lexicographers, but as analysts of extra-linguistic entities; they wished to analyze the universals *truth* and *goodness* and so they sharply separated their proper concerns from those of the man who makes dictionaries and the man who reads them.[1] It was as important for them, therefore, that these universals exist as it is important for zoologists that there be animals.

In the nineteenth century, John Stuart Mill had expounded a theory of meaning from which we can profitably take our point of departure in introducing the problem of universals as it was conceived by some in the twentieth century, for Russell described universals as the meanings of what Mill called general names. Mill had set forth his views in his *System of Logic*, freely admitting

[1] See, for example, Russell, *Philosophical Essays* (New York: Longmans, 1910), pp. 170–171; and Moore, *Principia Ethica* (Cambridge University Press, 1903), p. 6.

his dependence on older literature, particularly on scholastic writers. But in spite of the old origins of his views, he expressed them in an extremely influential book that became a standard reference on this subject, and so it is useful to take off from Mill's views.

Mill made three distinctions that bear directly on our concern in this chapter: (a) a distinction between singular names and general names, (b) one between concrete names and abstract names, and (c) another between nonconnotative and connotative names.

(a) While the distinction between singular names and general names can be *illustrated* by 'Socrates' and 'man', it is a distinction that is not too clearly *defined* by Mill. He spoke of the singular name as one "which is only capable of being truly affirmed . . . of one thing"[2] and of the general name as one which is capable of being truly affirmed of an indefinite number of things. There is a certain obscurity in the expression 'capable of being truly affirmed of', but the distinction is sufficiently clear for our purposes.

(b) "A concrete name," says Mill, "is a name which stands for a thing; an abstract name is a name which stands for an attribute of a thing."[3] Here it should be realized that Mill uses the word 'thing' quite narrowly, for his examples of concrete names are 'John', 'the sea', and 'this table'. Had he used the word 'thing' more broadly, somewhat in the way that 'entity' is sometimes used, he could not have made the distinction as he did, since in that case an abstract name would also name a thing—an abstract thing or entity. What Mill has in mind here, as is evident from other parts of his *System of Logic,* is a conception of *thing* as a proper sub-category of the category *entity,* namely *concrete* entity. For this reason his semantic distinction between two kinds of names—concrete and abstract—depends on a prior metaphysical distinction between two kinds of entities—concrete and abstract. A concrete name names a concrete entity and an abstract name names an abstract one. It should be repeated that 'thing' is used narrowly in Mill's explanation of what concrete and abstract names are, because it is not always so used by him. For example it is not used so narrowly in his statement of the distinction between a singular

[2] *A System of Logic* (New York: Longmans, Green, new impression of January 1947), p. 17.
[3] *Idem.*

name and a general name. When he says that a singular name is one that may be affirmed truly of "one thing", that one thing may be abstract; it may be an attribute as it is when referred to in the sentence 'Courage is a virtue'. Here 'courage' is a singular name of an abstract entity, and for this reason the classifications *singular-general* and *concrete-abstract* cut across each other. There are singular names which are abstract like 'courage', singular names which are concrete like 'John', general names which are abstract like 'virtue', and general names which are concrete like 'courageous'.

(c) Mill also distinguished between connotative and non-connotative names. He says that "a non-connotative term is one which signifies a subject only, or an attribute only. A connotative term is one which denotes a subject, and implies an attribute. By a subject is here meant anything which possesses attributes."[4] Again the method of drawing the distinction is not invulnerable; nevertheless something of what Mill had in mind may be gathered from his illustrations and some of the things he says about them. Before turning to that it will be useful to set down a few millian generalizations in which some of his basic semantic terms appear. First, *all concrete general names are connotative.* Second, *all abstract general names are connotative.* Therefore, *all general names are connotative.* Mill held that words like 'white' and 'virtuous' connote attributes. When we predicate the word 'white' of a snowball, "we convey the meaning that the attribute whiteness belongs to" it, he said in an extremely important passage.

There is a possible ambiguity on the *denotation* of general terms that is best explained here, since it is relevant to our treatment of Russell's views on universals to follow. When Mill says that the word 'man' denotes, he usually speaks of it as denoting each man, for example, Socrates, Plato, and Aristotle. There are passages, of course, in which he does suggest that 'man' has a single denotation that is the class of all men, but this is not the most typical statement of his point of view. It is this ambiguity of the word 'denotes' which leads later logicians to say that *the* denotation of the word 'man' is the class of all men.[5] On their view the predi-

4 *Ibid.,* p. 19.
5 See, for example, Alonzo Church, "Carnap's Introduction to Semantics," *Philosophical Review* (1943), 52:298–304.

cate 'man' *con*notes the attribute of being a man, while it *de*notes the class of all men; thus the predicate has *one* connotation and *one* denotation and they are distinct because an attribute is not identical with any class that corresponds to it; an attribute is a different *kind* of entity in spite of sharing the abstractness of a class. On the other hand, anti-platonic logicians who wish to avoid postulating abstract entities wherever possible have recently reverted to something like Mill's view of the way in which general terms name; they say that the general term denotes, not a class, but each individual of which it is true.[6] It should be pointed out, therefore, that in this chapter we are concerned mainly with criticizing arguments in favor of the existence of attributes or meanings.

Those who distinguish classes and attributes, and who treat the class of vixens as the denotation of 'vixen,' do well to distinguish between statements like (1) 'All and only vixens are female foxes' and (2) 'The attribute of being a vixen is identical with the attribute of being a female fox'. In sentence (1) the word 'vixen' has as its denotation the class of vixens, while *the attribute of being a vixen* is what Mill would call its connotation. On the other hand, in sentence (2) the attribute of being a vixen is *denoted* by the expression 'the attribute of being a vixen', as I think Mill would have agreed, and we may say without being too misleading that while this second sentence "deals with" attributes, the first does not. This has great significance for the discussion of Russell's early theory of universals, his theory of the a priori, and for a number of problems that arise in connection with Moore's conception of philosophical analysis.

2. *The confusions of Russell*

"Suppose, for instance, that I am in my room. I exist, and my room exists; but does 'in' exist? Yet obviously the word 'in' has a meaning; it denotes a relation which holds between me and my room. This relation is something, although we cannot say that it exists *in the same sense* in which I and my room exist. The relation 'in' is something which we can think about and understand, for, if we could not understand it, we could not understand the sentence 'I am in my room.'"

[6] See W. V. Quine, *Methods of Logic* (New York: Henry Holt, 1950).

This passage from Russell's *Problems of Philosophy*[7] presents for our inspection almost all of the fundamental issues surrounding the argument for universals in the early twentieth century. First of all, it allows us to see something of the nature of the universals whose existence Russell asserted. Secondly, it permits a discussion of the ambiguity of the word 'denotes' as Russell used it. Thirdly, it, together with other passages in the same book, introduces the related question: '*About* what is a sentence like 'I am in my room?'' and hence the question 'What is meant by the word 'about' or the phrase 'deals with' in such contexts?' since Russell says and implies throughout the *Problems of Philosophy* that such a sentence is *about* me, my room, and the relation of being in, that it *deals with* all of them, that it *concerns* them, and that it *involves* them. Fourthly, it permits us to discuss the relation between meanings and understanding.

For reasons that are irrelevant to our concern in this chapter, Russell was inclined to use a relational sentence like 'I am in my room' as an example, and hence a relation as the universal for whose existence he was arguing. But because of the irrelevancy of these considerations and because a nonrelational example like that provided by 'Socrates is a philosopher' is easier to deal with, I use it and examples like it in the discussion to follow, for Russell thought that 'Socrates is a philosopher' also implied the existence of universals, and the main issues are not changed by the change in illustration.

Russell was thinking of universals as attributes throughout *The Problems of Philosophy* (*whiteness* and *triangularity* are his favorite examples), and it is just because he construes universals as attributes that his use of the word 'denotes' in the above passage, a use which would dictate his saying that the word 'philosopher' *denotes* the attribute of being a philosopher, is so misleading. The tradition of Mill may waver between saying that the general term 'philosopher' denotes each philosopher and saying that it denotes the class of all philosophers, but it would never have allowed the confusion of saying that the word 'philosopher' in the

---

7 (First ed.; New York: Henry Holt, 1912). The passage quoted is on p. 90 of the impression of 1950 (New York: Oxford University Press), whose pagination is different from the first edition's. I use the later pagination in all of my citations.

sentence 'Socrates is a philosopher' *de*notes the *meaning* of the word 'philosopher', simply because the meaning of this general term, when it is construed as the attribute of being a philosopher, is for Mill the *connotation* of the term and a term doesn't denote what it connotes in one and the same context. What denotes the attribute of being a philosopher is an expression like 'philosopher-hood' or the phrase 'the attribute of being a philosopher' in a sentence like 'Socrates possesses the attribute of being a philosopher'. One might argue, of course, that Russell was inaugurating another usage, but there is no warning of this and moreover no clear statement of what he does mean by 'denotes' in this context.

This brings us to the difficult word 'about' and the phrase 'deals with'. If we regard the sentence 'Socrates is a philosopher' as being *about* or as *dealing with* Socrates, this is because the word 'Socrates', which is subject of the sentence, denotes Socrates in Mill's sense. But if we then say that the sentence 'Socrates is a philosopher' also deals with or is about the universal *philosopherhood*, we get ourselves into Russell's predicament. Instead of maintaining that all the entities which the sentence concerns are *de*noted in Mill's sense by components of the sentence, Russell maintains that a sentence like 'Socrates is a philosopher' is about one entity (Socrates) which is *de*noted by one of its components and about another (philosopherhood) which is *con*noted by one of its components. Of course, Russell *says* that things like philosopherhood are *denoted* by the general term 'philosopher', but not in any clearly understandable sense of the word 'denote' and certainly not in any sense justified by previous terminology.

The considerations which apply to Russell's first line of defense also apply to a second that he has frequently erected. He has maintained that even if we surrender the view that 'This is white' is about the universal whiteness, and adopt instead the view that we can define 'white' in terms of the predicate 'resembles', we are left with the universal *resemblance*. But just as the sentence 'This is white' is not *about* the universal *whiteness,* so 'This resembles that' is not *about* the universal *resemblance,* and for the very same reason.[8]

---

[8] See Quine's review of Russell's *Inquiry into Meaning and Truth* in *Journal of Symbolic Logic* (1941), 6:29–30.

The chief criticism of Russell's 1912 argument for the existence of universals is that the word 'philosopher' in the context 'Socrates is a philosopher' does not *de*note the attribute of being a philosopher, and therefore his argument is less genuinely puzzling than, say, the argument for the existence of concrete *physical* objects that begins with the premise 'I am in my room' and concludes that this premise couldn't be true unless there were physical objects. This, as we shall see, is virtually the argument offered by Moore for the existence of physical objects, an argument, incidentally, that Russell appears to reject in the *Problems of Philosophy* itself. The problems surrounding Moore's proof will be treated in the next chapter so I will not consider them here. However, it is worth noting that while an argument for the existence of physical objects that begins with non-epistemological premises or nonpsychological premises like 'I am in my room', 'Socrates is a philosopher', 'The Eiffel Tower is tall', or 'Here is a human hand' is capable of generating a certain amount of plausibility, the parallel argument for the existence of universals used by Russell in the *Problems* is based on an ambiguity in the use of the word 'denotes' that is quickly dispelled as long as we hold fast to some of Mill's distinctions.

3. *The structure of Russell's argument for universals*

The fact that Russell himself must add: "The relation 'in' is something which we can think about and understand, for, if we could not understand it, we could not understand the sentence 'I am in my room' " is indicative both of confusion and of his need for an epistemological or psychological premise. This confusion can best be dispelled by saying that while the statement 'I understand the word 'philosopher' ' *might* be covertly *about* the attribute of being a philosopher—we will challenge this later—'Socrates is a philosopher' is neither overtly nor covertly *about* the attribute. 'I understand the word 'philosopher' ' is an epistemological statement which does not follow logically from the statement 'Socrates is a philosopher', so that if the barest essentials of Russell's argument were to be written down, using our illustration instead of his, it would run as follows:

(a) Socrates is a philosopher;

(b) I understand the word 'philosopher';

therefore,

(c) There exists an attribute.

Now the connection between (a) and (b) is not deductive in character but rather like what was has been recently called 'pragmatic implication' by some, the sort of relation that holds between 'Socrates is a philosopher' and 'I believe that Socrates is a philosopher'. A man who asserts (a) implies (b) in some sense though (a) does not imply (b) logically, and therefore we are vindicated in our feeling that (a) could hardly be a premise from which the existence of attributes follows by strictly deductive steps, in our feeling that (b) is the really vital premise in the argument, and therefore in our conclusion that the step from (b) to (c) is the most serious step of serious platonists. It is the (b)-(c) form of the argument which I associate with the tradition of Frege, and it may be called the epistemological argument for attributes. With the crucial steps intermediate between (b) and (c) we shall be concerned later.

4. *The structure of Frege's argument*

Frege offered arguments for the existence of meanings that frankly begin with statements containing phrases like 'know a priori', from which an epistemological argument for meanings is extracted.[9] The initial impulse, which sends Frege to his distinction between the sense and the denotation of expressions like 'the evening star' and 'the morning star' and hence to his conviction that *there are* senses, is his belief that unless we make such a distinction the different "cognitive values", as he called them, of the two statements 'The evening star is the evening star' and 'The evening star is the morning star' will not be evident. In other words, one of Frege's reasons for invoking the semantic distinction between sense and denotation is his belief that it flows from and supports the epistemological distinction between the a priori and

---

[9] See his "Über Sinn und Bedeutung," *Zeitschrift für Philosophie und philosophische Kritik* (new series, 1892), 100:25–50; translated by Herbert Feigl under the title "On Sense and Nominatum" in H. Feigl and W. Sellars, eds., *Readings in Philosophical Analysis* (New York: Appleton-Century-Crofts, 1949); also translated by Max Black under the title "On Sense and Reference" in P. Geach and M. Black, eds., *Translations from the Philosophical Writings of Gottlob Frege* (Oxford: Blackwell, 1952).

the a posteriori. An attempted demonstration of the existence of senses for 'the evening star' and 'the morning star' that parallels Russell's attempted demonstration of the existence of meanings would begin with ' 'The evening star is identical with the morning star' is known a posteriori' as one premise and with ' 'The evening star is identical with the evening star' is known a priori' as another. The argument might then run: How can one be known a priori and the other not, unless one (though not the other) is seen to be true merely by virtue of our understanding the terms, i.e., by grasping the meanings of the terms (as distinct from grasping a ball of matter)? And if we must grasp meanings when we understand words, naturally there must be meanings for us to grasp. Once again the notion of understanding plays a crucial role in arguing for the existence of meanings, even though the more conspicuous philosophical aim is to preserve the distinction between knowledge a priori and knowledge a posteriori.

While Frege is mainly concerned with an illustration involving singular names, i.e., 'the evening star' and 'the morning star', his point has been generalized by his admirer Alonzo Church to cover our concern with the meanings of general terms.[10] The classic counterpart to Frege's pair of sentences is the pair 'All and only men are men' and 'All and only men are featherless bipeds'. In the latter case, it is argued by some that the word 'men' and the phrase 'featherless bipeds' have the same denotation—the class of all men or, alternatively named, the class of all featherless bipeds—while they do not have the same sense. On the other hand 'men' obviously has the same sense as 'men', and therefore while 'All and only men are men' is known a priori, 'All and only men are featherless bipeds' is known a posteriori. The parallel to the alleged demonstration of the existence of a sense as distinct from a denotation of 'the evening star' is the alleged demonstration of the existence of a sense as distinct from a denotation of general terms like 'men' and 'featherless biped'.

5. Epistemology and semantics

We should observe certain illuminating parallels between the pair of terms 'a priori' and 'analytic' and the pair 'understandable'

10 See note 5 above; also Carnap, *Meaning and Necessity* (Chicago: University of Chicago Press, 1947).

and 'meaningful'. The passage from the first member to the second in both pairs is characteristic of this whole period of philosophy in which epistemological premises are used in the extraction of ontological conclusions. "How is a priori knowledge possible?" we ask, and the answer emerges: "Because in knowing things a priori we express our knowledge in statements that are true by virtue of the *meanings* of the component terms." "How is understanding possible?" we ask, and we are told in reply: "Because the terms we understand are meaningful, i.e., full of meanings that are there to be grasped."

This step raises several questions, of which the most pressing is: How do philosophers think they get from the statement that we sometimes know things a priori and that we sometimes understand, to the statement that meanings exist? One of the chief problems in the superficially well-charted but wild sea of ontology turns about just this question. Do the "facts" of psychology or epistomology, like the fact that we *do* understand terms and that we *do* have something like what is traditionally called 'knowledge a priori', point deductively to conclusions like 'There are meanings'? The argument: ' 'Man' is understandable; therefore 'man' has a meaning; therefore there is at least one meaning', has a deductive ring. But is it the only way in which the case for meanings can be put? So far I have held that of the two arguments considered, *only that* which starts epistemologically is capable of developing a deductive argument for the existence of *meanings* that is not subject to elementary confusion, but shortly I will try to show that even if we *do* start with epistemological premises, it is not likely that we can concoct a convincing deductive "proof" of the existence of meanings.

It might be asked why so much emphasis is being laid on an epistemological proof, why the argument is construed as proceeding from premises like 'I understand the word 'philosopher' ' rather than from the semantic premise 'The term 'philosopher' has meaning'. This is because the argument for the existence of meanings which *begins* with a statement like 'The term 'philosopher' has meaning' is so unpersuasive as to make it unfair to construe it as part of a view which we are criticizing. Furthermore, in this respect we are being historical. Statements in the theory of meaning, like 'The word 'philosopher' has meaning' and ' 'All philosophers are men' is analytic', are usually offered as clarifications of ' 'Philosopher' is understood' and ' 'All philosophers are men' is known a priori', respectively. In the beginning are the acts of understanding and knowing a priori. They are the philosophical data which the notions of *meaningfulness* and of *analyticity* are supposed to illuminate. In a sense the issues resemble one that has arisen in theology. One can imagine (one knows) philosophers who abandon arguments for the existence of God that take off from statements about the material universe as premises, like 'Here is a human hand', and who rather begin with the psychological "fact" that men worship. In this respect their *terminus a quo* is like that of ontologists who embark from the facts of understanding and knowing a priori and sail on to meanings. Imagine a theologian who said: 'Men do worship, surely you can't deny *that*. But one can't worship without worshipping something, therefore an object of worship exists. And if an object of worship exists, God exists. Therefore God exists.' In moving deductively from the act of worship to the existence of objects of worship, such a theologian resembles the philosopher who uses a deductive epistemological argument for the existence of *meanings,* and in moving from the statement that an object of worship exists to 'God exists', he makes a step resembling that made by the philosopher who "deduces" that attributes or universals exist from the fact that meanings exist.

6. *The failure of the epistemological argument for meanings*

After having praised the epistemological argument faintly, that is, by comparison with the non-epistemological argument, I want to show why even *it* cannot supply us with a deductive proof of the existence of either meanings or universals. This brings us back to a part of Russell's crypto-epistemological argument purposely neglected in Section 3. In our consideration of that argument we called attention to the fact that the step from a singular non-epistemological statement like (a) 'Socrates is a philosopher' to (b) 'I understand the word 'philosopher' ' is not deductive but rather a case of pragmatic implication. For that reason (a) may be omitted from the so-called proof altogether, since most people would be willing to accept (b) as true and would therefore be quite willing to begin a proof with it as premise. But when we examine the step from (b) 'I understand the word 'philosopher' ' to (c) 'There are attributes', we see that this really involves several debatable steps that ought to be made explicit. The first is from (b) to (b₁) 'I grasp the meaning of the word 'philosopher' '; the next is to (b₂) 'There are meanings of general terms'; the last step is to (c) 'There are attributes'. That is the dark journey from the epistemological premise to the ontological conclusion.

In its original philosophic setting, the connection between 'I understand the word 'philosopher' ' and 'I grasp the meaning of the word 'philosopher' ' might have been viewed in one of at least two ways. It might have been conceived as a purely factual connection, established by taking two looks at one's self, so to speak— first to see whether one has understood the word and second to see whether one has grasped a meaning at the same time. But it is plain that this purely causal view of the relation is not sufficient to establish the *deductive* step from (b) to (b₁), so we can put it aside. But in that case we should be obliged to say that sentence (b) and sentence (b₁) are logically equivalent, or that the biconditional statement joining them is *analytic*. Now even a philosopher with the greatest sympathy for the concept of analyticity would find it hard to accept *this* as the foundation of platonism. To be told that 'I understand the word 'philosopher' if and only if I grasp the meaning of the word 'philosopher' ' is true by virtue of the meanings of *its* terms, among them the highly metaphorical 'grasp', is more than even the most patient and charitable students of 'analytic' could possibly grant. A similar difficulty presents itself when we examine the step from (b₂) to (c) of Section 3.

If we should say that 'I grasp the meaning of the word 'philosopher' ' presents the correct analysis of 'I understand the word 'philosopher' ', as an analytic philosopher of the earlier period might say, and if the former should be expanded even further into 'There is something that I grasp which is the meaning of the word 'philosopher' ', we should be saddled with *two* difficulties: elucidating the highly metaphorical notion of *grasping* and elucidating the notion of *being the meaning* of a word. The irony is that we find the word 'understand' much clearer than the terminology that is invented for its clarification, and so we rightly think of the explanations of Molière's physician when we are presented with Russell's platonic theory of universals. To be told that opium puts us to sleep because it possesses the dormitive virtue is in many ways similar to being told that we understand the word 'philosopher' because we grasp the meaning which it expresses; it is similar to being told that we know a priori that the evening star is the evening star because we see the self-identity of the meaning of 'evening star'. Nor is it very different from being told that 'good' is indefinable because the meaning of 'good' is simple. Grasping meanings, seeing their identity, and seeing their simplicity is far more obscure than the processes or facts they are supposed to clarify. That is one of the ironies of platonistic analysis, and that is why it is expendable.

The view that the statement 'I understand the word 'philosopher' ' is synonymous with 'I grasp the meaning of the word 'philosopher' ', which in turn is synonymous with 'There is something that I grasp which is the meaning of 'philosopher' ', and that this establishes the existence of meanings, may be compared with the following argument: 'I do this altruistically' is synonymous with 'I do this for the sake of someone else', which in turn is synonymous with 'There is something that is the sake of someone else and I do this for that thing', therefore there are *sakes*. A believer in *sakes* will behave just as a platonist does when we point out that we don't see, feel, or smell *sakes*: he will accuse us of blindness. 'How can you expect to see, feel, or smell a thing that is essentially different from stars, chairs, and cheeses?' he will ask. But what, then, is the relation between us and *sakes*? Do we *grasp* them too as we grasp meanings? Or do we do something else to them? The point is that no reference to these sakes really illuminates the notion of altruistic behavior, any more than a reference to platonic *meanings* elucidates the notion of understanding. Better to stumble about with our supposedly unclear notions of understanding, knowing a priori, and behaving altruistically than to propose such analyses, explanations, or accounts. Of all the "analyses" bequeathed to us by the age of meanings, those which introduce queer entities are the most suspicious. They are all modeled after the reasonable analysis of what it means to say that Jones is a father. To say this is to say that Jones is a male and that there is someone whom Jones begat. Here no new *kind* of entity has been introduced for which we must invent a relation comparable to grasping a meaning or to whatever it is that we do to a sake. The son is as seeable, as touchable, and as smellable as the father, but meanings are unholy ghosts. The inflationary introduction of queer entities is best abandoned in philosophy as the early moderns abandoned occult qualities in physics. Instead of trying to *account* for the epistemological fact of understanding by inventing occult entities, we had best take the fact of understanding as unanalyzed or try to explain it, clarify it, illuminate it from a more helpful point of view.

CHAPTER III

The Existence of Physical Objects

1. *Three views on the existence of physical objects*

While both Moore and Russell seemed to think that one could give arguments for the existence of meanings—evidently of a deductive nature—they differed about the possibility of proving the existence of matter or of physical objects. Indeed, one can think of the history of analytic reflection on the existence of physical objects as divisible into three positions that span a half-century: that of Russell in *The Problems of Philosophy,* where he denied that one could prove their existence; that of Moore in his "Proof of an External World", where he offered such a proof;[1] and that of logical positivists who not only maintain that no such proof is possible but go further and say that the statement 'Physical objects exist' is meaningless and hence not susceptible of proof, disproof, or skepticism. In this chapter the first two views will be considered. They not only illustrate more general philosophical differences between Moore and Russell but also provide another example of the fact that their controversies are often the controversies which their positivistic descendants sought to dissolve rather than mediate.

2. *Russell's skepticism*

It is somewhat remarkable that many philosophers who have treated the existence of meanings as self-evident or who have offered proofs of their existence have at the same time denied the self-evidence of the existence of physical objects and have developed great doubts about the possibility of proving their existence. This is often the product of the strange combination of platonism

[1] Annual Philosophical Lecture, Henriette Hertz Trust, British Academy, 1939, *The Proceedings of the British Academy,* vol. 25.

and kantianism that was fairly prevalent in the pre-positivistic period of analytic philosophy. It is most strikingly illustrated in the early writings of Russell and is worth examination not only for its own sake but also for the light it throws on the later development of the subject. At the very time when he advanced what we have construed as a confused deductive argument for the existence of universals, Russell rejected a parallel argument for the existence of physical objects *as he conceived them then*. That is to say, he did not think that a deductive *proof* of the existence of physical objects could be given. And yet one might suppose that if the true statement 'I understand the word 'in' ' is thought to entail the existence of the meaning of 'in' and hence the existence of at least one universal, the true statement 'I am in my room' might be supposed to entail the existence of my room and hence the existence of at least one physical object. But in spite of this, and even in spite of a faint suggestion of such an argument, Russell says elsewhere in the *Problems* that the statement that there are physical objects does not follow from statements that are more certain than itself, and this is his chief reason for not offering a deductive proof of the existence of physical objects.

3. *The theory of descriptions and the theory of proper names*

Russell's views on the existence of external objects as they were set forth in the *Problems of Philosophy* were intimately connected with his theory of definite descriptions. A descriptive phrase, it will be recalled, is an expression like 'the first president of the United States', 'the tallest building in New York City', 'the author of *Waverly*', and 'the winged horse captured by Bellerophon'. Now Russell's theory of definite descriptions as usually understood is a theory according to which such descriptive phrases are to be eliminated in the manner indicated in an earlier chapter. It may be regarded as a general recipe for eliminating expressions of the form 'the so-and-so', where 'so-and-so' is a predicate like those used in the above examples. As such it must be distinguished from another theory of Russell's to the effect that most proper names are disguised descriptions. "Common words, even proper names, are usually really descriptions. That is to say, the thought in the mind of a person using a proper name correctly can generally only be expressed explicitly if we replace the proper name by a description."[2] This theory takes as its definienda ordinary proper names and translates them into descriptive phrases, whereas what is commonly called Russell's theory of descriptions takes as its task the elimination of the descriptive phrases themselves. It is important to distinguish these two theories not only because they are obviously different but because many philosophers have accepted Russell's theory of descriptions without accepting his theory of ordinary proper names (as I shall call the other theory from now on).

4. *Two uses of the theory of proper names: neutral and belligerent*

Having made this distinction between Russell's theory of descriptions and Russell's theory of ordinary proper names, it is important to make a distinction between two uses to which the theory of proper names is put by Russell. We may distinguish two kinds of linguistic replacements or translations that Russell makes by means of his theory of proper names, one of which is epistemologically neutral and the other of which isn't. A good example of an epistemologically neutral translation is that whereby Russell replaces 'Bismark' by 'the prime minister of Germany in 1863'. Here nothing is done that bears on one's theory of knowledge in the conventional sense; it is a replacement to which no one could object out of subjectivistic, idealistic, or dualistic scruples. But, says Russell when he proceeds to unite his theory of proper names and his theory of perception *of 1912,* if someone other than Bismarck thinks and says of Bismarck that Bismarck is a diplomat, "what this person [is] acquainted with [are] certain sense-data which he [connects] . . . with Bismarck's body. His body, as a physical object, and still more his mind [are] only known as the body and the mind connected with these sense-data. That is, they [are] known by description."[3] In short, a statement like 'Bismarck is a diplomat' is first to be replaced by means of Russell's theory of proper names (in an epistemologically belligerent way!) and then the result is to be replaced with the help of the theory of descriptions. We are asked first to transform 'Bismarck is a diplomat' into something

2 *Problems of Philosophy,* p. 54.
3 *Ibid.,* p. 55.

like 'The one and only physical object connected with this smell, this color, that sound, etc., is a diplomat', and then to call the theory of descriptions into play in order to give us at the end of our efforts a statement like 'There exists exactly one physical object which is connected with this smell, this color, that sound, etc., and which is a diplomat'. By means of this double play we convert an ordinary singular statement like 'Bismarck is a diplomat' into a highly complex statement which *contains as a conjunct* the statement 'There is *at least* one physical object connected with this smell, this color, that sound which is a diplomat'. The fact that this existential statement or something like it is a conjunct of what Russell regards as the most accurate expression of the proposition normally expressed by 'Bismarck is a diplomat' is of great importance. Precisely because it is a conjunct of the ordinary proposition 'Bismarck is a diplomat' when the latter has been "thrown into logical form", we can't prove this conjunct by deduction from 'Bismarck is a diplomat' without begging the question. And precisely because the object whose existence is asserted is hidden and kantian in nature, we can't "know" that object "by acquaintance".

5. *Why the platonic meaning fares better than the thing-in-itself*

We now see why the kantian and early russellian physical object fares so badly by comparison with the platonic meaning, and yet our examination of the latter shows it to be much more like the kantian thing-in-itself and much more mysterious than Russell or other platonists have supposed. Clearly the sentence 'There is something that I grasp which is the meaning of the word 'philosopher' ' bears a relation to 'I understand the word 'philosopher' ' which is very like the relation that 'There is exactly one physical object which is connected with this smell, this color, this sound, etc., etc., and which is a diplomat' bears to 'Bismarck is a diplomat'. Why, then, didn't Russell try to "prove" the existence of physical objects as he did the existence of universals or meanings? The answer, I think, is that he did not see the similarity of the two situations. Even if he had not sought a proof, even if he had tried to translate 'Bismarck is a diplomat' and 'I understand the word 'philosopher' ' with no intention of *proving* the existence of physical objects or meanings, I think Russell would have held that the truth of the statement 'I grasp the meaning of 'philosopher' ' showed that we were *acquainted* with meanings, whereas he would have held that the corresponding analysis of 'Bismarck is a diplomat' showed that we were *not* acquainted with physical objects. The meaning is therefore put by Russell into the same company as the sense-datum which is known by "acquaintance", while the physical object is behind the iron curtain in kant-land and known only by "description". Hence those who say that it exists must justify their statement in some other way. In Russell's case it was justified by what we may call "pragmatic" considerations (though he didn't call them that), so that in 1912, when he was attacking William James for his doctrine of "transatlantic truth", Russell was using a variant of that doctrine in the metaphysical clutch. For Russell had said: "The way in which simplicity comes in from supposing that there really are physical objects is easily seen. If the cat appears at one moment in one part of the room, and at another in another part, it is natural to suppose that it has moved from the one to the other, passing over a series of intermediate positions. But if it is merely a set of sense-data, it cannot have ever been in any place where I did not see it; thus we shall have to suppose that it did not exist at all while I was not looking, but suddenly sprang into being in a new place . . . Thus every principle of simplicity urges us to adopt the natural view, that there really are objects other than our selves and our sense-data which have an existence not dependent upon our perceiving them."[4]

6. *Moore's proof*

In the history of analytic philosophy there has been less agreement on physical objects than on meanings, as I have said, and this is borne out not only by Russell's own later abandonment of his kantian views for more phenomenalistic ones, but also by the fact that G. E. Moore later tried to offer a proof of the existence of physical objects. His attempt at a proof is not only interesting in its own right but helps us clarify by contrast Russell's very different view of 1912. Moore's proof is supposedly aimed at Kant, who had said in his preface to the second edition of *Critique of Pure Reason:* "It still remains a scandal to philosophy . . . that the existence of things outside of us . . . must be accepted merely on *faith,* and that, if anyone thinks good to doubt their existence, we are unable

4 *Ibid.,* pp. 23–24.

to counter his doubts by any satisfactory proof." And because it was directed against Kant, Moore's attack *might* be regarded as an attack on the Kant-like views which Russell was defending in the *Problems of Philosophy*. They face each other, therefore, as the two characteristically pre-positivistic views on the existence of the external world, and provide us with a controversy from which positivists fled or which they hoped to dissolve by attention to our use of language, the empiricist criterion of meaning, and the notion of analyticity.

The main issue between the Russell of the *Problems* and Moore of the "Proof" is not whether physical objects do exist but whether we can *prove* that they exist. Moreover, both disputants share the conviction that the statement (a) 'There are physical objects' is meaningful in precisely the sense in which (b) 'There are human hands' is meaningful. What they may be construed as arguing about is whether (a) can be deduced from other statements which are known to be true, in fact, about whether (a) can be deduced from (b) in a manner that supplies a proof of (a).

Moore treats Kant's phrase "things outside of us" as synonymous with "things to be met with in space", another kantian phrase, and then tries to prove the existence of physical objects as a subclass of Kant's "things to be met with in space". And all he does is to deduce from the fact that there are mountains, stones, planets, houses, chairs, tables, and pieces of paper the desired conclusion that there are physical objects. That is all. It is made more dramatic in a typically moorean way by beginning with premises that Moore's audience would have denied only at the risk of meeting the face that J. M. Keynes has described so well.[5]

(1) 'Here is one human hand' (uttered while Moore is waving one of his hands).

(2) 'Here is another human hand' (uttered while Moore waves his other hand).

From these two premises Moore deduces the statement:

(3) 'Two human hands exist.'

---

[5] "Moore . . . was a master of this method—greeting one's remarks with a gasp of incredulity—*Do* you *really* think *that,* an expression of face as if to hear such a thing said reduced him to a state of wonder verging on imbecility, with his mouth wide open and wagging his head in the negative so violently that his hair shook. *Oh!* he would say, goggling at you as if either you or he must be mad; and no reply was possible" (*Two Memoirs,* London: Hart-Davis, 1949, p. 85).

At this point he introduces what may be regarded as an assumption of the analyticity of the statement 'All human hands are physical objects', or, alternatively, the rule: 'From the statement 'There are two human hands' we may deduce the statement 'There are two physical objects.' ' And after appealing to this he is home, having safely demonstrated that which was to be proven in a rigorous way—the existence of things in an external world!

Moore is aware, of course, that many philosophers would feel that he has not given a satisfactory proof of the statement in question, for one thing because some philosophers have understood the phrase 'proof of an external world' as including a proof of things which he hasn't attempted to prove. Many of these philosophers, he says after offering his own proof, would demand a proof of what he asserted when he held up his hands and said 'Here's one hand and here's another'. But what they really want, according to Moore, is not merely a proof of these two propositions but "something like a general statement as to how any propositions of this sort may be proved". Moore readily admits that he hasn't given this, and indeed says: "If this is what is meant by proof of the existence of external things, I do not believe that any proof of the existence of external things is possible."[6] For one thing, in order to prove "Here's one hand and here's another', he says he should need to prove that he is not dreaming, and this he cannot do.

The other objection to his procedure Moore treats somewhat differently. It is put forward by philosophers who hold that if you cannot give a proof of the premise 'Here's one hand and here's another', then you do not *know* it to be true, their point being that while the conclusion might *follow* from the premise, only a conclusion which follows from a premise known to be true is one that is thereby proven. This view Moore rejects simply by saying that he can know things which he cannot prove, and that he does know that 'Here is a human hand' is true.

7. Russell's skepticism and Moore's proof contrasted

I think that Russell of the *Problems* was the kind of philosopher to whom Moore alludes after Moore offers his proof, because I think that the Russell of that book would have denied that he

[6] Moore, "Proof of an External World," p. 29 (see note 1 above).

knew that a human hand was being waved before his face by Moore, and that his interpretation of Moore's two premises would have been strictly analogous to his own interpretation of 'Bismarck is a diplomat'. Moore's statement about his hands and that of Bismarck's friend about Bismarck would have been viewed by Russell as singular statements "about" a physical object, and in each case Russell would have said that the person asserting them asserts them on the basis of insufficient evidence. Russell would have denied that Moore *knew* that he was waving a hand, as Russell denied that Bismarck's friend could ever "really know" that Bismarck was a diplomat. For this reason Russell in the *Problems* falls into the class of philosophers who grant that Moore's conclusion follows from his premises but who deny that Moore has *proven* the conclusion through his failure to *know* the premises. This might be what Russell is getting at when he says in the *Problems* that the statement that physical objects exist follows from no statement that is more certain than itself. And probably because Russell in 1912 also worried about the difficulty of not being able to prove that he was not dreaming, he too does not seek "something like a general statement as to how any proposition of this sort may be proved".

If Russell in the *Problems* can be represented as having denied that Moore knew his (Moore's) premises to be true, did Russell grant that Moore's *inference* was formally *like* that used in proof even though the premises were not known? Could Russell's attitude be expressed by his saying to Moore: "If only you knew the premise to be true, you might have *proven* that physical objects exist?" I don't think so, for there is reason to believe that Russell's interpretation of 'Bismarck is a diplomat' would have forced him to label Moore's inference as a case of begging the question. In other words, I think that the Russell of 1912 would not only refuse to allow that Moore knew the premises but in addition might have held that *the deduction proceeds so trivially as to prevent the argument from being a proof even if the premises were known*. The point is that a russellian translation of Moore's premise would contain the very existential conclusion that Moore wishes to demonstrate. 'Here's a human hand', like 'Bismarck is a diplomat', would have been viewed by Russell as expressing in a poor way what would best be expressed by a sentence beginning with a descriptive phrase, and this sentence would have gone into russellese as 'There exists exactly one physical object connected with such-and-such sense-data'. This in turn would be decomposed into 'There is at least one physical object connected with such-and-such sense-data and there is at most one physical object connected with such-and-such sense-data', and in this form the existential conclusion desired would appear so conspicuously in the premise as to render the "proof" worthless: the point being that 'There is at least one physical object connected with such-and-such sense-data' contains in a proof-damaging way the statement 'There is at least one physical object'.

The fallacy known as "begging the question" is not easy to define. For what *is* the logical relation that a consequence must bear to a premise in an *alleged* proof in order to justify the charge of begging the question? We can give examples, of course. The question is begged, presumably, when the premise is a conjunction of which the conclusion is a conjunct, and it is also begged when the conclusion is one of the premises. But suppose the premise is Russell's translation of Moore's statement. There might be no doubt that the reasoning 'There is exactly one physical object connected with such-and-such sense-data, therefore there is at least one physical object connected with such-and-such sense-data' does *not* furnish the basis for a proof, because the conclusion is (in a sense that needs elaboration) a conjunct of the premise. But how about the case which is most crucial for us, namely the step from 'There is at least one physical object connected with such-and-such sense-data' to 'There is at least one physical object'? I should say that this inference also creates suspicion because it is like the "proof" of 'There is at least one man' from the premise 'There is at least one thing which is a man and which is tall'. Moreover, it won't help to say, as Moore says in his own account of *his* argument, that the premise is more "specific", or that the conclusion might have been true even when the premise was false, for the example of begging the question listed above has this characteristic. It might be true that a conjunction was false while one of the conjuncts was true; it might be that a man existed though no tall man existed.

Under the circumstances it would seem that we must move onto very slippery terrain and say that an argument begs the question when no one can *know* the premise without knowing the conclusion. Could anyone satisfy himself that Bismarck was a diplomat without simultaneously or beforehand satisfying himself that a physical object existed? Could anyone satisfy himself that Moore was waving a human hand without simultaneously or beforehand satisfying himself that a physical object existed? I think how similar this problem is to the one that Mill wrestled with when he charged the syllogism with begging the question. Can one know that all men are mortal without knowing that Socrates is a mortal? What modes of inference furnish adequate underpinnings for a proof? I will not enter this vexed question here, but it is sufficient to say that a theory according to which ordinary singular statements like 'Bismarck is a diplomat' and 'Here is a human hand' are translated into russellese at the very beginning of our philosophical speculations renders them unfit to function as premises in a *proof* of the existence of physical objects.

It follows that while we may abstractly distinguish two sets of philosophers who might disagree with Moore—those who say he doesn't know his premises to be true, and those who deny that his conclusion follows from them in a proof-making way—it turns out that Russell, as we have construed his views in the *Problems,* falls into *both* categories, and therefore poses a dilemma that is directed against every proof of the kind offered by Moore. Either we know the premises or we don't. If we don't know them we can't prove the conclusion, and if we do know them we shall be assuming that which is to be proven and hence begging the question. One fact worth repeating here is that Russell claims that we don't know the premise just because it contains a conjunct which asserts the existence of the *hidden* cause of sense-data. It is the presence of this existential assertion as a part of the premise itself, therefore, that causes both difficulties. It makes it impossible for us to know the premises to be true and it forces us to beg the question when we try to prove the existence of physical objects in a moorean way.

It should be realized, of course, that the russellian analysis of the premise, while it torpedoes any effort to prove the existence of physical objects in a moorean way, still allows us to say that a man who believes that a human hand is here is *committed* to a belief in the existence of physical objects. It is this which still allows Moore to carry out a number of his other well-known moves. When he refutes those who *deny* that there are physical objects by saying 'Here's a human hand', he can refute them even if he accepts Russell's translation of 'Here's a human hand', for the denial of the existence of physical objects is inconsistent with 'Here's a human hand' even when translated into russellese. I suggest that this is part of the reason why Moore's "Proof of an External World" is less popular than his "Defence of Common Sense".[7] In the latter he is at his best, because he is attacking those who deny that there are physical objects by pointing out propositions which they believe and which are inconsistent with 'There are no physical objects'. But the fallacy of begging the question calls attention to the fact that this logical relationship between propositions p and q is no guarantee that we can use one of them as the premise in a proof of the other, and the latter is precisely what the "Proof of an External World" attempts. It is a more positive paper; it tries to *prove* a belief of common sense, while the "Defence" merely defends one against philosophers who grant too much to common sense to begin with.

8. *Russell's philosophical method and Moore's contrasted*

We should not leave this comparison of the two views on the existence of physical objects without noticing a very fundamental aspect of the whole problem. It should be realized that Russell refuses to use as a premise in a philosophical argument a statement from ordinary language like 'Here's a human hand' before translating it into language using descriptive phrases. And once he translates these statements in this way, the existential conclusion which Moore wants to prove becomes so conspicuous a component of the premise that any "proof" moving from this premise to the existential conclusion must be regarded as a case of begging the question. Therefore, Russell is forced to consider the premise itself, and it is this premise which he neither knows nor can prove. Moore, on the other hand, is not willing to regard the premise as

[7] *Contemporary British Philosophy*, J. H. Muirhead, ed., 2nd. ser. (New York: Macmillan, 1925), pp. 193–223.

a statement which *must* be analyzed into the language of descriptive phrases, particularly by means of Russell's belligerent theory of proper names. In this way Moore is able to treat it as a proposition which is distinct from the existential conclusion to be proven, and as a proposition which does not contain the conclusion in a way that justifies the charge that he is begging the question.

The difference between Moore and Russell on this point may also be formulated by saying that Russell insists on throwing the premise "into logical form" before performing any deductions, particularly those that are of philosophical importance. It is as if the machinery of philosophy and logic could not get started until the statements of ordinary language were converted into materials for logical deduction, and yet once this initial polishing has been done, the result is a statement from which the existence of physical objects follows in a trivial way. One is tempted to ask, therefore, whether Russell doesn't accomplish in the first polishing step, in the throw into logical form, what Moore accomplishes directly. Russell moves into the language of descriptions and then into the language of existential quantifiers, while Moore moves directly from the statement of ordinary language to the existential conclusion, bypassing the middle, sentence-polishing step of Russell. In the end they both have traveled the same circuit, from 'Bismarck is a diplomat' and 'Here's a human hand' to 'Physical objects exist', only Russell's logical translation swallows Moore's conclusion into itself with one gulp. It is for this reason, one might say, that Moore's proof seems trivial when put into russellese. 'Here's a human hand' turns out to say 'There exists a physical object' plus something else, so that we seem to beg the question when we try to prove the existence of physical objects in Moore's way.

This also brings out a fundamental point in Moore's philosophy. Moore would hold that he might know 'Here's a human hand' without being in a position to analyze its "meaning". I am not saying that he *would* reject Russell's analysis of 'Here's a human hand', but rather that he would assert with confidence that he knew the proposition he expressed by waving and saying 'Here's a hand' at his lecture whether or not he had succeeded in analyzing it into *any* terms, Russell's or anybody else's. And for this reason he might perfectly well bypass the russellian step and go to his conclusion with an air of "proof".

Russell, however, is incapable of such forbearance when it comes to sentences of ordinary language. For him 'Here's a hand' is not logical tender and must be converted into the gold of existential quantifiers and variables. In the *Problems* he was obliged to analyze what we mean by our ordinary claims of empirical knowledge and concluded that in every such case we claim to know propositions which contain as integral parts propositions asserting the existence of kantian unknowables. The point is, then, that when Russell concludes that "the table is the physical object that *causes* certain sense-data", the physical objects *he* had in mind were, as he says, like Kant's. This is why he resists any effort to "prove" ordinary empirical statements referring to them. He thinks of proof as beginning with premises that can be known with certainty in the way he claims to know the truth of sensory reports. But if he will begin only with premises known with certainty in this sense, he can't in the very nature of the case prove by deductive steps a proposition which asserts the existence of a physical object conceived as the cause of the sense-data. He cannot even begin such a proof. This is fundamental in the 1912 russellian avoidance of proofs of the existence of physical objects.

This point may also be brought out by comparing the two uses of the theory of ordinary proper names—the epistemological and the epistemologically neutral use. Starting with the name 'Bismarck', Russell could move in either of two directions. Either he could use the descriptive phrase 'the prime minister of Germany in 1863' or 'the physical object causing such-and-such sense-data'. Suppose he had chosen the first, epistemologically neutral translation, rather than the second. In that case the translation might be thought of as closer to Moore's intent. Naturally, charges of question-begging parallel to those presented earlier would still be possible. But the russellian sentence which would translate a sentence like 'The prime minister of Germany in 1863 is a diplomat', even if it ran: 'There is exactly one physical object which is prime minister of Germany in 1863 and it is a diplomat', would not bear upon its face its unknowability in the way that the epistemologically belligerent translation does. Russell would not have converted the proposition into terms that make the roots of his kantianism evident. The physical object that is prime minister of Germany in 1863 and the physical object causing such-and-such sense-data are different to this extent: Russell might cheerfully acknowledge that he "knows" of the existence of the former while speaking with the vulgar; indeed this is what "knowing" it by description amounts to. But he held that we "really" don't know that it exists; its existence we can neither know nor prove. Nevertheless, the two descriptive phrases mentioned describe the same object. Indeed, Russell's epistemology of 1912 is succinctly formulated as the generalization of just such an identity. He argues that the descriptive phrases 'the physical object who is prime minister of Germany in 1863' and the descriptive phrase 'the physical object causing this color, that sound, that smell' describe the same thing, but that the latter is a more articulate way of referring to that thing, that somehow it gets to the object by a clearer and more explicit route. For this reason, when ordinary sentences like 'Bismarck is a diplomat' are translated by the epistemologically *belligerent* theory of proper names, it becomes apparent not only that an existential assumption lurks within the ordinary man's statement but also that this assumption involves something as deep as a physical object behind a sensory veil that can never be pulled aside.

That Russell is also willing to speak in an unphilosophical way about physical objects is evident in the passage: "Suppose for instance, that I am in my room. I exist and my room exists." Here there is no kantianism. He seems to imply that he knows that he is in his room and that it *follows* in a way that might be used in a moorean proof, that his room and he both exist. But let him go into the epistemological mood, translating 'I am in my room' by using existential quantifiers and the key phrase 'causing such-and-such sense-data', and we are right back where we started. All the agnosticism will be revived and Moore's claim that he *knows* that he is in his room or that he is waving a hand will be resisted. What this shows, I think, is that the fundamental difference between the Moore of the "Proof" and the Russell of the *Problems* on the existence of external objects is one that centers about the fact that when Russell is agnostic he is thinking of physical objects in a "philosophical" way—as hidden kantian causes of our sense-data, while Moore is not, in spite of Moore's attempt to answer Kant. In a sense, therefore, what Moore tries to prove the existence of, and what Russell denies that we can prove the existence of, can be identified with each other only on the theory that physical objects are inaccessible causes of sense-data, the theory we have previously called epistemologically belligerent. In fact, Russell's physical objects are the very things whose existence phenomenalists deny, while they rarely deny the existence of the philosophically innocuous physical objects of which Moore spoke.

9. Why the platonic meaning should not fare better than the thing-in-itself

In this chapter we have called attention to the two-pronged character of Russell's implicit rejection in 1912 of the kind of proof of the existence of physical objects that Moore came to offer in 1939: one stressed the fact that the russellian translation already contains the existential conclusion that Moore wants to demonstrate in a way that supposedly forces Moore to beg the question; the other stressed the fact that the physical object is behind the kantian curtain. With the issues arising out of the first criticism we shall be concerned in the next section but we need not argue here against the doctrine of things-in-themselves. In passing we might observe that the doctrine that the physical object is known only by description was adopted by Russell at a time when he also supposed that *meanings* were known by acquaintance. But the fact is that platonic meanings and kantian things-in-themselves are very much in the same boat. The sentence 'There is something that I grasp which is the meaning of the word 'philosopher'' stands to 'I understand the word 'philosopher'' in much the way that 'There is an (unknowable) physical object which is connected with this smell, this color, that sound, which is a diplomat' stands to 'Bismarck is a diplomat'. I conclude that platonic meanings are to be avoided on grounds analogous to those that lead us to avoid the kantian thing-in-itself. Neither of them really brings us to a clearer understanding of what we mean when we say that we understand a word or what we mean when we say that Bismarck is a diplomat, and yet what is curious about the history of analytic philosophy is the fact that belief in meanings has survived so much longer than belief in things-in-themselves.

The fact that ordinary people do speak about Moore's un-

kantian physical objects suggests the question: Is there an unpla-
tonic version of the meaning of a word that might be equally acceptable to philosophers using nothing but ordinary language?
There might be, but it is extremely important to realize that the
notion of meaning *as it is used by the platonist* is much more ten-
dentious than Moore's commonsensical use of the notion of physical object. Moore is speaking up for all those who think that they
have hands, but the meanings for which platonists speak are used
more technically. Meanings must support the theory of a priori
knowledge, they must be public, nonmental, graspable, and they
must exist in some other realm or sense. Plainly they need more
defense than they can get by using Moore's methods.

10. *The validity of a Russell-like criticism of Moore's proof*

Now we may ask: Is the criticism of the moorean proof which
is based on Russell's theory of proper names justified? Are all of
our common sense statements, like Moore's 'Here's a human hand',
synonymous with statements which contain Moore's conclusion in
a way that makes his "proof" fallacious? As we have already seen,
this depends on the validity of the epistemologically belligerent
version of Russell's theory of proper names. But is it valid? We
recall that Russell said in 1912: "proper names . . . are . . . really
descriptions. That is to say, the thought in the mind of a person
using a proper name correctly can generally only be expressed
explicitly if we replace the proper name by a description"; and by
this I take him to mean that the proper names he speaks of are
synonymous with descriptive phrases. But *is* every ordinary proper
name like 'Bismarck' *synonymous* with a descriptive phrase like
'the physical object causing such-and-such sense data'? I should
think that philosophers who have no doubts about the notion of
synonymy would answer 'No'. Not only is the epistemologically
belligerent version not defensible; neither is the epistemologically
neutral version according to which 'Bismarck' is *synonymous* with
'the prime minister of Germany in 1863'. The point is that *no* ordinary proper name is synonymous with a descriptive phrase (for
those who use 'synonymous with' confidently). The proof is simple
and depends on Russell's theory of descriptions itself. If some
proper name, say 'N', were synonymous with some descriptive

phrase, say 'the so-and-so', then the identity-sentence 'The so-and-so = N' would be analytic, that is, true by virtue of the meanings of its component terms. But Russell's theory of descriptions assures us that *any* sentence beginning with the phrase 'the so-and-so' is to be construed as a sentence which asserts in part that there are so-and-so's, and that such a sentence is *not* analytic. To say that 'Scott' is synonymous with 'the author of *Waverley*' is to say that 'The author of *Waverley* = Scott' is analytic. But this sentence says in part that someone wrote *Waverley* and is therefore not analytic, not determined to be true by examining its meanings alone.

At most we can say that 'Scott' *denotes* the same thing as 'the author of *Waverley*'; at most we can say that 'Bismarck' denotes the same thing as 'the Prime Minister of Germany in 1863'; at most we can say that 'Bismarck' *denotes* the same thing as 'the physical object causing such-and-such sense-data'; at most we can say that the subject of Moore's premise *denotes* the physical object causing Moore's sense-data at that moment. And if this is the most we can say, we cannot say that Moore's premise contains his existential conclusion in a question-begging way. Russell's translation is not synonymous with Moore's original.

11. *Why Moore's proof is unconvincing*

Does this mean that Moore's proof is convincing? To answer this usefully we must recall that Moore's proof contained two parts: one that led him from 'Here's a human hand' to 'There exists a human hand' and a second that led him from 'There exists a human hand' to 'There are physical objects'. Only the first concerns us here.

If I say, 'Here's a human hand', you may counter by saying, 'What? I don't see anything'. To help you I may say, 'The thing (physical object) I'm waving. Don't you see it?' But this shows that I presuppose the existence of a thing of which I say 'It's a human hand' in a sense of 'presuppose' recently discussed by P. F. Strawson.[8] The point is that we can make a statement by using a sentence like 'Here's a human hand' if and only if we (and our hearers) believe that there is something to which 'here' refers. For Strawson,

[8] *Introduction to Logical Theory* (New York: John Wiley, 1952), pp. 174ff.

therefore, the existence of the thing to which 'here' refers is "pre-supposed" in a special sense, and for this reason Moore's first utter-ance would seem pointless to a person who didn't believe that Moore was talking about *something*. Once the person is persuaded that Moore is waving *something*, he knows not what, the person may look a little more closely and see that it's a hand, but the dis-covery that it's a hand *may* take place well after he accepts the fact that Moore is talking about something. The point, then, is that Moore needs assent to *some* existential statement even before he can gain assent to 'Here's a human hand'. The audience's formu-lated responses might occur as follows: (a) Moore's waving some-thing; (b) it's a hand. Therefore the audience accepts the existence of something spoken about before it accepts any thing else. How it formulates this first acceptance is another matter. It may formu-late it as 'Moore's waving something' or 'Moore's trying to get me to attend to something', but it must formulate some such existen-tial statement quite early in the game. If the audience said: 'Moore's mad. He's waving nothing at all!' it would hardly be interested in looking further to see whether Moore was right in saying that the thing he waved was a hand.

What I am trying to bring out is the fact that *some* existential premise is presupposed here even though we do not construe this premise as a conjunct of the "analysis" of 'Here's a human hand'. Therefore, if the first part of Moore's proof were to incorporate this premise, it would read: (a) Something's being waved by Moore; (b) whatever he's waving is a hand; therefore, (c) some-thing's a hand. In other words, the conclusion 'There is at least one human hand' can only be deduced from a set of premises of which at least one is existential. This is a very traditional thesis but a sound one. And so while the russellian attempt to show that *Moore's* premises comprise one asserting the existence of physical objects is not supported, a related comment is in order: namely, that Moore doesn't *prove* the existence of hands without his presupposing the existence of something that can be waved. And what can be waved but a physical object?

One can now see why such a "proof" of the existence of physi-cal objects as Moore's seems so unconvincing. Anyone who was skeptical enough about the existence of physical objects to seek a proof of that would probably be just as skeptical about the statement that Moore was waving something.

12. *The conclusion of this chapter and the last*

In the light of the last chapter and this, we venture to say that the age of meaning produced no very convincing deductive proofs of the existence of meanings or physical objects. Its failure to do so led a later generation to abandon such proofs and to ask whether the existential statements of philosophy might be fundamentally different from those of the sciences and everyday life. In the next chapter we shall examine the attempt to provide a special sense of 'exists' for such statements; in the one following that we shall examine the view that they are all analytic and the view that they are distinguished through asserting that the universe of discourse is not empty; in Chapter VI we shall consider the more revolutionary thesis that they are all meaningless.

CHAPTER IV

The Use of 'Exists'

1. *Three views on the use of 'exists'*

Up to now we have concentrated on arguments for the existence of universals and physical objects, arguments that emerge in the writings of the earlier figures in the history of the analytic movement. We have distilled two that parallel each other—one that allegedly proves the existence of at least one meaning by accepting as a premise some true statement containing the word 'understand' or the phrase 'know a priori', another that allegedly proves the existence of at least one physical object by accepting as a premise some statement like 'Here is a human hand'. In this chapter we shall look into the notion of existence involved in these "proofs". It may be helpful to begin by quoting two memorable passages in which Russell explains his view that a universal like the relation *north of* does not exist in the same sense in which the physical objects Edinburgh and London exist.

"If we ask 'Where and when does this relation exist?' the answer must be 'Nowhere and nowhen.' There is no place or time where we can find the relation 'north of.' It does not exist in Edinburgh any more than in London, for it relates the two and is neutral as between them. Nor can we say that it exists at any particular time. Now everything that can be apprehended by the senses or by introspection exists at some particular time. Hence the relation 'north of' is radically different from such things. It is neither in space nor in time, neither material nor mental; yet it is something."[1]

"We shall find it convenient only to speak of things *existing* when they are in time, that is to say, when we can point to some

[1] *Problems of Philosophy*, p. 98.

time *at* which they exist (not excluding the possibility of their existing at all times). Thus thoughts and feelings, minds and physical objects *exist*. But universals do not exist in this sense; we shall say that they *subsist* or *have being,* where 'being' is opposed to 'existence' as being timeless. The world of universals, therefore, may also be described as the world of being. The world of being is unchangeable, rigid, exact, delightful to the mathematician, the logician, the builder of metaphysical systems, and all who love perfection more than life. The world of existence is fleeting, vague, without sharp boundaries, without any clear plan or arrangement, but it contains all thoughts and feelings, all the data of sense, and all physical objects, everything that can do either good or harm, everything that makes any difference to the value of life and the world. According to our temperaments, we shall prefer the contemplation of the one or of the other. The one we do not prefer will probably seem to us a pale shadow of the one we prefer, and hardly worthy to be regarded as in any sense real. But the truth is that both have the same claim on our impartial attention, both are real, and both are important to the metaphysician. Indeed no sooner have we distinguished the two worlds than it becomes necessary to consider their relations."[2]

Russell's view in these passages lies between two positions that have been taken in the history of speculation about the word 'exists'. At one extreme there is a view that certainly may be attributed to John Stuart Mill, according to which the word 'exists' is univocal; I shall call this view 'univocalism'. At the other extreme is the view that the word 'exists' has more than two uses; indeed that it has as many distinct uses as there are categories; I shall call this 'multivocalism'. Russell seems willing to stop at two uses of 'exist' and so the most felicitous name for his view appears to be 'duovocalism'.

While for Russell in *The Problems of Philosophy* the grand break comes at the line between universals and nonuniversals, Gilbert Ryle, one of the most vocal and most recent exponents of multivocalism, appears willing to say that both within the class of Russell's universals and Russell's nonuniversals there are breaks

[2] *Ibid.,* pp. 99–100.

that entail a shift in the meaning of 'exists'. Thus he says, for example: "It may be true that there exists a cathedral in Oxford, a three-engined bomber, and a square number between 9 and 25. But the naïve passage to the conclusion that there are three existents, a building, a brand of aircraft and a number soon leads to trouble. The senses of 'exists' in which the three subjects are said to exist are different and their logical behaviors are different."[3] Here numbers and brands, both of them species of universals on Russell's view and hence said by him to exist in the same sense, are said to exist in *different* senses by Ryle. And elsewhere Ryle says:

"It is perfectly proper to say, in one logical tone of voice, that there exist minds and to say, in another logical tone of voice, that there exist bodies. But these expressions do not indicate two different species of existence, for 'existence' is not a generic word like 'coloured' or 'sexed.' They indicate two different senses of 'exist,' somewhat as 'rising' has different senses in 'the tide is rising', 'hopes are rising', and 'the average age of death is rising'. A man would be thought to be making a poor joke who said that three things are now rising, namely the tide, hopes, and the average age of death. It would be just as good or bad a joke to say that there exist prime numbers and Wednesdays and public opinions and navies; or that there exist both minds and bodies."[4]

Here *minds* and *bodies* are said to exist in different senses, again contrary to the quoted passage from Russell in the *Problems of Philosophy*.

In a neglected part of his *System of Logic*,[5] Mill not only defends univocalism but also expresses a number of worries over it that have reappeared in more recent literature on this question. Mill is faced with (what he regards as) a terminological problem arising from the fact that he wants to divide the class of namable things into three categories: *feelings, substances,* and *attributes* ('feelings' is synonymous with 'states of mind' for Mill). His trouble lies in not being able to find a concrete term corresponding to the abstract term 'existence' which will be broad enough to embrace

[3] *Philosophical Arguments* (Oxford: Clarendon Press, 1945), pp. 15–16.
[4] *The Concept of Mind* (London: Hutchinson's University Library, 1949), p. 23.
[5] Bk. 1, ch. 3, "Of the Things denoted by Names," especially sec. 2, "Ambiguity of the most general names."

these three categories as subclasses of the grandest category of all. One difficulty is that obvious candidates among common nouns, like 'object' and 'thing', are usually understood as denoting only substances. Mill, therefore, wants a word like 'entity' (although he thinks it is also sullied), which will permit him to say that *whiteness,* for example, is an entity without implying that it is a substance. He is troubled by precisely the thing that troubles Carnap at one point in his *Meaning and Necessity.*[6] Both want to avoid what Carnap calls "hypostatization or substantialization or reification". Now what is this sin? Carnap, like Mill, thinks that it consists in saying that all entities are things or substances. It is *not* hypostatization from Carnap's point of view to say that attributes are *beings* or *entities,* but Mill carries his terminological anxiety even to the point of fear about using the predicate 'is a being' as the most general of all, because, he remarks, "if we were to say, extension, colour, wisdom, virtue, are beings, we should perhaps be suspected of thinking with some of the ancients, that the cardinal virtues are animals; . . . We should be supposed, in short, to believe that Attributes are Substances." And Russell, by making the word 'exists' an elliptical shorthand for 'exists in space and time', treats it, not as Mill uses the word 'exists' in the following passage, but rather as Mill uses the phrase 'is a thing': "When we have occasion for a name which shall be capable of denoting whatever exists . . . there is hardly a word applicable to the purpose which is not also, and even more familiarly, taken in a sense in which it denotes only substances. But substances are not all that exists; attributes, if such things are to be spoken of, must be said to exist; feelings certainly exist. Yet when we speak of an *object,* or of a *thing,* we are almost always supposed to mean a substance. There seems a kind of contradiction in using such an expression as that one *thing* is merely an attribute of another thing."[7]

2. *Duovocalism: the doctrine that 'exists' has two uses*

Russell's duovocalism in the *Problems* deserves special attention because, as might already be evident, it is compatible with the kind of univocalism advocated by Mill. The fact that Russell him-

---

[6] See *Meaning and Necessity*, pp. 22–23.
[7] Mill, *System of Logic*, p. 30. And yet "such *things* are to be spoken of" by Mill.

self says of being north of that "It is neither in space nor in time, neither material nor mental; *yet it is something* [my italics]" suggests that even Russell thinks there is a generic notion of which his *exists* and *subsists* are species, so to speak. It suggests that Russell might be obliged to accept a univocalistic view, were it understood that a univocalist merely maintains that, in the sentences 'The relation *north of* is something', 'Edinburgh is something', 'Russell's mind is something', the phrase 'is something' is used univocally. In adding that "we shall find it convenient only to speak of things existing when they are in time", Russell says nothing of great philosophical importance from the point of view of the univocalist. From that point of view, once we have gotten to see that the relation *north of* is something just as Edinburgh is, we *may*, if we wish, now say that the relation *north of* is so different from Edinburgh that we would do well to say that one *sub*sists while the other *ex*ists, even though they are both something in the same sense of 'are both something'. This would be a good deal like the sort of instruction that a parent might be forced to give to a child who had just come to realize what men and women have in common. After the child had discovered that men and women are both men from the point of view of their biological class, the parent might tell him that because males and females are so very different it is customary to use two different words—'men' and 'women'—for them. To dispel confusion, however, he would have to remind the child that it is, unfortunately, also customary to call *all* animals of the class *man* 'men' and therefore to use the word 'men' in a general and a special sense. Is this very different from what goes on when one decides to apply the word 'exists' only to things in space and time, even though one commonly applies it more generally? I don't think so; both situations are similar insofar as we are led to use 'exists', after the fashion of 'man', in a general and a special way. But why should the fact that one thing exists in space and time, while another does not, make it convenient for Russell to say that only the first exists and that only the second subsists? Reasons that are no more indicative of a profound philosophical point than those which impel us to call only males 'men' and only females 'women' in certain contexts; or those which impel us to call males handsome and females beautiful even though we think that there is some univocal predicate that can be applied to both of them; or those that impel us to use 'church' sometimes as meaning *place of worship* and sometimes as meaning *Christian place of worship*. The discussion reminds one of the sports writer who could invent similar distinctions (of little philosophical interest) in the case of the obviously logical word 'class', which is in this respect very much like 'exists': "We all know that lots of wolves together make a pack, lots of lions a pride, and then there is a gaggle of geese, a shoal of fish and a bevy of (what else?) beauties. Add these impertinent ones by Smith: 'A yammer of radio announcers . . . a gangle of basketball players . . . a grouse of ball players . . . a Braille of umpires . . . a doze of race stewards . . . a dawdle of baseball magnates . . . a venality of managers . . . a quiescence of fighters . . . a dissonance of commissioners . . . a scheme of jockeys . . . a prevarication of golfers . . . a vagrance of amateur tennis players . . . an indigence of writers (sports) . . . a congealing of editors."[8]

In concluding our discussion of Russell's view, we may repeat that the crucial statement in the passage quoted from him is the following: "It [the relation *north of*] is neither in space nor in time, neither material nor mental; yet it is something." From this statement one infers that being something is a genus of which being in space and time and being something not in space and time are species. We can therefore say that there is a correspondingly general expression, namely 'There is at least one', which we can put before the phrase 'physical object' and before the word 'universal'. In both of the resulting sentences, 'There is at least one physical object' and 'There is at least one universal', the phrase 'there is at least one' is used in the same sense, and this is reflected in the fact that we can use logical notation and symbolize these two sentences as follows: '$(\exists x)$ (x is a physical object)' and '$(\exists x)$ (x is a universal)'. Now, if Russell was prepared in the *Problems of Philosophy* to symbolize the two sentences as indicated, then he should have granted that the symbol '$(\exists x)$', read in English as 'there is an x such that', is used in the same way in both cases. The alternative view, according to which it means one thing in one context and another in the other, is as doubtful and pointless as the view that

<hr/>

[8] "Books of the Times," *New York Times,* July 10, 1954.

the copula 'is a', as it appears in both contexts before the predicates 'universal' and 'physical object', is used in two different senses.

3. *Forestalling a possible misunderstanding*

A few remarks should be added in order to forestall a misunderstanding. If we hold that physical objects exist in space and time, we can certainly form an expression like 'exists in space and time' which will not replace the unqualified expression 'exists'. And if Russell could make some sense of the phrase 'out of space and time', he might form a third expression like 'exists out of space and time'. This is not denied. We would then have three terms: 'exists', 'exists in space and time', and 'exists out of space and time', no one of which could be replaced by any other in the trio. I suggest, in fact, that using the term 'exists' quite generally is tantamount to using Russell's 'is something', using the second tantamount to using 'exists' narrowly, and the third term could replace Russell's 'subsists'. I also suggest that the parallel in the case of 'man' is this: The biologist's use of 'man' as a generic term (which I will write in capitals from now on when it is used generically) is analogous to my completely general word 'exists' and Russell's 'is something'; the ordinary use of 'man' as meaning *male* is analogous to the use of 'exists in space and time' and Russell's special use of 'exists'; and finally the use of 'woman' is analogous to the use of 'exists out of space and time' and Russell's 'subsists'. For purposes of easy reference I will write these down in three adjoining columns, using Russell's phrase 'space and time' rather than what might best be read 'space-time' in the light of contemporary physics.

List I	List II (Russell's)	List III
(1) exists	(1′) is something	(1′′) MAN
(2) exists in space and time	(2′) exists	(2′′) man
(3) exists out of space and time	(3′) subsists	(3′′) woman

Now I suggest that the word 'exists' in List I is a term that Mill might have been contented with, instead of looking for common nouns like 'object', 'thing', 'entity', though I sympathize with his motives for avoiding them. (Maybe 'existent' is the common noun he sought.) In each column above, no term is replaceable by any other, but in each column the notion expressed by the first term is generic in the sense that it appears as a component of, or of some expansion of, the second and third. I also suggest that List II is less illuminating than List I for someone who thinks that whatever exists or subsists (in the List II sense) *is something*. For similar reasons, List III is less illuminating than List IV below.

List IV

$1'''$: MAN
$2'''$: male MAN
$3'''$: female MAN

4. *An alternative approach to some uses of 'exists'*

After all of this, however, it should be observed that we are not forced to say that the word 'exists' or the phrases 'there are', 'there exists', and others like them, are *always* used in ordinary life in a way that is profitably or clearly rendered from a philosophical point of view by straightforward translation into modern logical symbolism. The latter is likely to clarify only one of the many ways in which these words and phrases are used in ordinary language. It is quite satisfactory for straightforward paraphrase of 'There is at least one red thing', 'There is at least one horse', or 'There is at least one chair in that room'. Such illustrations seem to raise no profound philosophical puzzles when they are rendered with the help of logical symbolism as indicated. But the matter is somewhat different when we come to sentences like 'There is a difference in age between John and Tom' or 'There is a possibility that James will come'. Here, of course, we can, *if we wish*, translate these sentences respectively into '$(\exists x)$ (x is an age-difference and x is between John and Tom)', and '$(\exists x)$ (x is identical with the possibility that James will come)'. But if we do choose to translate them in this way, we will not clarify them. On the contrary, we will be saddled with the conclusion that there are in the universe different sorts of entities like red objects, prime numbers, age-differences, and possibilities. Such a conclusion is unwelcome to some philosophers, either because they think they understand it and think it false, or because they think it nonsensical. Thinking that such a conclusion is unwelcome—for whatever reason—they are inclined to say—and rightly—that if you want to translate the original sentences of ordinary language into statements which are clear and acceptable, it won't do to take the obvious way out, so to speak: it won't do to use the more or less obvious pattern of translation illustrated by translating 'There is at least one red thing' in the manner indicated above.

A similar feeling may be voiced, as Russell does, by saying that 'there is' in 'There is a possibility that James will come' is not used in the same sense as 'there is' in 'There is a red thing', but this is a very dangerous way of speaking, given the philosophical motives in question. For in spite of protestations to the contrary, it gives the impression that it is quite all right to translate 'There is a possibility that James will come' into '($\exists x$) (x is identical with the possibility that James will come)', provided only that you recognize that the phrase '($\exists x$)' means something different from what it means in '($\exists x$) (x is red)'. One might just as well introduce a new existential quantifier. And yet if the philosopher who operates in this way is asked just how this difference of meaning between these two quantifiers is registered, he cannot answer clearly.

How, then, can we clarify these puzzling sentences and yet avoid the unwelcome conclusion that there are possibilities and age-differences in our universe, without adopting something like Russell's device of saying that possibilities and age-differences exist in one sense and human beings in another? Before answering, let us consider our examples.

In the case of 'There is a difference in age between John and Tom', we might begin by saying that we understand the relational predicate 'is as old as' and that we test statements of the form 'x is as old as y' without having to see that x has some queer thing called an age, that y has one, and that these ages are identical. In that event, the belief of the ordinary man that there is a difference in age between John and Tom would be rendered in language that is not misleading by saying instead, simply, 'It is not the case that John is as old as Tom'. We might offer an analogous translation of 'There is a possibility that James will come' in which we replace it by some statement about the statement 'James will come', for example by the statement that this statement is not certainly false. But having clarified the original puzzling statement in this way, it is misleading to sum up our attitude toward the situation by saying that 'there is' is used in one sense in the case of 'There is a man' and in another in the case of 'There is a difference in age between John and Tom'. For what we have done is to show that we *need not assert the existence* of age-differences or the existence of possibilities in communicating what we want to communicate. Now I do not deny that some philosophers are eager to translate these puzzling statements into a notation which parallels that of '$(\exists x)$ (x is a man)', because they really believe that possibilities and age-differences exist along with men. Such philosophers are not being addressed at this point. Here I appeal to those philosophers who, in my opinion, want to say the right thing, but who say it in a way that is not calculated to avoid confusion. Their point of view must be distinguished from that of Russell in the *Problems of Philosophy* in spite of the fact that he too speaks of the different senses of 'exists'. Russell did *not* treat the statement 'There are universals' in a manner analogous to that in which we have just treated 'There is a difference in age between John and Tom' and 'There is a possibility that James will come'. In effect, Russell adopted the translation of 'There are universals' into '$(\exists x)$ (x is a universal)' (though he doesn't say so in so many words), and he also adopted a similar translation of 'There are physical objects'. He made no effort to elucidate the former in any way analogous to that in which we have tried to elucidate our examples. On the contrary, he wanted *to prove* that universals exist, but then, recognizing their queerness, was driven to saying that they exist in another sense. The result is a deliberate effort to distinguish two expressions of the form 'there exist', having all of their so-called logical properties in common and yet differing in sense. But, as we have seen, even that effort was undercut by Russell's tendency to use the phrase 'is something' univocally.

5. *The multivocalism of Ryle*

Having distinguished two kinds of philosophers who *say* that there are different senses of the word 'exists', I now wish to turn to the views of Gilbert Ryle on this difficult subject because he too talks of 'exists' as having different senses. I should like to say in advance that while certain substantive philosophical views expressed in Ryle's *Concept of Mind* resemble the clarifications offered in the earlier handling of 'There is a difference in age between John and Tom' and 'There is a possibility that James will come', Ryle's own formulation of his philosophical procedure sometimes suggests that his own multivocalism is merely a generalization of Russell's duovocalism.

The passages which give strongest support to this second interpretation of Ryle are those I have already quoted from his *Philosophical Arguments* and his *Concept of Mind*. There we have an explicit statement that 'exist' has different senses, indeed many more senses than Russell assigned to it. In these passages one gets the impression that Ryle thinks that there are many different "categories" and that we assert the non-emptiness of those categories in as many different senses of 'exist' as there are categories. Moreover, Ryle seems to avoid anything like Russell's general notion of *being something* and seems, therefore, to have conducted a more consistent and thoroughgoing attack on univocalism. When we say 'There exist minds' and when we say 'There exist bodies', according to Ryle, we use two different senses of 'exist', "somewhat as 'rising' has different senses in 'the tide is rising', 'hopes are rising', and 'the average age of death is rising' ", and he adds that uttering the conjunctive statement 'There exist bodies and there exist minds' is about as funny as saying 'Three things are now rising, namely the tide, hopes, and the average age of death'.

The following discussion of Ryle's views is divided into two parts. I wish to show in this section that some things he says suggest that he merely espouses a generalization of Russell's duovocalism—and these things I will criticize adversely. Then I will try to show in the next section how Ryle's general view might be defended by treating the statement 'There are minds' in a manner analogous to that in which we treated 'There is a difference in age between John and Tom' and similar examples. Indeed, I think that this may be the main direction of Ryle's work.

In considering Ryle's view it is useful to begin with a distinction drawn by Quine between two kinds of existential statements.[9]

9 "Designation and Existence," *Journal of Philosophy*, vol. 36 (1939); reprinted in Feigl and Sellars, *Readings in Philosophical Analysis*. See pp. 44–45 of the latter.

On the one hand there are *singular* existence statements of the form
'There is such a thing as so-and-so', and on the other *general* existence statements of the form 'There are so-and-so's'. The idea of a
singular existential statement is illustrated by

>   (a) There is such a thing as Edinburgh

and by

>   (b) There is such a thing as being north of.

The general existential statement is illustrated by

>   (c) There are cities in Scotland

and by

>   (d) There are relations.

Now statement (a) is not profound but it is clear and true. I
shouldn't imagine that anyone would protest or be alarmed at
hearing someone utter it. But (b) is just the sort of thing that a
philosopher (like Russell) was moved to *argue* for; moreover it is an
example of the sort of thing that philosophers say and defend
while trainmen don't. And yet a trainman might easily say in answer to the question 'Is there such a place as Edinburgh?' that
there is, and only a bit of straightforward questioning on the part
of a philosopher might lead that trainman to say that if there is
such a *place* as Edinburgh, then there is such a *thing* as Edinburgh.
There is a parallel difference between (c) and (d). In other words,
(c) is to (d) as (a) is to (b) in this respect. Statements (a) and (c)
are ordinary or semi-ordinary, while (b) and (d) are philosophical
jargon.

While (b) 'There is such a thing as being north of' is, like (d)
'There are relations', more "philosophical" than examples (a) and
(c), (d) is the more "philosophical" of the pair (b) and (d). This
may be more evident if we compare the parallel examples of 'There
is such a thing as manhood' and 'There are attributes'. The second
of this last pair is much more likely to cause puzzlement than is the
first. I leave aside the reasons for this, since, as a matter of fact, I
suspect that most ordinary people who do accept 'There is such a
thing as manhood' accept it because they think it means neither

more nor less than 'There are men'. But it doesn't for platonists, since the very reasons that lead them to assert the existence of whiteness and *north of* should lead them to assert the existence of unicornhood even though there are no unicorns. The point is that they say manhood exists, it will be recalled, merely because they understand the term 'man', so that the mere fact that they understand the term 'unicorn' *should* lead them to assert the existence of unicornhood.

If we make this distinction between singular existence statements and general existence statements, it is possible to discuss the issues at stake between Mill's univocalism and an extension of Russell's duovocalism by concentrating on either kind of statement. For (a) 'There is such a thing as Edinburgh' and (b) 'There is such a thing as *north of*' (the two singular existence statements) and (c) 'There are cities in Scotland' and (d) 'There are relations' (the two general existence statements) can be translated into logical jargon as the following respectively:

(a′) (∃x) (x is identical with Edinburgh.)

(b′) (∃x) (x is identical with being north of.)

(c′) (∃x) (x is a city in Scotland.)

(d′) (∃x) (x is a relation.)

Now, as I see it, one issue between univocalism and multivocalism (or duovocalism) can be stated in either of the following two ways:

(1) Is the symbol '(∃x)' as it occurs in (a′) used as it is used in (b′)?

(2) Is the symbol '(∃x)' as it occurs in (c′) used as it is used in (d′)?

In answer, I should say that *all* occurrences of it are used in the same way. Nevertheless, I recognize that someone who immediately translated 'There is such a thing as *manhood*' by '(∃x) (x is a man)' or who, in the same spirit, translated (b) 'There is such a thing as being north of', not by (b′) above, but by (b′ ′) '(∃x) (∃y) (x is north of y)', would be *tempted* to say that the phrase 'there is such a thing as' in (b) is used in a different sense from the same phrase in (a). Why? Simply because *the pattern* of translation advocated would be different. Statement (a)'s translation into (a′) follows the pattern of taking the singular name of a concrete object and prefacing '(∃x) (x is identical with' to it. But clearly the philosopher who translated (b) by putting in its place not (b′) but (b′′) would follow an entirely different pattern. It is this difference of *pattern* of translation, then, that causes some philosophers to say that the original phrase 'there is such a thing as' means something different in context (b) from what it means in (a). I should say at once that there are no insuperable objections to speaking in this way, provided we understand each other. Nevertheless, we must be perfectly clear about the difference between a strict duovocalism like Russell's, in which 'There is such a thing as being north of' is *not* rendered by 'Some things are north of others', and one in which it is. Were we prepared to take certain risks, we might say that Russell "really" says that 'there are' is used in different senses, while the hypothetical philosopher last considered does not. I suspect that Ryle is more like this hypothetical philosopher than he is like Russell, no matter how much like Russell Ryle may sound. For the moment, however, I shall concentrate on those statements by Ryle which are dangerously like Russell's.

There is another point that might be made by reference to the distinction between singular and general statements of existence. It arises from something that Ryle says in a passage previously quoted. He says that we must assert the existence of minds and bodies in "different logical tones of voice" because the conjunction of 'There are minds and there are bodies' sounds absurd and punnish, like 'She came home in a flood of tears and a sedan chair' and 'Three things are now rising, namely the tide, hopes, and the average age of death'. This suggests that what Ryle might be worried about are conjunctions not of *singular* but rather of *general* existence statements, which contain "category-words" like 'minds', 'bodies', 'universals', etc., as their predicates. (When I say that a general existence statement contains something as its predicate, I mean merely that it is like 'There are cities in Scotland' in containing the expression 'cities in Scotland' as its predicate.)

Now it may very well be that Ryle's dismay over 'There are

minds and there are bodies' is stimulated not by the fact that it is
a conjunction of *existential* statements but by the fact that it is a
conjunction of two *general* existential statements. This would be
confirmed if hearing Russell conjoin two singular existential statements like 'There is such a thing as Edinburgh' ['Edinburgh is
something'] and 'There is such a thing as being north of' ['Being
north of is something'] did not cause us to suppose he was telling
jokes, as, of course, it doesn't. So even if 'There are physical objects
and there are meanings' were to leave us in stitches, still, if 'There
is such a thing as Edinburgh and there is such a thing as being
north of' didn't, we might conclude that the source of mirth was
not in the double occurrence of 'there are' but rather in the expressions 'physical object' and 'meaning'. However, once the conjunction 'There are minds and there are bodies' is thought to be
funny because of combining a reference to such differently described things, then, of course, we can point out that even *within
one category* there will be pairs of species which are such that
the conjunctive assertion of the fact that they both contain members would raise a titter. For example, if one were to say after read-
ing Lewis Carroll, "Yes, there are cabbages and there are kings
and there are bits of sealing wax," one might be thought to be
mildly funny, but that would not justify our thinking that 'there
are' was being used in three different senses. The point is that
sometimes the humor (or attempt at it) comes from punning on
a word like 'rising' or 'in' and sometimes from the discrepancy of
the subject matter involved, as in the case of 'exists'.

    So far I have argued that if minds and bodies *are* very different
sorts of things and if physical objects and meanings are, it would
not follow that the strangeness or comic quality of a conjunction of
general existential statements containing these categorial predicates would prove that 'there exists' was being used in different
senses in one sentence. On the contrary, the very phrase 'different
sorts of things' suggests that they are species of the genus *thing*,
just as cabbages and kings are. And, moreover, when Ryle speaks
of "categories" he gives the impression that there are different
pigeonholes in the desk that makes up everything. Why, then, *must*
someone who says, 'There is something in category *A*' use 'there is'
in a sense different from that in which he uses it when he says,
'There is something in category *B*'?

One principle which Ryle seems to use when he says that 'there are' has two meanings in the context 'There are minds and there are bodies' appears to be this: No expression that can be combined with one categorial predicate like 'body' to form a true statement is synonymous with the same expression combined in the same way with another categorial predicate like 'mind'. Thus Ryle says that 'I bought a left-hand glove and I bought a right-hand glove and I bought a pair of gloves' illustrates this situation because gloves and pairs are in different categories. According to Ryle's view, the last occurrence of 'I bought' must differ in sense from the first two because pairs are bought in a sense different from that in which single gloves are bought. And similarly, I suppose, with 'There are right-hand gloves and there are left-hand gloves and there are pairs of gloves'. Similarly with 'There are bodies and there are minds' and with 'There are bodies and there are universals'. But, of course, Ryle must say that the situation is different with 'There are kings and there are cabbages and there are bits of sealing wax'. This last involves no multivocality of 'there are', so that the question naturally arises: What distinguishes the last case from the others?

And furthermore, which is the fundamental notion? Is it the nonsynonymy of the different occurrences of 'there are' or is it the categorial difference of 'mind' and 'body'? Are the predicates 'body' and 'mind' seen to be different categorial predicates on the basis of our seeing the multivocality of 'there is a' as prefixed to both of them, or do we come to see that 'there is a' is multivocal as prefixed to each of them because we know that they each represent a distinct category? I confess that I can *see* neither directly. I know that cabbages are not kings and, conversely, I know that universals are not physical objects; but I don't see that the first is a noncategorial mutual exclusion while the second is a case of two categories excluding each other. For this reason I can't use this as a basis for concluding that while 'There are cabbages and there are kings' involves no pun, 'There are minds and there are bodies' does.

Now I don't deny that there are some things that one can say truly about universals that one can't say truly about physical objects, for I think the statement 'Johnson kicked a physical object' is true, while 'Johnson kicked a meaning' is not. But if a man were to say 'Johnson kicked a physical object and Johnson kicked a meaning', and for some strange reason insisted on regarding the conjunction as true, he might add that 'Johnson kicked' meant something different the second time it occurred in the conjunction from what it meant the first time, because, as he might say, "Of course, we don't kick meanings in the sense in which we kick physical objects". I think that the contrast between a cartesian who uses the devices of modern logic and Ryle (in one of his moods) may now be stated fairly clearly. The simple-minded logistic cartesian who is also a logistic platonist would say that minds, physical objects, and universals, all exist in the same sense—even though they are very different sorts of things. Mill is a case in point. He would therefore leave himself open to the attack of another philosopher, who might then flatly deny or query the meaningfulness of the statement that universals exist as well as the statement that minds exist. But Ryle, who is certainly not a cartesian but who sometimes seems bent on so construing 'There are minds' in such a way as to allow it to be true, thinks he is forced to say that 'there are' is here used in a sense which is different from that in which it is used in 'There are bodies'. And sometimes, as I have said, this leads to language which is dangerously like Russell's in the *Problems of Philosophy*.

In concluding this discussion of one interpretation of Ryle's multivocalism—his tendency to speak without qualification about 'exists' as having different senses—I should like to reiterate my own positive view on this point. Once a philosopher decides to assert the existence of minds or meanings without providing further clarification or translation of his assertion, or worse, once he goes so far as to adopt anything like the quantifier of modern logic in formulating his existential statements, he will find it difficult to speak of the different senses of 'exist' without confusing the issue. Indeed he may even find himself defeating his own ends. For consider the following statement: 'There are exactly two places at which the phrase 'there are' occurs in the sentence 'There are minds and there are bodies', *and* there are exactly two meanings of 'there are' expressed in that sentence'. This is one (admittedly dangerous) way of expressing Ryle's fundamental thesis. But does he suppose that in saying this we are making a pun on 'There are exactly two' because in one case we count physical ink marks

(Category A) and in the other meanings (Category B)? I should think not, because the very thesis to the effect that 'there are' is ambiguous implies that two distinct ink marks have two distinct meanings in the *same* sense of 'two'. Here, by Ryle's own standards, the two occurrences of the phrase 'two distinct' have two distinct meanings in turn, thereby making it impossible for him to say that the number of occurrences of 'there are' is two in the same sense as the number of meanings of 'there are' is two.

And finally, it should be repeated that a duovocalist like Russell in the *Problems* is bent on *proving* the existence of universals to ordinary men who believe in the existence of physical objects but not in universals. Is it not strange, then, that Russell should say to the ordinary man that he is proving the existence of universals in another sense of 'exists'? Think how unpersuasive it would be to argue as follows: "You think that only articles of clothing are capes, but you are wrong. Some bodies of land are too, only in a different sense of 'cape'." If a philosopher is going to be clever and prove that there are more things than an ordinary man thinks there are, he should not change the meaning of 'there are' in the middle of the argument. Something similar is clearly relevant in theology.

6. *How Ryle might dispense with multivocalism*

Very often in the *Concept of Mind* Ryle suggests that the puzzling sentence 'There are bodies and there are minds' might be profitably replaced by what I shall write as 'There are bodies and there are bodies that behave mentally'. I am not so much interested now in the truth or philosophical usefulness of Ryle's thesis when formulated in this (oversimplified) way as in its implication for his approach to the notion of existence. And therefore I will not pause to discuss the difficult expression 'behave mentally', which is telescopic in the extreme. What I wish to point out is that this translation or replacement of a puzzling statement by another one which is presumed to be less puzzling should not lead us to say that 'there are' in 'There are minds' has a different sense from the same expression in 'There are bodies'. For the effect of this translation resembles the effect of our suggested translations of 'There is a difference in age between John and Tom', 'There is a possibility that James will come', and 'There is such a thing as manhood' (where the last is translated, symbolically, into '($\exists x$) (x is a man)'). And what is the general effect of these translations of existential statements of ordinary language? From our present point of view they all *free us from the need to assert the existence* of things like age-differences, possibilities, and attributes, insofar as they allow us to say what some of us want to say, without ever having to admit *their* existence in the way that we cheerfully admit the existence of men. Moreover, we are saved from having to say that the phrase 'exists' applies to some "entities" in one sense and to others in another "sense". And because it seems to me that Ryle's philosophy of mind needs no such appeal to different senses, I see no reason for his concluding that 'there exist' when it precedes 'minds' means something different from what it means when it precedes 'bodies'—unless that is merely understood as a way of saying that, while it's all right to translate 'There are bodies' into '($\exists x$) (x is a body)' and to stop there, it's not only not all right to do something analogous with 'There are minds', but you've got to translate it according to some other pattern.

Here we are reminded of the non-platonic rendering of 'There is such a thing as manhood' discussed earlier. A non-platonist might refuse to render it '($\exists x$) (x is identical with manhood)' and to stop there, though he might be quite willing in the case of 'There is such a thing as Edinburgh' to render it as '($\exists x$) (x is identical with Edinburgh)' and stop. He paraphrases the puzzling statement (whether correctly from a broader philosophical point of view doesn't interest us now) by using a different pattern of translation: he renders it as '($\exists x$) (x is a man)'. And this is something like what the Ryle-like translator of 'There are minds' does when he paraphrases it as 'There are bodies that behave mentally' and ultimately as '($\exists x$) (x is a body and x behaves mentally)'.

In passing we might observe certain differences within the class of clarifying translations just considered. In some cases, as in the translations of 'There are minds' and 'There is such a thing as *manhood*', we do not free ourselves from asserting existence altogether, for in the translation we continue to assert the existence of bodies of a certain kind and of men. But when we move from 'There is a difference in age between John and Tom' to 'It is not the case that John is as old as Tom', we move to a nonexistential statement altogether. This difference merely underscores the fact that philosophical clarification of statements which seem to commit us to the existence of things that don't exist, or which seem to imply existential statements we don't understand, can be accomplished by different patterns of translation. The temptation is to suppose that the original contexts *use* the word 'exists' differently if the pattern of translation is different, but I think this way of speaking should be resisted. The whole thing may be described in a clearer and less puzzling way.

7. Conclusion

It should not be concluded from this chapter that 'exists' or 'there are' *must* always be used in exactly the same way. That would be absurd. One conclusion is that the use of 'there are' which is symbolized by the existential quantifier of modern logic— '($\exists x$)'—is clear, and that with its help a large number of ordinary and scientific statements of existence may be formulated. But there are some existential statements in ordinary language which, when translated according to the simple pattern whereby we go from 'There are men' to '($\exists x$) (x is a man)', merely have their puzzling nature exposed. If they are so translated, therefore, it can only be to dramatize their peculiarity and to show that something further must be done. This can sometimes take the form of further translation which clarifies and removes puzzlement by removing the need to postulate obscure entities or nonentities.

Some very serious philosophical problems involving existence have not been mentioned in this chapter. They arise from a consideration of existential statements in ordinary language or science which cannot be paraphrased in a way that quiets our anxieties. The existential statements of arithmetic fall into this group. They explicitly assert the existence of numbers, they are naturally rendered by the use of the existential quantifier, and yet they are not easily translated into statements which do not assert the existence of puzzling things, or which assert the existence of nonpuzzling things. Here, it might be said, we must surely distinguish a new sense of 'exists', for one thing because we cannot contextually eliminate the existential quantifier, and for another because arithmetic is a priori true. We cannot deny that this raises a profound philosophical problem, but we must question the argument in favor of distinguishing a new sense of 'exists'. It amounts to saying that arithmetical statements like 'There are prime numbers between 5 and 50' are a priori true and therefore that the phrase 'there are' is used differently in arithmetical statements from the way in which it is used when we say 'There are mountains in Alaska', which is not a priori. Whatever merit there may be in the claim—and I admit none—this argument for it is fallacious. Frege provides its refutation implicitly when he says that the phrase 'is identical with' is used in the same way in the context 'The evening star is identical with the evening star' and in the context 'The evening star is identical with the morning star', even though the first is a priori true and the second not.[10] Furthermore, he does not conclude that a conjunction of his two statements is like 'She came home in a flood of tears and a sedan chair'. His example is instructive because the phrase 'there is', like 'is identical with', is a logical constant and can therefore appear in a statement of any epistemological status. Think how absurd it would be to conclude that the logical constant 'or' is used differently in the law of excluded middle from the way in which it is used in 'She fell or she was pushed', just because one is "a priori" and the other not. 'There are' is in the same boat as 'or'.

In the next chapter we shall consider an unsuccessful attempt to deal with so-called philosophical statements of existence in a way that resembles this approach to the existential statements of mathematics.

[10] "On Sense and Nominatum" in Feigl and Sellars.

CHAPTER V

Categories and Postulates

1. *Are the existential statements of philosophers "analytic"?*

In arguing against what was called multivocalism, I argued against a sweeping way of separating philosophy and other disciplines, for I maintained that some who assert the existence of meanings, minds, physical objects, numbers, ghosts in machines, or ghosts out of machines *may* all be interpreted as using the phrases 'there are', 'there is', 'there exists', 'there exist' in the same way. In this chapter I want to begin by considering the view that existential statements of philosophers (*qua* philosophers) are distinguished by being analytic, that is to say, the view according to which typically philosophical existential statements—like 'There are meanings', 'There are minds', 'There are physical objects', 'There are numbers', 'There are ghosts in machines', 'There are ghosts out of machines', etc.—are analytic. Since the predicates in these existential statements are usually construed by those who maintain such a position as "category-words", we are in effect denying one alleged difference between so-called category-words and others. In this way we are continuing the argument begun in the last chapter, since our criticism of multivocalism is also directed against the view that we may single out the existential statements of philosophy or metaphysics or ontology as a class and say that they are all justified or rejected in a special way. This does not involve us in a grand and noble defense of *all* metaphysical statements, for one thing because metaphysicians contradict each other, but it does commit us to a rejection of several sweeping (and often pejorative) characterizations of metaphysics and ontology.

After considering this view of philosophical existential statements, I shall turn to another which is closely related to it but nevertheless different, the view that these statements assert that there are members in a theory's universe of discourse, while non-philosophical existential statements are narrower in their reference.

It is of some historical interest to point out that my criticism of Ryle's multivocalism in the last chapter was directed at more descriptively oriented philosophers in the analytic tradition, at philosophers who hold that we can detect the multivocality of 'there is' by examining its use in ordinary language. In this chapter, however, I shift my attention to philosophers like Carnap, who use the machinery of modern logic in the course of their "rational reconstruction" of ordinary and scientific language. I think mainly of them as the philosophers who regard a statement like 'There are numbers' as peculiarly philosophical by comparison with 'There are prime numbers between 5 and 50', for example, and who therefore maintain some intrinsic epistemological difference between the existential statements of philosophers and those made by ordinary men and scientists. This said, however, it should be acknowledged that philosophers more wedded than Carnap is to ordinary language have said something similar about the differences between philosophy and science, and conversely that logicians (like Russell in a later phase) aiming at reconstruction have often defended multivocalism. The choice of who should be taken as the representative of what inadequate view, is dictated by a belief that the philosophers of ordinary language have offered more interesting defenses of multivocalism, while the reconstruction-minded logicians have been more fruitfully wrong in trying to distinguish philosophy and science by the methods to be considered in this chapter.

My own aim in all of these matters, as will be evident, is not to repudiate the linguistic or epistemological data, so to speak, for whose explanation or clarification multivocalists have invented their many meanings of 'exists'. My aim is to show that these many meanings are either unnecessary or more obscure than the data they are supposed to clarify. This is one of the most important themes of this book, as it runs through my criticism of platonism and multivocalism. The two doctrines to be considered in this chapter will be criticized on related grounds. Here the utility of the ideas of analyticity and category will be examined.

2. *Some elementary logical notions*

In an earlier chapter we introduced some of the devices of modern logic, especially Russell's theory of descriptions, in treating some of the problems concerning existence. The limited degree to which logical terminology was used then was in part a reflection of the limited degree to which it was used in discussions of ontology in the period of the early Russell and Moore. But more recent issues surrounding this question, notably those growing out of positivistic reflections, are conveyed most effectively by using some devices of mathematical logic. Theoretically, all that is involved might be communicated without these devices (for how else do we get to understand them except by translating into language that we already understand?), but the gain in clarity and economical expression *after* the mountain has been climbed is worth the climb. Those who have done this once need not read this section.

The most conspicuous feature of logical paraphrase is the fact that the final result in some cases is an expression made up of what are called variables, logical constants, and nonlogical constants. Thus the traditional 'Some men are mortal' becomes 'There is an x such that x is a man and x is mortal'; and in the latter expression 'there is' (sometimes symbolized as '∃' as we saw in the last chapter) and 'and' are logical constants, 'x' is a variable, and the expressions 'man' and 'mortal' are nonlogical constants. The English sentence which is closest to this formula in logical notation is 'There is at least one thing which is both a man and mortal', and if this is borne in mind, the strangeness of the expression 'there is an x such that x is' may be diminished for readers not familiar with mathematical usage.

As a result of writing the sentence in this way it becomes possible to distinguish two of its main parts conveniently: the part that merely reads 'x is a man and x is mortal', which is an expression that is sometimes called a *sentential function,* sometimes a *propositional function,* sometimes a *statement matrix,* sometimes a *statement-form,* sometimes an *open sentence;* and the part that reads 'there is an x such that', which is sometimes called the *existential operator* and more often these days the *existential quantifier.* A sentential function is distinguished by the fact that we cannot say that it is true, but neither can we say that it is false. The point is that since the 'x' functions as a blank, a person who utters 'x is a man and x is a mortal' is not referring to anything, so that we are not in a position to say whether he speaks truly or falsely. And yet this sentential function is *close* to a sentence in that one of two things may be done to it which swiftly makes it a sentence: either we may replace the variable 'x' wherever it occurs by a name of something, e.g., 'Socrates'—in which case we get the sentence 'Socrates is a man and Socrates is mortal'—or we may prefix the quantifier 'there is an x such that' and get a sentence that expresses in logical notation what is also expressed by 'There is something which is a man and mortal' and 'Some men are mortal'. We might also have prefixed what is called a universal quantifier, the expression 'for every x' (sometimes symbolized '(x)'), and thereby have constructed the sentence: 'For every x, x is a man and x is mortal', which in more ordinary language would read 'Everything is a man and mortal', a false sentence but just for that reason a comprehensible one. It should be added that when a sentential function like 'x is a man and x is mortal' appears in a sentence like 'There is an x such that x is a man and x is mortal', the occurrences of 'x' in that sentential function are said to be *bound* in it, whereas in the unquantified sentential function itself the 'x' is said to be *free*. We needn't concern ourselves with a general definition of freedom and bondage here, since they are available in all good logic texts.

Most recent texts on mathematical logic distinguish several parts of the subject. One part is concerned with laws of logic which permit us to infer 'Something is a man' from 'Some men are mortal', and such laws are parts of what is called the theory of quantification because they are laws governing the notion of existential quantification. It is plain that, in order to determine whether the conditional statement (a), 'If there is an x such that x is a man and x is mortal, then there is an x such that x is a man', is true, and therefore the basis of a valid deductive inference of its 'then'-clause from its 'if'-clause, we must reckon with the peculiarities of the quantifier 'there is an x such that'. This is necessary because another conditional sentence, differing from this one only in that it contains 'there is *no* x such that' rather than 'there *is* an x such that', would not be true. That is to say, from the statement that there is nothing that is both a man and mortal, it *doesn't* follow that there is nothing which is a man; while from the statement that something is a man and mortal, it does follow that something is a man.

It should be evident that the words 'man' and 'mortal', unlike the quantifier 'there is an *x* such that' and 'and', do not occur *essentially*[1] in sentence (a) because, from the point of view of the logician, any other pair of predicates put in their place would also yield a *true* conditional sentence. For this reason some logicians when they write down the *laws* of the theory of quantification are given to writing down sentences more *general* than (a) in order to indicate explicitly that they can formulate principles governing not only one inference involving 'man' and 'mortal' but *every* inference of a certain form. The first step in the direction of formulating this principle is to remove the words 'man' and 'mortal' from (a) and to replace them by variables drawn from another segment of the alphabet, e.g., '*P*', '*Q*', etc. This will result in a *sentential function* like 'If there is an *x* such that *x* is *P* and *x* is *Q*, then there is an *x* such that *x* is *P*'. And now to this some logicians prefix the pair of universal quantifiers 'for every *P* and for every *Q*', to get a sentence which is a law of logic:

(A) For every *P* and *Q*, if there is an *x* such that *x* is *P* and *Q*, then there is an *x* such that *x* is *P*.

3. *Quine and ontology*

Now we come close to the problem of ontology as it arises for contemporary logicians, since some, like Quine, have asked: What sorts of things are these *P*'s and *Q*'s and these *x*'s? And once it is said that these are properties or classes in the case of the *P*'s and *Q*'s (we have seen from our discussion of Russell on universals that 'classes' would be a better answer), and that these are physical objects in the case of the *x*'s, Quine says that this theory (or the person who accepts it) is *committed* to classes or properties and to physical objects. Thus he says: "In general, *an entity is assumed by a theory if and only if it must be counted among the values of the variables*

---

[1] For a detailed discussion of the idea of essential occurrence, see Quine, "Truth by Convention," *Philosophical Essays for A. N. Whitehead* (New York, 1936), pp. 90–124; reprinted in Feigl and Sellars.

in order that the statements affirmed in the theory be true [his italics]."[2] And elsewhere:

"There is certainly commitment to entities through discourse; for we are quite capable of saying in so many words that *there are* black swans, that *there is* a mountain more than 9,000 meters high, and that *there are* prime numbers above a hundred. Saying these things, we also say by implication that there are physical objects and abstract entities; for all the black swans are physical objects and all the prime numbers above a hundred are abstract entities."[3]

It should be realized that when one says that a person holding a theory is committed to the existence of abstract entities and physical objects, one is neither approving nor disapproving of his holding that theory. The question whether his speaking in such a way as to be committed to those entities is justified is a very different one from the question whether he *is* committed to them. It is a question of "what there really is" for Quine, as opposed to a question of what we *say* there is. In his more recent writings on the subject Quine has improved his formulation of this point, if only because his early, sloganized version of the thesis—"To be is to be the value of a variable"—wrongly suggests to some that we need only find out what are the values of the variables of our system in order to find out what *there really is*. That slogan might have been less misleadingly formulated as "To be presupposed by a given theory is to be the value of a variable in that theory", at the expense of not being a slogan comparable in brevity to Berkeley's "To be is to be perceived". The question whether there really are physical objects is settled, according to Quine, by an evaluation of a theory that is committed to an ontology of physical objects.

This approach, I suggest, is very close to that of Moore in an important respect. It will be recalled that Moore attempted to prove that there are physical objects by adducing as premises 'Here's a human hand' and 'Here's another', but in proving his conclusion he had to go by way of a lemma, so to speak, namely the statement 'There are human hands'. Now Quine's conception of

[2] *From A Logical Point of View* (Cambridge: Harvard University Press, 1953), p. 103.
[3] "On Carnap's Views on Ontology," *Philosophical Studies*, vol. 2 (1951), p. 67.

a defense of the existence of physical objects makes use of the connection between what may be called Moore's lemma and Moore's conclusion (but not that between Moore's premise and the lemma). For Quine implies that if you justify your acceptance of 'There are human hands', you will have justified your acceptance of 'There are physical objects' *on the assumption that all human hands are physical objects*. By contraposition, if you reject the view that physical objects exist you should withdraw the statement that there are human hands or disallow the statement (or the rule-counterpart of) 'All human hands are physical objects'. How you justify 'There are human hands' or 'All human hands are physical objects' is another matter.

4. *'Analytic' is not enough*

Now it is plain that on most views the statement 'There are human hands' would *not* be an analytic statement, so that if the justification of 'There are physical objects' had to be carried out via a justification of 'There are human hands', you would have to do more than examine meanings. Moreover, even if you did not have a lemma like 'There are human hands' through which you could move, and therefore had to establish 'There are physical objects' directly, so to speak, you could not say that *it* was true by virtue of the meaning of its terms. The point is that the predicate 'is a physical object' occupies no privileged position by virtue of the semantical status of the sentence 'There is an x such that x is a physical object'. This sentence is as synthetic as 'There is a human hand', and therefore the predicate 'is a physical object' is on a par with less general and noncategorial predicates like 'is a human hand'.

From this conclusion even positivists should not flinch, since it seems like a natural consequence of their desire to distinguish between analytic arithmetic and synthetic physics. In spite of my own distrust of the notion of analyticity, I see no reason for the most confirmed user of it to object to what I have said, provided he is willing to use the phrase 'physical objects'. I conclude, therefore, that even those who accept the distinction between analytic and synthetic as clear enough for philosophical purposes are forced to conclude that while some general existential statements containing "category-words" are analytic, others are synthetic. It follows that the distinction between analytic and synthetic is not sufficient for drawing the line between a statement like 'There are physical objects' and 'There are books', nor is it sufficient for making a sharp distinction between the method of establishing 'There are physical objects' and establishing 'There are minds', since both are synthetic. The net effect of this, in conjunction with our defense of the univocality of 'there exists' in the last chapter, is to question the most powerful arguments for the contrast between category-words and other predicates, or between some category-words and others. We are therefore rapidly on our way to denying that there is any intrinsic distinction between category-words and other predicates.

5. *The universe of discourse is not enough*

I now wish to consider another proposed distinction between so-called categorial predicates like 'number' on the one hand and predicates like 'cabbages' and 'kings' on the other. There are mathematical systems in which one finds statements like 'There is an n such that n is prime and n is greater than 100'. When they are constructed by a mathematician in an axiomatic way, the mathematician will often begin by announcing that the class of numbers is his universe of discourse, and for this reason some philosophers are inclined to think that this initial decision to take numbers as the universe of discourse somehow confers a peculiar epistemological status on the predicate 'number', one that distinguishes it from noncategorial predicates. It is sometimes suggested that this decision to "take" numbers as the universe of discourse reflects some special quality of the existential statement 'There are numbers' and that this distinguishes it from 'There are cabbages', because, I suppose, it is rare to build systems of cabbage-ology in which one announces gravely that one is taking cabbages as one's universe of discourse. What I should like to bring out, however, is that the decision to take numbers as the universe of discourse does not of itself reflect the analyticity of 'There are numbers', precisely because a cabbage-ologist might make a similar decision without *thereby* making 'There are cabbages' true by virtue of the meaning of its terms. Stated generally, the decision to quantify over a certain class of entities C does not of itself confer analyticity on the sentence 'There are C's'. This may be brought out more clearly by certain logical considerations.

If we avail ourselves of a logic like Quine's in *Mathematical Logic,* which is in the Zermelo tradition, we need not use the kind associated with the theory of types.[4] That is to say, we don't feel obliged to mark off typographically different kinds of variables, as the author of a mathematical text would if he were to express the fact that there are prime numbers greater than 100. *He* might say 'There is an n such that n is a prime and n is greater than 100', in which case his variable 'n' would be very different from our 'x'. He might begin with a statement that his universe of discourse is the class of natural numbers and then use the variable 'n' rather than our 'x'. But a *philosopher* who is conscious of some of the ontological issues involved might very well wish to bring out the logic of the situation explicitly, and therefore wish to write, not '$(\exists n)$ (n is prime and n is greater than 100)', but rather '$(\exists x)$ (x is a number and x is prime and x is greater than 100)' in order to express the same theorem. One cannot imagine any serious objection to this procedure, except, of course, a total rejection of the kind of logic we use. But with this sort of dispute between logicians we are not for the moment concerned. It seems hard to believe that the kind of issue we have been considering is simply a matter of whether we choose a logic in the Zermelo tradition or one in the tradition of Whitehead and Russell; so we assume, therefore, that whatever issues might arise between these two logics are neutral with respect to the questions we are discussing. It is hard to believe that a logic with a theory of types is either "more natural" or philosophically superior. The theory of types is an *ad hoc* device introduced in order to avoid a paradox, but like so many *ad hoc* devices to which people are driven for reasons of convenience, it is sometimes construed as though it were divinely ordained. Furthermore, Quine has shown that even its acceptance is not enough to sustain the attitude maintained by those philosophers who wish to drive a wedge between predicates that they call categorial ("universal words" in the terminology of Carnap) and those that are not categorial. This is not to deny that there might be serious differ-

4 *Ibid.,* p. 70.

ences between predicates like 'is a number', 'is a cabbage', 'is Scotch', and 'is a physical object' if the latter were in our language, but they would have one similarity: they would all denote *sub*classes of the universal class in a logic like the one we have adopted. In keeping with our view that 'there exists' is univocal and generic, we have deliberately avoided any undemocratic distinctions as between predicates. Naturally, some are wider than others, but this is irrelevant; some noncategorial predicates are wider than other noncategorial predicates.

Once we have adopted this method of quantification, we are not *obliged* to ticket the so-called category of the entity we are concerned with, since that is not more "essential" to the entity than any other predicate that applies to it. For example, after writing down '($\exists x$) (x wrote *Waverley*)', we are not *obliged* to go back and cross this out and replace it by '($\exists x$) (x is a person and x wrote *Waverley*)', although we may if we wish. Indeed, this is true even if we use a logic containing the theory of types. If we want to say that at least one *person* wrote *Waverley*, we can say it in so many words by including the predicate 'is a person' in our vocabulary and then appropriately inserting it into an existential statement. But if we want to say neither more nor less than 'Something wrote *Waverley*', we may do that too. This is the sort of freedom we have, and it helps us understand a mistake into which proponents of the opposite approach are liable to fall.

Suppose a little axiom system is couched in language that Russell uses in illustrating his theory of descriptions: (1) At least one *person* wrote *Waverley*; (2) at most one *person* wrote *Waverley*; and (3) *whoever* wrote *Waverley* was Scotch. This formulation might stem from our conviction that only a person could have written *Waverley*, a conviction to which we might give voice by making up a new kind of variable 'p' for persons. While *we* realize, of course, that wherever we now write '($\exists p$) (p is a person)' we might just as well have written '($\exists x$) (x is a person)', and therefore would never call the former sentence analytic, we can well imagine a philosopher fallaciously arguing that because '($\exists p$)' is synonymous with 'there is a person such that', it follows that '($\exists p$) (p is a person)' *is* analytic. Once again it is our task to show that such a statement would be absurd even if the notion of analyticity were unexceptionable.

What is at the root of this puzzle? I think it becomes obvious as soon as we examine a sentence like '($\exists p$) (p is a person)' in terms of a more general method of writing quantifiers, and this is best done by first translating it into English. It would then read 'There is a person who is a person', and if we translate this into the more general notation we get:

(a) '($\exists x$) (x is a person and x is a person)'.

Notice the 'and'. Clearly (a) is not analytic if '($\exists x$) (x is a person)' is not, because the latter and (a) are logically equivalent. The non-analyticity of (a) is parallel to the non-analyticity of 'It is raining *and* it is raining' as distinct from '*If* it is raining, *then* it is raining'. It is granted, of course, that the universally quantified statement '(p) (p is a person)' might be called analytic, but this should not faze us since *its* translation into our notation is

(b) '(x) (If x is a person then x is a person)',

which is logically true and quite compatible with the fact that (a) is not analytic, since (a) is not deducible from (b) without the assumption that there is a person.

6. *Carnap, ontology, and analyticity*

I suspect that there are philosophers like Carnap who would fully acknowledge that 'physical object' is not categorial in the sense intended, because they would admit that 'There are physical objects' is not analytic. But such philosophers might continue to say that 'There are numbers' is analytic and, hence that 'number' is a category-word. If they did, they would have to support their claim of analyticity on grounds other than the fact that the class of numbers is the universe of discourse of a given system. *And what this brings out is the difference between being an existential statement that is analytic and being one that asserts the existence of members in the universe of discourse.* The second characteristic does not imply the first, and obviously the first does not imply the second as ordinary (allegedly analytic) mathematical existential statements like 'There are prime numbers greater than 100' show.

In trying to demonstrate the analyticity (and the triviality) of 'There is an n such that n is a number', Carnap says that it "is immediately seen from the rule which states that words like 'five' are substitutable for the new variables",[5] or alternatively that it is a consequence of the analytic statement '5 is a number', which is a trivial consequence of that rule. And yet the "rule" which states that words like 'five' are substitutends of a variable becomes far less trivial when it is couched in a language that does not absorb the notion of number into the variable itself. The issue is quite like that which emerged in our discussion of the quantifier '$(\exists p)$' when that is read 'there is a person p such that'.

In order to make the point clearer, it might be useful to turn to an analogous situation in connection with words like 'Pegasus' and 'Bucephalus'. Imagine someone who was constructing a framework for the thing-language (physical object-language) about to provide the list of words that are analogous to 'five' in the case of the theory of natural numbers. Now he could of course list *both* 'Pegasus' and 'Bucephalus' as such expressions; in which case 'Pegasus is a physical object' and 'Bucephalus is a physical object' would play roles analogous to 'Five is a number' insofar as either one of them would be regarded as statements from which 'There is an x such that x is a physical object' would follow. But plainly this leads to difficulties of a kind intimately connected with the purpose of Russell's theory of descriptions. For if there is no such thing as Pegasus (as there isn't), then 'Pegasus' does not name anything and cannot figure as the replacement of 'a' in existential generalization, i.e., an inference of the form:

$$\ldots\ldots a\ldots\ldots$$
$$\text{therefore, } (\exists x)\ldots\ldots x\ldots\ldots$$

We may conclude, therefore, that a rule of the thing-language which is analogous to the rule in the theory of numbers "which states that words like 'five' are substitutable for the new variables" is a rule that is rightly promulgated only after it is known that 'Bucephalus' names something. But is the matter any different in the case of the theory of natural numbers? No. The person who builds a framework for the theory of natural numbers *might* also engage in investigations analogous to those of the man who makes

[5] "Empiricism, Semantics, and Ontology," *Revue internationale de Philosophie,* vol. 11 (1950); reprinted in Linsky, *Semantics and the Philosophy of Language.* See pp. 212–213 of the latter.

up the vocabulary of the thing-language. It only requires a little imagination to see how he might be *forced* into similar investigations. Suppose that Greek mathematicians had been as fanciful as ordinary Greeks and had had a mathematical mythology in which a brief word like 'bigprim', explained as 'the even prime bigger than 2', appeared. Now consider a logician who is constructing his framework. He has just listed 'one', 'two', 'three', 'four', 'five', etc., and an ordinary Greek asks, "But what about 'bigprim'?", just as a Greek *might* have asked about 'Pegasus' when the list was being made out for the thing-language. What would the logician ask? No doubt, "What do you mean by 'bigprim'?" To which he receives the answer, "The even prime bigger than 2". What would the logician say? I should have thought he would say, "There's no such thing as bigprim", and rightly so. But how does he know that there is no such thing as bigprim? By knowing that there is no even prime greater than 2, i.e., by knowing some mathematics of precisely the kind that he's trying to build a framework for. And how does he know that there *is* such a thing as five? In a similar way.

Since we have called attention to a similarity between the rules that introduce names into the vocabularies of the thing-language and the theory of natural numbers, it is important to connect this with the difference that is emphasized by those who regard the distinction between analytic and synthetic as a clear one. They might point out that while 'There is an x such that x is a horse belonging to Alexander and no other horse belongs to Alexander' is a true *synthetic* existential statement that guarantees the namehood of 'Bucephalus', 'There is such a thing as the successor of 4' (or some such sentence as would serve to guarantee the namehood of 'five') is *analytic*. By 'guaranteeing namehood' I mean guaranteeing that the expressions name something.

Now the effect of admitting *the possibility* of such a difference even while granting the similarities for which I have been arguing is to make it perfectly clear once again that the mere fact that a sentence is existential and "categorial" does not make it analytic. For if the language in question contained the phrase 'physical object', the sentence 'There are physical objects' would be a synthetic consequence of 'There is an x such that x is a horse'. And even if the word 'Bucephalus' has been treated as short for 'the *physical* object which is the horse of Alexander', all statements containing the latter description would also be synthetic for containing an existential conjunct.

If there is a serious difference between 'There are physical objects' and 'There are numbers', it is the same difference as that which allegedly exists between 'The Eiffel Tower is a physical object' and '5 is a number'. Therefore the contrast between the analytic and the synthetic in its most plausible form cannot sustain the contrast between ontology and non-ontology. For, as we shall see, the innocuous way of identifying the analytic is to say that it is the class of statements which are logical truths or deducible therefrom by definitional rules of the kind that help Russell and Whitehead deduce a statement like '5 is a number' from logical truths. In this case the logical truths are specified not epistemologically but rather by the fact that only variables and certain constants like 'all', 'neither-nor', and 'is a member of' appear in them essentially. Now some among the existential truths that are called ontological can be deduced from truths of logic so conceived, namely, 'There are numbers'. But so can some that are not usually called ontological, like 'There are prime numbers greater than 100'. And in that broad class of existential truths which *cannot* be deduced from logic there are also those that are sometimes called categorial or ontological, like 'There are physical objects' and 'There are minds', as well as those that are not categorial, like 'There are books' and 'There are mountains'. If one does not push the issue far enough back to see whether such statements are deducible from the so-called truths of logic, one cannot draw any metalinguistic line between the mathematical existential statements and the nonmathematical existential statements beyond the obvious line—one contains predicates *like* 'number' and 'prime number', the other *like* 'ships', 'sealing wax', and 'physical objects', which should go without drawing. In a later chapter, therefore, we shall push the issue further back not simply out of an interest in distinguishing *existential* statements that are analytic, but in order to explore this distinction as applied to *any* statements, for we have now seen that the logical constant 'there is' does not differ radically from other logical constants like 'is identical with'. Knowing only that a statement begins with an existential quantifier, like knowing only that it contains an identity-sign, gives us no clue as to whether it is analytic or synthetic. And this is true even when its predicate denotes the universe of discourse.

7. *The categorial and the noncategorial: a dubious distinction*

In regarding the existential quantifier as univocal and as merely very general, we restore a kind of democracy between so-called categorial predicates and others by showing that *any* predicate can be made categorial. We may construct systems in which our basic logic is supplemented by a decision to take numbers as a universe of discourse or to take cabbages as our universe of discourse. We may take persons as our universe of discourse and then say that some person wrote *Waverly,* or we may take our logic's universal class as our universe of discourse and then say that some entity in this neutral sense wrote *Waverley.* In the former case the extralogical predicate we choose to make fundamental may then be notationally absorbed, so to speak, into the quantifier. It is we who make the decision to take what certain predicates denote as our universe of discourse. If we make a class C our universe of discourse in a given system, *we* make 'C' a categorial predicate, and this involves, in effect, making 'There are C's' a postulate. The point is that the distinction between categorial predicates and noncategorial predicates is as fluid and relative as the notion of postulates.[6] We make our categories like our postulates with an eye to getting somewhere. And just as there are no points which are intrinsically starting points, so there are no statements that are intrinsically assumptions, or predicates that are intrinsically categorial. But while making an existential postulate ("I postulate that there are C's") is a free act, we may be called on to justify such free acts. Whether some existential postulates like 'There are numbers' may be justified by reference to some anterior pedigree and hence 'analytic' in a clear sense, we will discuss later. I may anticipate by saying that I don't think so, but I will have accomplished my main purpose in this chapter if I have shown that making numbers or physical objects our universe of discourse *of itself* confers no dignity on them that we could not confer on cabbages. In this chapter we

6 Quine, *From A Logical Point of View,* p. 35. See also R. M. Martin, "On 'Analytic'," *Philosophical Studies* (1952), 3:42–47.

have shown that no predicate has reason to bow before the predicate 'physical object' or the predicate 'number'; hence we have continued our opposition to a distinction between intrinsically categorial and intrinsically noncategorial predicates.

Having so far shown that the existential statements of philosophers are not distinguished from others on the score of using 'exists' strangely, or on the score of being uniformly analytic, or on the score of asserting the non-emptiness of universes of discourse, I now wish to consider the charge that they are uniformly meaningless. In passing it should be observed that the act of postulation, whereby we *make* certain sentences postulates and *take* certain classes as our universe of discourse, is of fundamental philosophical importance, not only in its own right but also as a clue to other acts of philosophical legislation.

CHAPTER VI

Metaphysics and the Criterion of Meaning

1. *Are the existential statements of philosophy meaningless?*

We now come to another effort to distinguish radically between the existential statements of philosophers and those of science and common sense: the effort to show that certain existential statements are meaningless. In the twentieth century logical positivism is distinguished not only by its active use of the notion of analyticity but also by its attempt to analyze the concept of an empirically meaningful statement. Both of them have been applied by positivists in a somewhat similar way, that is to say, as devices whereby positivistic hostility to metaphysics might be given rigorous expression and support. Thus, if metaphysics pretends to formulate knowledge, a positivist asks of it: What kind of knowledge?—which amounts to asking: What kind of statements does a metaphysician make? In answering their own question, many positivists come to the conclusion that metaphysical statements are either pretentiously disguised versions of statements which might just as well appear in the works of empirical scientists, for example in the works of sober cosmologists (if there are any); or that they are disguised analytic statements and hence derivable from logic; or that they are at best *putatively* meaningful utterances that can be fitted into neither of these categories. The effort is to strike through all the masks of metaphysics and thereby to carry out the practical implications of the thesis that all serious cognitive language falls into the domain of the empirical or the formal sciences.

The contrast between the views of Russell in 1912 and those of Moore with which we began our considerations of the problem of existence may serve to clarify the roots of the view that the questions 'Do physical objects exist?' and 'Do meanings exist?' are meaningless. We have already seen that while Moore asserts 'There are physical objects' in a sense that makes it follow immediately from 'There are human hands', Russell's approach of 1912 is quite different, in part because of his kantian view of the nature of physical objects. It is worth reminding ourselves of this contrast in the present context, because it is against the assertion that the kantian physical object exists that positivists usually direct their energies. The philosopher like Moore who says that physical objects exist simply because human hands exist does not arouse suspicion so much as positivistic amusement, but the philosopher like Kant or Russell who is prepared to deny or be skeptical about Moore's premise and conclusion is the object of scorn. He is the ontologist who imagines that there is a wall, a curtain, or a veil behind which the physical object may or may not exist, and who maintains that we can never really know whether it does or doesn't exist just because of the wall's power to cut off our vision into the true nature of things-in-themselves.

The contrast between the Russell-Kant approach and Moore's has been converted by Carnap into a distinction between two types of question, what he calls an external question and an internal question, as we have already said:

"Are there properties, classes, numbers, propositions? In order to understand more clearly the nature of these and related problems, it is above all necessary to recognize a fundamental distinction between two kinds of questions concerning the existence or reality of entities. If someone wishes to speak in his language about a new kind of entities, he has to introduce a system of new ways of speaking, subject to new rules; we shall call this procedure the construction of a *framework* for the new entities in question. And now we must distinguish two kinds of questions of existence: first, questions of the existence of certain entities of the new kind *within the framework;* we call them *internal questions;* and second, questions concerning the existence or reality *of the framework itself,* called *external questions.* Internal questions and possible answers to them are formulated with the help of the new forms of expressions. The answers may be found either by purely logical methods or by empirical methods, depending on whether the framework is a logical or a factual one. An external question is of a problematic character which is in need of closer examination."[1]

For Carnap the question 'Are there prime numbers greater than 100?' is a question which is internal to the framework or the theory of natural numbers, while 'Are there authors?' might be regarded as internal to the language or framework of empirical common sense. The true answer to the first question Carnap regards as analytic; the true answer to the second he thinks is synthetic. We have nodded to this provisionally, but have admonished those who say that just as the "categorial" statement 'There is an n such that n is a number' is trivial and analytic in the theory of natural numbers, so its categorial counterpart 'There is an x such that x is a physical object' is trivial and analytic in the theory of common sense, the framework of the thing-language, or whatever you wish to call it. But that is all behind us now, for now we wish to investigate these "external questions" of which Carnap speaks, since they are indeed problematic in character.

Carnap says that as distinct from questions like 'Are unicorns real or imaginary?' in which the "concept of reality . . . is an empirical, scientific, non-metaphysical concept" (because the question is equivalent to the question 'Are there unicorns?'), there is the "external question of the reality of the thing world itself". In contrast to the question 'Are unicorns real?' "this question is raised neither by the man in the street nor by scientists, but only by philosophers. Realists give an affirmative answer, subjective idealists a negative one, and the controversy goes on for centuries without ever being solved."[2] Here we are shown what might be called the disreputable ancestry of the "external question". It is here that we see the positivistic criterion of meaning in operation, since such a bald question is rejected as meaningless by *some* who accept that criterion. Carnap is more charitable than most, so that after suggesting that the question which has been debated for centuries by realists and subjective idealists is quite disreputable, he adds a sort of homily, a bit of advice on how to legitimize it. He begins by

---

[1] Carnap, "Empiricism, Semantics, and Ontology" in Linsky, *Semantics and the Philosophy of Language,* pp. 209–210.

[2] *Ibid.,* p. 210.

saying, "It cannot be solved because it is framed in a wrong way."[3] Realists and idealists should not look a gift horse in the mouth, for it appears that what they ask in their wrong-headed way can be given expression in a way that neatly avoids the strictures of empiricism. "Those who raise the question of the reality of the thing world itself have perhaps in mind not a theoretical question as their formulation seems to suggest, but rather a practical question, a matter of practical decision concerning the structure of our language."[4] Here we have a characteristic positivistic move, calculated to remove the sting from the original aspersions, to subtract insult from injury. It is very much like the move of some positivistic theorists of ethics, who assign ethical sentences "emotive meaning" after denying them "cognitive meaning"; in ontology we are urged to withdraw so-called metaphysical statements as cognitively meaningless and to recognize that what we are doing is adopting a decision to build a certain kind of framework.

2. *Postulation and the criterion of meaning*

Two questions must be distinguished. First, what are these decisions that we make when we start to build a framework? And second, what prompts us to say that the old ways of discussing the existence of physical objects, meanings, universals, etc., are meaningless? The second will be our main concern in this chapter.

Turning to the first question, we should recognize that the results of the last chapter prevent us from saying that the assertions of existence which contain so-called categorial predicates are always analytic. What we *have* concluded is that some of them are postulated and others are not. But we have also denied that the postulated existential statements will be intrinsically categorial in any clear sense. Moreover, our logic contains one expression that we use for asserting existence, and it is univocal. Whatever predicate 'C' is then introduced into the system as the name of a universe of discourse—whether it be the allegedly "categorial" predicate 'physical object' or the "noncategorial" predicate 'human hand'—must be accompanied by an associated existential statement 'There is at

[3] *Idem.*
[4] *Ibid.*, p. 211.

least one *C'*, which we postulate. In some cases we postulate the existence of things called physical objects and in some cases the existence of things called human hands. The point is that while we recognize Carnap's desire to distinguish between questions like 'Are there meanings?' and questions like 'Are there human hands?' the only legitimate basis for it that we can recognize is the distinction between postulated existential statement and nonpostulated existential statement. Using a metaphor, we may say that we accept the distinction between building a house and furnishing it, but reject the implication that the traditionally categorial existential statements like 'There are physical objects' are always imbedded in the walls and foundation of the house itself, while more ordinary existential statements are always part of its furnishings. If we begin with a relatively pure logic, i.e., one that has not yet introduced its "categories", we are free to choose our categories without selecting them from the conventional stock. Once we have adopted this view of the distinction between a postulated existential statement and non-postulated existential statement, we are freed from almost all of the more recent dichotomies between ontology and empirical science. According to the view which I am defending, the selection of the existential postulates of a given system involves a decision, just as all postulation does.

The serious question is whether some postulations are to be justified in a peculiar way. In the remaining sections of this chapter I wish to consider the root of the view that these fundamental decisions are matters of value rather than matters of fact, and the conviction that, as usually formulated by philosophers, the traditional counterparts of these decisions, for example, blunt metaphysical assertions to the effect that universals or physical objects do or do not exist, are "empirically" or "cognitively" meaningless sentences. By turning to the positivistic literature on empirical meaning, I wish to show that what might be thought to be a positivistic "discovery" that ontological statements in their traditional philosophical form are "meaningless" is itself the product of a decision, so that far from there being a linguistic "fact" which impels Carnap to transform the problem of ontology into a question of estimating the value of certain decisions, this transformation is itself connected with a more fundamental decision to use the word 'meaningful' in a certain way. If one thinks of the positivist's term 'meaningful' as a clear, descriptive predicate, one has the impression that Carnap has looked at the statements of traditional philosophers, has discovered that they lack something called "empirical meaning", and on the basis of this metalinguistic discovery has advised them to ask another question, one that is at best a substitute for the "meaningless" question debated by idealists and realists. As we shall see, the situation is complicated because of recent shifts in the empiricist or positivist theory of meaning itself.

3. *Logical positivism and metaphysics*

The hostility to metaphysics on the part of logical positivists is somewhat different from what is at most indifference to it in the writings of the early figures of the analytic movement. In the case of the early Russell, for example, we find this remark: "I have confined myself in the main to those problems of philosophy in regard to which I thought it possible to say something positive and constructive, since merely negative criticism seemed out of place. *For this reason, theory of knowledge occupies a larger space than metaphysics in the present volume* [my italics]."[5] Now we know that there are many passages in *The Problems of Philosophy* which deal with metaphysical questions in the traditional sense—notably those on appearance and reality and those involving the problem of universals. But in the remark just quoted there is enough self-consciousness about the inconclusive character of metaphysical considerations to suggest that Russell is something of a forerunner of the positivistic attack on metaphysics. A. J. Ayer says: "The traditional disputes of philosophers are, for the most part, as unwarranted as they are unfruitful. The surest way to end them is to establish beyond question what should be the purpose and method of a philosophical enquiry."[6] This leads to an attempt on Ayer's part to set down a clear distinction between meaningful, nonmetaphysical statements on the one hand and meaningless, metaphysical statements on the other. Here metaphysics is not to be avoided as a particularly controversial or destructive subject (as it is by Rus-

---

[5] Preface to *The Problems of Philosophy.*

[6] A. J. Ayer, *Language, Truth, and Logic* (New York: Dover Publications, 1950, first published in 1936), p. 33.

sell) but rather as a subject in which *meaningless* statements are made. A kind of rationalistic therapy is offered to metaphysicians, since Ayer hopes to persuade them by argument that an entire class of questions over which they puzzle fruitlessly are *nonsensical* rather than merely difficult.

The vigorous thesis 'All metaphysical statements are meaningless' is a good deal like 'All men are mortal' in form, and when we examine defenses of the latter statement we usually expect inductive evidence. In its crudest form this consists in giving a series of examples like 'Plato is a man and mortal', 'Aristotle is a man and mortal', and so on. Such a construal of the anti-metaphysical thesis of positivists would make it a universal empirical statement. But this is not what its proponents always maintain. Very rarely do they defend the thesis in this way. Usually what is done is to produce some good solid statement like 'This desk is brown' and to say 'But surely this is meaningful!' And then what is done is to produce something like 'The Absolute enters into, but is itself incapable of, evolution and progress' as a horrible example of metaphysics. It is then held that the former is comprehensible and understandable and possessed of "literal meaning" while the latter is not. This being assumed, the next move consists in providing a criterion which will make of 'This desk is brown' a meaningful statement and of 'The Absolute, etc.' a meaningless statement. It is then maintained that something similar can be done for all sentences of the kind illustrated by 'This desk is brown', namely, that they can be shown to be meaningful by use of the criterion in question, whereas sentences like the one using the word 'absolute' can be shown to be meaning*less*. From here it is an easy step to holding that *all* metaphysical statements are meaning*less* on the basis of the criterion, whereas all scientific statements are meaning*ful*.

Now what happens when a criterion is presented according to which decent scientific sentences are meaningless? The criterion is revised. What happens when atrocious metaphysical sentences turn out to be meaningful? The criterion is revised. But how do we know whether the offending sentence *is* scientific or metaphysical? This is never made clear and we are not expected to push too far in this direction. For obviously if we were clear about what a metaphysical and scientific sentence was in the first case we wouldn't be looking for this criterion. The fact is that we have to begin with some strong suspicions and hostilities toward certain sentences which we can't understand because we can't check them, and strong attachments to others that we can understand and check. And since our understanding of a meaningful sentence is supposed to be not merely a subjective matter but rather a reflection of something objective about the sentence, a positivist is led to suppose that if we try hard enough we will be able to produce an objective characterization of all and only understandable sentences and *ipso facto* of all the incomprehensible ones.

What I wish to get at is the root of the desire to find a criterion of meaning. It begins with puzzlement about certain kinds of disputes which philosophers engage in without obvious consensus or success, and is followed by an effort to produce some formula which will show that a solution could *never* be reached. The search for a criterion of meaning, therefore, is motivated by considerations much like those which motivate some philosophers in seeking a criterion for analyticity. In the case of meaningfulness a criterion is supposed to show us that we are wasting our time in trying to supply arguments for certain statements at all, whereas in the case of analyticity a criterion is supposed to help us pick out the statements for which it is fruitless to give *empirical* arguments.

The problem of finding a criterion for applying the term 'meaningful' resembles that of finding a criterion for 'analytic' in more than a methodological way, since the notion of analyticity has intimate logical connections with that of meaning. This is evident from the fact that the usual characterization of analytic statements is that they are true by virtue of the meanings of their terms, while the parallel characterization of meaningful expressions is that they *have* meaning. But it is as helpful to rest with this unanalyzed characterization of 'meaningful' as it is to rest with the parallel definition of 'analytic'—i.e., not helpful at all. Such an approach to meaningfulness at its best leads an empiricist to a halfway house, for even a hardened empiricist who is willing to visit with meanings temporarily can only exhibit his empiricism by pushing on to the view that a meaningful statement is one whose justification depends on sense experience, one which is capable of experiential test, one which is known a posteriori. As it stands, even this is too vague and too epistemological for some empiricists, so the search for a semantic criterion must continue until an exact metalinguistic formulation of the notion of an a posteriori statement is found. When it is viewed in this light, one sees a certain symmetry in the master plan of logical positivism. On the one hand the a priori true and the a priori false are identified with the analytic and the self-contradictory respectively and hence with the logical in the broadest sense; on the other, the whole class of statements which are either a posteriori true or a posteriori false are identified as the class of empirically meaningful statements. For this reason the empiricist criterion of meaning stands to the a posteriori as the criterion of analyticity does to the a priori, and therefore it is evident that if modern positivism fails to give a decent account of either analyticity or meaningfulness, we must take a qualified view of its contribution to modern philosophy. Like so many organized movements it may have to be praised for its temper rather than its dogma, or for its emphasis on the importance of language rather than for what it says about language.

4. *The criterion of meaning, natural language,
   and "rational reconstruction"*

The most interesting aspect of the similarity between the positivistic approach to meaningfulness and the positivistic approach to analyticity is the fact that, in the case of meaningfulness as in the case of analyticity, there are positivists who think that the criterion they seek is one which can be arrived at by studying the logical behavior of linguistic expressions in natural language, and there are those who don't. It is worth examining the approach of the first group in order to see why some positivists have supposed that it must lead to a sense of hopelessness that can only be removed by turning to artificial languages. Perhaps the most acute student of this problem, C. G. Hempel, has set forth in a remarkably clear way the frustration of those who have sought rigid criteria of meaningfulness without resorting to artificial languages. In the remainder of this section I shall summarize what he has shown, and then consider the implications of his results for the problem of existence in particular.

According to Hempel, the basic notions in the empiricist theory of meaning are the notions of observable characteristic, observable predicate, and observation-sentence:

"A property or a relation of physical objects will be called an *observable characteristic* if, under suitable circumstances, its presence or absence in a given instance can be ascertained through direct observation. Thus the terms 'green,' 'soft,' 'liquid,' 'longer than,' designate observable characteristics, while 'bivalent,' 'radioactive,' 'better electric conductor,' and 'introvert' do not. Terms which designate observable characteristics will be called *observation predicates*. Finally, by an *observation sentence* we shall understand any sentence which—correctly or incorrectly—asserts of one or more specifically named objects that they have, or that they lack, some specified observable characteristic."[7]

It should be realized that this notion of observation-sentence is illustrated by sentences like 'The Eiffel Tower is taller than the buildings in its vicinity', which appear in what Carnap calls 'the thing-language'. It is not to be confused with that notion of observation-sentence which is illustrated by those highly deintellectualized sentences of phenomenalists like 'Green here now', in which neither a name of a physical object nor an objective predicate appears.

Most of the empiricist theories of meaning which are presented as devices for picking out the meaningful sentences in natural language—both ordinary and scientific—and which are ultimately rejected by Hempel, take the following form: they are attempts at defining '*S* is meaningful' (where *S* is a statement in scientific or ordinary language) by reference to different logical relations that might hold between *S* and a set of observation-sentences. One such theory which some positivists reject is the view that defines a meaningful statement as subject to what is sometimes called "complete verifiability in principle". In logical terminology this theory says that a sentence *S* has empirical meaning if and only if it is not analytic and follows logically from a finite and logically consistent class of observation sentences. The requirement that the sentence

---

[7] C. G. Hempel, "Problems and Changes in the Empiricist Criterion of Meaning" in Linsky, pp. 164–165.

not be analytic is a product of the positivist conviction that an analytic sentence is not *empirically* meaningful and the awareness that it follows from *any* statement; the requirement that the observation-sentences make up a class of mutually consistent statements acknowledges the fact that an inconsistent class of statements would imply *any* statement.

The difficulties in this formulation reported by Hempel are typical and worth stating in detail; a moral may be extracted from them without reënacting kindred failures. First of all, this criterion would rule out as meaningless all sentences of universal form and hence all scientific laws, simply because no universal sentence follows logically from a finite set of observation sentences. Second, whereas a universal statement like 'Everything is O', where 'O' is an observable predicate, would be meaning*less* on this criterion, its contradictory, the existential statement 'There is a non-O', would be meaning*ful*. And finally, it would lead us to say that if S is meaningful on the criterion because it is a consequence of a finite class of observation-sentences, then the alternation of S and any other sentence, say N, would be meaningful.

Now suppose that N is a sentence like 'The absolute is perfect' (to use Hempel's rather forceful illustration of a meaningless sentence), which could not pass muster before the criterion in its own right. We would, nevertheless, be forced by this criterion to say that 'S or N' is meaningful, i.e., to say that an alternation of a meaningful and a meaningless sentence is meaningful. Such a situation is intolerable to a positivist, and in reaction it has been claimed that the objectionable sentences emerge as meaningful only because too many sentences are candidates to begin with. That is to say, since (a) every sentence in natural language can be a substituend for the sentential variables in logical laws, because logical laws are indifferent to the philosophical status of sentences (as is illustrated by the fact that they allow the meaningless 'Socrates is a man or the Absolute is perfect' to be a logical consequence of the meaningful 'Socrates is a man'), and since (b) the positivist sees no way of preventing a logical consequence of a meaningful sentence from being called meaningful, his conclusion is that the source of infection is somehow present in region (a). In other words, he cannot expect a philosophically neutral technique—

formal logic—to keep out philosophically objectionable sentences, so he himself must keep them out from the very beginning.

He therefore suggests that we reverse our procedure. Instead of looking out on a sea of ordinary sentences and trying to describe what relation a meaningful sentence and only a meaningful sentence bears to observation-sentences, we now *propose* to *call* certain expressions meaningful to begin with and to *call* others meaningful if and only if they bear specified relations to those that were first called meaningful. In this way the criterion of meaning does not rise up from natural language, but is handed down in a legislative way. The theorist of meaning specifies a certain list of observable predicates or sentences which he *labels* as meaningful, and he then specifies certain ways of generating other expressions which will embarrass him neither by allowing anything like 'The Absolute is perfect' to emerge as meaningful nor by forbidding perfectly meaningful expressions out of excessive positivistic zeal.

5. *The decision to make certain expressions meaningless*

Given this view of empirical meaning, how do we come to reject as meaningless the ontological debates of idealists and realists? How do we come to reject the statements of traditional philosophers that matter is or isn't real? Simply, it would seem, by so arranging our list of meaningful terms so that the predicates 'physical object', 'meaning', etc., as construed by the philosophers who use them in an objectionable way, neither appear on the list nor stand in suitable relations to those which are on the list. And what can be said to the philosopher who protests against the list precisely because these terms can't or don't appear on it? Nothing beyond the fact that he, poor fellow, wants to speak a language which is not that of empirical science. But what if institutionalized empirical science should change tomorrow? Could that suffice to admit, say, the expression 'thing-in-itself' or 'The Absolute'? I don't know what empiricist theorists of meaning would say to that, but it is obvious that they do occasionally trim the sails of the theory of meaning or tack with scientific winds, so they might well consider an alteration of this kind. What must be emphasized is the fact that they do no more than *resolve* to apply the word 'meaningful' to certain terms. They say, in effect, if a predicate is observable then it is to be *called* meaningful. They don't say that there is a property called observability which is correlated with another one called meaningfulness. It's not as if they were asserting a universal statement of the form 'All observable predicates are meaningful' which could be refuted by producing a counter-example. They *elect* to call terms meaningful which are observable, and they indirectly elect to call others like 'thing-in-itself' meaningless. In effect, they decide to *call* rather than *find* the debates of realists versus idealists meaningless and add that they are right in calling them meaningless.

How different is this from saying as the moral philosopher does that certain things ought not to be done? Not altogether different. The moralist says that acts of stealing ought not to be committed; the theorist of meaning says that 'thing-in-itself' ought not to be called meaningful. The point is that we set up a rule which allows us to give as a reason for calling an expression meaningful the fact that it is observable, just as a moral rule allows us to give as a reason for saying that something ought not be done the fact that it is an act of stealing. Incidentally, it would seem that stealing is a fairly clear notion by comparision to being an observable predicate, so that far from sniffing at the obscurity of ethical rules, positivistic theorists of meaning should recognize the respects in which ethical rules might even be clearer than their own, and should study them for whatever insight they give into the kind of decision, decree, or legislation to which the positivistic theorist of meaning is committed.

We see therefore that another predicate has been added to the list of those philosophical terms which we apply by fiat. The last chapter revealed the extent to which 'postulate' is such a term; this one produces 'empirically meaningful'. To be a postulate is to be called a postulate, and to be meaningful is to be called meaningful. What we shall see in later chapters is how the recent history of speculation on analytic statements gives rise to a similar conclusion. Then we will turn to ethics for analogical light on the justification of some of the decisions involved.

6. *Summary of conclusions on existence*

In concluding this part on existence we sum up our results as follows. We have seen that there is no reason to believe that the phrase 'there exists' is as multivocal as some philosophers have made out; we have rejected the view according to which existential statements which are "categorial" are all of them analytic on the (obscure) view of an analytic statement as one which is true by virtue of the meanings of its terms; we have come to suspect this formulation of analyticity because of our unwillingness to accept various arguments for the existence of meanings; we have come to see that the theory of empirical meaning on the basis of which certain positivists are led to treat certain ontological disputes as meaningless is itself the product of a decree or a decision to use the word 'meaningful' in a certain way. We have argued that so-called categorial predicates may or may not denote universes of discourse, and in this respect are quite similar to other predicates. In passing we have focused on the act of postulation or assumption as a piece of legislation. To be meaningless is to be called meaningless in a certain language, just as to be a postulate is to be called a postulate in a given system. Logicians make postulates of certain statements, and the positivist makes certain expressions meaningless. But why should the positivist make certain expressions meaningless? We see the absurdity of supposing that there is some objective property of statements which forces us, out of respect for "semantic reality", to call them postulates, and positivists admit that there is no objective property of meaningfulness which forces them to call certain expressions meaningless. In the second part of this book we shall see a similar pattern in the development of thinking about the a priori and the analytic; in it we shall develop some important similarities and differences in the uses of 'postulate', 'analytic', and 'meaningful'. In the third part we shall compare and contrast the ways of justifying philosophical legislation and moral action.

PART II

WHAT MUST BE

CHAPTER VII

A Pre-Positivistic View
of the A Priori

1. *A priori knowledge and the existence of universals*

The development we have just witnessed in connection with the problem of existence has a parallel in the closely related history of recent reflection on a priori knowledge. Just as the discussion of understanding in the analytic literature of the twentieth century begins with a belief in the existence of meanings and then develops into a more pragmatic, more conventionalistic tendency to appeal to rules, proposals, and decisions, so the literature on a priori knowledge develops in a similar way. If anything, the pattern is more conspicuous. Once again we select the early Russell as the representative of the age of meanings. We will then turn to the contribution of the linguistic age, when it was supposed that notion of the a priori could be identified with a concept of analytic that might be applied to sentences of ordinary language. Finally, we will conclude with a discussion of the attempt to solve the problem by an appeal to artificial languages in the age of decision.

We have been led to see one connection between the problem of universals and that of the a priori by virtue of the fact that some philosophers (usually under the influence of positivism) have held that an ontological statement like 'There are universals' is analytic and hence a priori. But there is another and older connection which is in some ways more interesting. We have had a glimpse of it in Frege's conclusion that there are *senses* or meanings in addition to denotations, on the ground that the distinction between the a priori and a posteriori would be difficult to maintain without the postulation of such senses (which some construe as attributes when they are the senses of general terms). A similar point of view appears in the statement of Russell in 1912 that a priori statements "deal exclusively with" universals conceived as attributes. It is predicated on the assumption that every statement must "deal with" some things, or be "about" some things which must be known and whose properties or relations must be known in order for us to know whether the statement about them is true. But now a question arises: why are a priori statements described not merely as statements which *deal with universals,* but as statements which deal with them *exclusively?* One answer is that Russell had already construed the a posteriori statement 'I am in my room' as dealing with a universal, so that it was necessary to add the qualification "exclusively" in order to distinguish a priori statements from others, but there is another which is more illuminating and more closely connected with the classic problem of the a priori. Russell was also influenced by the traditional view that a priori statements are *necessary,* and he therefore concluded that a mere examination of the finite number of things to which, say, the terms 'black cat' and 'cat' apply would not establish the necessity of the a priori statement 'Every black cat is a cat'. Thus the a priori statement was said to be about universals and about them only, for two reasons. Russell thought (1) that we *can* discover that the a priori statement 'Every black cat is a cat' is *true* and necessary merely by examining the relation between the universal *the attribute of being a black cat* and the universal *the attribute of being a cat,* and (2) that we *can't* discover that it is necessary by examining the black cats Jemimah, Archie, Tigress, and their friends. Another way of putting this point is to say that a statement like 'Every black cat is a cat' *says* more than what can be supported by an examination of millions of physical cats, but that it says no more than what could be established by examining two universals. We shall have occasion to examine this thesis in great detail.

Here it suffices to bear in mind two central assumptions of this point of view: namely that every statement deals with entities which are its subject matter, and also the assumption that a method of justifying the truth of a statement is not enough and must be supplemented by ways of establishing its modality. Between them they drove Russell to reject the view that physical objects are the entities with which a priori statements deal, and because he scorned what he regarded as the psychologistic mistake of construing a priori statements—in particular the laws of formal logic—

as laws of *thought,* he concluded that: "The fact seems to be that all our *a priori* knowledge is concerned with entities which do not, properly speaking, *exist,* either in the mental or in the physical world"[1]—namely with universals conceived as attributes. Although his view is quite different from those of later positivists, he shares one tendency with them, namely the conviction that in establishing a statement like 'Every black cat is a cat', we examine a different kind of entity from those to which the terms 'black cat' and 'cat' apply. In the case of Russell it was, rather, the attribute, and in the case of some positivists it is the linguistic expression itself. Moreover, Russell and some (not all by any means) positivists make a mistake which is not justified by these moves no matter what we think of the moves themselves: they all suppose that these entities which we must examine according to their theories are the entities with which the a priori statements "deal". Thus Russell's theory that a priori statements deal exclusively with universals and the parallel positivistic theory that a priori statements deal exclusively with linguistic expressions are equally mistaken. In this chapter we shall concentrate on the former in an effort to show some of its limitations and some of the issues which it generated in the later history of the subject. It turns out that Russell's theory of the a priori suffers from the same defects as the argument which leads him to postulate universals in his discussion of 'I am in my room'.

2. *Ordinary a priori statements not about attributes*

We have already seen the error of treating 'I am in my room' as though it were "about" three entities: me, my room, and the relation of *being in* (viewed intensionally), and the analogous error of treating 'Russell is a philosopher' as though it were "about" Russell and the attribute of being a philosopher. This kind of error runs throughout the doctrine of the a priori set forth by Russell at the same time, for if an a priori statement "deals exclusively with" universals, it differs significantly from a singular, a posteriori statement like 'I am in my room' simply by virtue of the latter's dealing only partially with universals. Russell held that an allegedly a priori statement like 'Every bald man is a man' deals with or is *about* the attribute of being a bald man and the attribute of being

[1] *Problems of Philosophy,* pp. 89–90.

a man, while it is plain that if our earlier animadversions on his interpretation of 'I am in my room' and 'Socrates is a philosopher' are justified, this is not true. Neither 'Socrates is a philosopher' nor 'Every bald man is a man' deals with *any* universals conceived as attributes. It might be plausible to say that the statement 'The attribute of being a bald man includes the attribute of being a man' deals with or is *about* these attributes, or even to say that 'Every bald man is *necessarily* a man' is covertly about the attributes in question. But the sentence 'Every bald man is a man' must not be confused with either of the other two, and the jump from 'Every bald man is a man' to either one of them in an effort to show that a priori statements deal exclusively with universals is as misguided as the conversion of 'This is white' into 'This has whiteness' in an effort to show that singular empirical statements deal partially with universals.

The classic problem of the a priori is to give an account of what we mean when we say that certain *nonmodal* statements like '7 + 5 = 12' are a priori and necessary, or an explanation of why it is that we say that they are necessary. And the property of being a priori or being necessary is best construed as a property of the statement said to be a priori, and not incorporated adverbially, as it were, into the statement itself. The distinction of being a priori is not always worn upon the statement itself. The necessity of the statement is something that might never have been seen by a person who knows exactly what the statement means. According to the classical view, this is what often makes the discovery of the a priori character of a statement a real discovery. A man comes to believe that a certain statement is true by going through all sorts of empirical tests until he sees or is made to see that the statement is a priori and therefore that another method *might* be employed. Consider Frege's statement, 'The evening star is the evening star'.[2] Surely it *can* be established by looking at the evening star, even though it needn't be. Those who deny this covertly replace Frege's statement by something like 'The evening star is necessarily the evening star', with which it is *not* synonymous. The role of the doctrine of the a priori should be to show me that I *might* have known the truth of

[2] "On Sense and Nominatum" in Feigl and Sellars, *Readings in Philosophical Analysis*.

the statement 'The evening star is the evening star' *without* engaging in experiment or observation, and not that I *couldn't* have known it through such experiment or observation. Before being instructed by the epistemologist, I might have done many things to establish the truth of the statement whose truth I did establish. What these many things are makes no difference. The fact is that the doctrine of the a priori is constructed in order to show me *another* way. But it does not follow from the fact that I *might* then come to see *the truth* of the a priori statement in another way that I did *not* validly establish its *truth* in my way. Nor does it make any difference that there are other statements *like* mine where my poor method might not avail. (I have in mind Frege's point against Mill that whereas counting pebbles might help with establishing '2 + 1 = 3', it won't avail when the numbers involved outrun the pebbles at our command.) What I am insisting on is the fact that the doctrine of the a priori is a doctrine that advises me of a method that I *might* use in order to establish truth but which, in some cases at any rate, I don't *have* to use. All this is connected with the point with which we began, namely that the statement traditionally presented to us *as* a priori is not a statement *of a priori–ness*.

The fact that looking does not establish the a priori–ness of 'The evening star is the evening star' is, therefore, no criticism of it; for the sentence it confirms asserts nothing about anything being a priori. The phrase 'a priori true' is traditionally replaceable by 'true and known to be true without recourse to experience', and 'a priori false' is replaceable by 'false and known to be false without recourse to experience'. Thus ' 'The evening star is the evening star' is a priori true' means that this statement is true *and* I can know it to be true without astronomical observation; while 'The evening star is the morning star', although true, cannot be established without observation and therefore is *not* a priori. But both statements are *true* in the same sense of 'true', and they are both true of the evening star. Similarly for the difference between 'All men are animals' and 'All men are mortal'; the first is true of all men and the second is true of all men, only according to some philosophers we can discover the truth of the first differently if we want to. Nevertheless we can, if we wish, support our acceptance of the first as we support our knowledge of the second. That is to say, we can treat 'All men are animals' as we treat 'All men are mortal'—by examining Socrates, finding out that he is a man and an animal, and then examining Plato, Aristotle, etc. Granted that we do not establish its a priori–ness or necessity in this way, but we are not *obliged to*. We are primarily interested in the *truth* of a priori statements, and the illusion that we *must* establish their a priori character in the course of establishing their truth is the result of the error against which I am arguing: the view that the a priori statement covertly involves the concept of the a priori.

One is tempted to say that there is no more reason to suppose that we should construe 'The evening star is the evening star' as synonymous with or replaceable by 'The evening star is necessarily the evening star' because the former statement is necessary, than there is for concluding that because 'The evening star is the morning star' is contingent, it is synonymous with 'The evening star is contingently identical with the morning star'. Indeed, philosophers who advocate such a translation would then find it as difficult to say that so-called synthetic statements can be supported by an examination of their ostensible subject matter as they now do in connection with necessary statements. For plainly to show not only that all men *are* mortals but also that they are contingently so is to assume a burden which no ordinary believer in the mortality of man is prepared to accept.

The introduction of words and phrases like 'necessarily', 'contingently', and the adverbial counterparts of 'a priori' and 'a posteriori' into the necessary, contingent, a posteriori, or a priori statement itself, while trying to find out what it "deals with", on the ground that this is what the statement "really means", is as wrong-headed as the effort to replace 'Socrates is a philosopher' by 'Socrates exemplifies philosopherhood', or 'Socrates is a man' by 'Socrates exemplifies manhood'. For just as the translation of the singular statement in this manner misleads us into supposing that the original is about attributes too, so the conversion of 'The evening star is the evening star' into 'The evening star is necessarily the evening star' transforms a statement which is true of the evening star into one that is presumably true of *the sense* of 'the evening star'. Analogously, the conversion of 'All men are rational animals' into "All men are necessarily rational animals' results in the misapprehension that the first is about intensions as the second might be in the case of each pair: 'Socrates is a man' and 'Socrates exemplifies manhood'; 'The evening star is the evening star' and 'The evening star is necessarily the evening star'. It was Frege who recognized this clearly in his notion of oblique contexts.[3]

If we take a sentence like 'All men are necessarily rational animals', we find that its truth does not survive the substitution of terms with identical extensions, for assuming that 'man' and 'featherless biped' are identical in extension, we cannot replace one for the other in the above context without producing the false statement 'All featherless bipeds are necessarily rational animals'. Quine has concluded that this shows that predicates like 'men' and 'rational animals' do not occur designatively in modal contexts and hence that quantification into such contexts is not ordinarily possible,[4] while Church has pointed out that one might generalize Frege's point of view and say that in such a context the word 'man' does not denote its *ordinary* denotation (i.e., the denotation it has in nonmodal contexts like 'All men are rational animals') but rather denotes what would ordinarily be its sense, namely, the attribute of being a man in the case of 'man' and the attribute of being a rational animal in the case of 'rational animal'.[5] The effect of Church's observation is to lead us to say that if we choose to regard 'All men are necessarily rational animals' as being about *any* entities or as dealing with them, it would be best to think of those entities as attributes. The situation is quite similar in the case of 'The evening star is necessarily the evening star', which, Church would say, is about the singular term's ordinary sense, namely, an *individual concept*.

This completes my effort to show the error in Russell's notion that a priori statements like 'Every bald man is a man' and '7 + 5 = 12' are about universals conceived intensionally, and my effort to show that this mistake is intimately linked with his belief in 1912 that 'I am in my room' deals with the relation of *being in*

---

[3] *Ibid.*, p. 87.

[4] "Notes on Existence and Necessity," *Journal of Philosophy*, vol. 40 (1943); reprinted in Linsky, *Semantics and the Philosophy of Language*.

[5] In a review of Quine's "Notes on Existence and Necessity," *Journal of Symbolic Logic* (1943), 8:45–47.

conceived intensionally. It does not touch the question as to whether he should have selected some other entities like classes as the subject matter of a priori statements, nor does it raise the question as to whether sentences which *do* contain expressions like 'necessarily' must be construed as being about attributes. That is a very different kind of problem, related to the matters discussed in Chapter II, Sections 4–6.

That Russell should have taken the position he took on the a priori in 1912 creates an irony that is worth mentioning, since it was Russell who in his *Introduction to Mathematical Philosophy* said of C. I. Lewis's modal notion of strict implication:

"The essential point of difference between the theory which I advocate and the theory advocated by Professor Lewis is this: He maintains that, when one proposition *q* is 'formally deducible' from another *p*, the relation which we perceive between them is one which he calls 'strict implication,' which is not the relation expressed by 'not-*p* or *q*' but a narrower relation, holding only when there are certain formal connections between *p* and *q*. I maintain that, whether or not there be such a relation as he speaks of, it is in any case one that mathematics does not need, and therefore one that, on general grounds of economy, ought not to be admitted into our apparatus of fundamental notions; that, whenever the relation of 'formal deducibility' holds between two propositions, it is the case that we can see that either the first is false or the second true, and that nothing beyond this fact is necessary to be admitted into our premisses."[6]

If in the *Problems of Philosophy* Russell had applied such a viewpoint to nonmathematical statements said to be a priori, he would not have needed to adopt the theory of universals or the theory of a priori in that book. For just as he would have eliminated expressions like 'strictly implies' from mathematics, he would also have eliminated expressions like 'is necessarily identical with' as parts of the a priori statements his theory is supposed to account for. And if he had done that as well as adhered to the distinction between connoting and denoting as bequeathed to him by Mill and Frege, he would never have been forced to postulate intensional

---

[6] P. 154.

universals as the *subject matter* of nonmodal a priori statements.

Our examination of Russell's early platonism helps underscore and perhaps explain what Russell observed with such surprise— namely that the ordinary man is not aware of the existence of universals. The theory of universals is a philosophical construction rather than something *obviously dictated* by common sense or *ordinary* language. In an earlier chapter we saw universals introduced because of a belief that they were demanded as the objects of the mental grasping that accompanies the understanding of words. Some philosophers say that we are not justified in saying that this page is white unless we know, as it were independently, that this page exemplifies whiteness; analogously they say that we can't detect the truth of a priori statements unless we see that something is related to something in a certain way, so attributes are introduced as the somethings. What they quietly assume, of course, is that there must be some clearly marked domain of entities which we "examine" in order to establish these a priori statements. But why should there be such a domain at all? Why should there be a clearly marked subject matter for each statement? This question can be put not only to platonists but also to their positivistic successors in the theory of the a priori, philosophers who maintain that what we have to inspect are not the attributes *being a bald man* and *being a man* but rather the linguistic expressions 'bald man' and 'man'.

It is worth noting again how in the case of both Frege and Russell the drive to universals originates epistemologically, i.e., by way of premises involving mental conduct verbs like 'understand' and 'known to be true without recourse to experience'. With the possible exception of a few ontological purists interested in existence for its own sake, most philosophers realize that the "discovery" that universals exist is no good-in-itself. Few struggle for a cause that might in the end win only grudging agreement ("So there *are* universals! So what?"). They have their eyes on bigger game—on the explanation of certain kinds of mental behavior. This is evident not only in Russell but also in Frege, as I have indicated. In each case the route is different, but they begin and end at the same place. Russell bluntly says that a priori propositions deal with meanings; Frege says more delicately that there are a priori propositions so there must be meanings, without making Russell's mistake of saying that the a priori proposition always deals with those meanings. Their course is just the reverse of that of traditional theologians who say that God exists, therefore theological knowledge exists; Frege and Russell say, rather, that a priori knowledge exists and therefore that universals exist.

3. *Understanding and the subject matter of statements*

A curious component of the early view of Russell is that according to it all a priori true statements deal exclusively with universals, but not all statements which deal exclusively with universals are a priori true. I am not thinking of the trivial point that some statements which deal exclusively with universals are false and hence not a priori true, like 'No man is a man'. The point is that not all *true* statements which deal exclusively with universals are a priori on the view in question. The exceptions are empirical generalizations like 'All men are mortal'. In 1912 Russell held that 'All men are animals' and 'All men are mortals' both deal exclusively with universals, in spite of the fact that one is a priori and the other not.

Naturally, they are both distinguished from 'I am in my room' and 'Russell is a philosopher' in that these last two do not deal with universals exclusively—only partially, because of the intrusion of Russell, me, and my room. Yet how are the two universal statements mentioned above distinguished from one another? They are distinguished, Russell says, by the fact that in one case (the a priori case) we can "see" the connection between the universals merely by attending to the universals, whereas in the other case we must, alas, look at particulars falling under these universals.

This is one of the most intriguing of all the views bundled together by Russell in 1912. The view that priori propositions are *about* universals can at least be explained in terms of the view that a priori true statements are statements of necessity like 'All men are necessarily rational animals', in which predicates like 'men' and 'rational animals' denote what would ordinarily be their senses, i.e., the attributes of being a man and being a rational animal respectively. And, no doubt, those who endow scientific laws with a kind of necessity might speak consistently, if they held a related view. But as Russell construed empirical generalizations, no such notion of necessity enters, since he regards scientific law as non-necessary. What operates in Russell's case is not so much the conviction that scientific laws contain some modal component, as the same old confusion that a statement is *about* those entities which we must grasp or be acquainted with in order to understand the statement. This was the view that dictated the conclusion that statements like 'Socrates is a man' are about a concrete Socrates and a universal manhood, but there the mixed nature of the subject matter—a physical object and a universal—presented no glaring paradox for a philosopher who appeared to hold that we must examine those things with which the statement deals in order to see whether the statement is true. There we have to look at an *existent* to see whether it is an example of a *subsistent* in order to see whether Russell is a philosopher or Socrates is a man. And in the case of a priori propositions, we can safely conduct our examinations without leaving the level of subsistents. But the empirical scientist is put in the strangest of positions. He makes generalizations which are about universals exclusively, and yet he can establish them as true only by examining the particulars that illustrate the universals. The real rationale of the position comes out in the following passage:

"One way of discovering what a proposition deals with is to ask ourselves what words we must understand—in other words, what objects we must be acquainted with—in order to see what the proposition means. As soon as we see what the proposition means, even if we do not yet know whether it is true or false, it is evident that we must have acquaintance with whatever is really dealt with by the proposition. By applying this test, it appears that many propositions which might seem to be concerned with particulars are really concerned only with universals. In the special case of 'two and two are four', even when we interpret it as meaning 'any collection formed of two twos is a collection of four', it is plain that we can *understand* the proposition, i.e. we can see what it is that it asserts, as soon as we know what is meant by 'collection' and 'two' and 'four.' It is quite unnecessary to know all the couples in the world: if it were necessary, obviously we could never understand the proposition, since the couples are infinitely numerous and therefore cannot all be known to us. . . . The statement made is about 'couple', the universal, and not about this or that couple. Thus the statement 'two and two are four' deals exclusively with universals, and therefore may be known by anybody who is acquainted with the universals concerned and can perceive the relation between them which the statement asserts."[7]

Within this passage we can find the two basic causes of Russell's difficulties. On the one hand, the confusion between the sense and denotation of a word pushed to the point where Russell holds that sentences are *about* the senses of their component terms in ordinary discourse; on the other, the view that we cannot understand a word without standing in some relation of mental grasping (Frege) or *acquaintance* (Russell) to a universal. Once Russell accepts the first principle he is forced to say that both the a posteriori generalizations of empirical science and the a priori generalizations *deal exclusively with, are concerned exclusively with, are about only* universals. But the semantic distinction, as one might call it, between "dealing exclusively with universals" and not dealing with them exclusively is sufficient only to draw the line between singular statements like 'Russell is a philosopher' on the one hand and both kinds of universal statements—a priori and a posteriori—on the other. In order to distinguish two species within the latter category, he must turn to another consideration, as he does in considering 'All men are mortal'. Here, as in the case of the arithmetical statement,

"we can *understand* what the proposition means as soon as we understand the universals involved, namely *man* and *mortal*. It is obviously unncessary to have an individual acquaintance with the whole human race in order to understand what our proposition means. Thus the difference between an *a priori* general proposition and an empirical generalization does not come in the *meaning* of the proposition; it comes in the nature of the *evidence* for it. . . . We believe that all men are mortal because we know that there are innumerable instances of men dying, and no instances of their living beyond a certain age. We do not believe it because we see a connection between the universal *man* and the universal *mortal*."[8]

[7] *Problems of Philosophy*, pp. 104–105.
[8] *Ibid.*, p. 106.

Here we can see tension between the principle that seems to motivate Russell's theory of the a priori, namely the principle that a statement is verified by examining only the entities with which it deals, and Russell's conception of how it is that we establish scientific laws. Had Russell not made the mistake of supposing that sentences are about the entities with which we must be acquainted in understanding them, and therefore *about* what Frege and Mill would have called the senses or connotations of their component terms, he would not have been put in this position. As it is, he must hold that while a discovery about the relation between universals cannot give us evidence about the world without our making existential assumptions, a discovery about the world can support a statement which deals exclusively with meanings.

4. *Logic and the synthetic a priori*

The characterization of the a priori that emerges from these pages of the early Russell, pages that continue to command great interest and support on the part of some philosophers, would run as follows: A statement is a priori true if it is (1) true, (2) deals exclusively with universals, and (3) can be seen to be true by seeing a connection between those universals with which it deals. But surprisingly enough, when he comes to discuss *analyticity,* Russell limits the analytic to truths like 'A bald man is a man' and 'A plane figure is a figure', both of them substitution-instances of 'Everything which is P and Q is Q'. What we are said to perceive in establishing the statement is the *containment* of the predicate-universal in the subject-universal. But where the truth is a priori and not of this form, as in the case of '$7 + 5 = 12$', we must perceive another kind of connection between universals, whose exact nature is never made clear. At best it may be described as the connection which holds between the universals with which an a priori true statement deals when that statement is not analytic. In short, the Russell of 1912 believed in the synthetic a priori. He supposed that there were two kinds of connections that might exist between the universals with which a priori propositions deal exclusively, and hence two kinds of a priori propositions.

Those who are not surprised need only be reminded of two things. First, that we are often told by historians of philosophy that it was *Principia Mathematica* by Russell and Whitehead that had undermined the view that arithmetical propositions are synthetic a priori, and second, that the three-volumed *Principia Mathematica* had begun to appear in 1910 while the *Problems of Philosophy* appeared in 1912. Now, the reasons usually given for describing the accomplishment of *Principia Mathematica* in this way are linked with a statement by Frege on the subject of analytic propositions which appeared in 1884. Frege says:

"The problem becomes, in fact, that of finding the proof of the proposition, and of following it up right back to the primitive truths. If, in carrying out this process, we come only on general logical laws and on definitions, then the truth is an analytic one, bearing in mind that we must take account also of all propositions upon which the admissibility of any of the definitions depends. If, however, it is impossible to give the proof without making use of truths which are not of a general logical nature, but belong to the sphere of some special science, then the proposition is a synthetic one."[9]

It is plain that if we can show that the propositions of arithmetic are deducible from those of logic by means of definitions, we have shown, as far as Frege is concerned, that the truths of arithmetic are analytic. It does come as something of a surprise, therefore, to find Bertrand Russell saying in 1912, after the beginning of the publication of *Principia Mathematica,* in which he and Whitehead had deduced arithmetic from logic in Frege's way, that "Kant undoubtedly deserves credit . . . for having perceived that we have *a priori* knowledge which is not purely 'analytic', i.e. such that the opposite would be self-contradictory",[10] and more particularly for his having perceived that "all the propositions of arithemtic . . . are 'synthetic', i.e. not analytic" because "in all these propositions, no analysis of the subject will reveal the predicate".[11] Russell even said that Kant had "pointed out, quite truly, that 7 and 5 have to be put together to give 12: the idea of 12 is not *contained* in them, nor even in the idea of adding them together".[12]

[9] *The Foundations of Arithmetic* (Breslau, 1884); English translation by J. L. Austin (Oxford: Blackwell, 1950), p. 4e.
[10] *Problems of Philosophy,* p. 82.
[11] *Ibid.,* pp. 83–84.
[12] *Ibid.,* p. 84.

What makes the Russell of 1912 hesitate to call the statements of arithmetic analytic? What permits him, nay makes him, endorse the kantian view of arithmetic when he had already built what most positivists regard as the greatest anti-kantian bomb ever constructed? In a sense the answer appears very simple. He construed the notion of analyticity so narrowly that some of the logical truths that he required in the derivation of mathematics from logic were not analytic. On this point Frege's remark quoted above and more recent formulations under his influence suggest a division of the problem of analyticity which not only illuminates Russell's views at that time, but also helps prepare the way for more recent discussions of the problem.

5. Recent discussions of analyticity

These recent discussions of analyticity[13] suggest that it is helpful to distinguish initially at least four kinds of statements. (1) Those which contain only logical constants and variables in an essential way, where for our present purposes 'logical constant' may be defined ostensively by pointing to words like 'and', 'or', 'every', and others; in short, the truths of the propositional calculus, quantification theory, and set theory. Standard examples of this sort of statement are the following:

'For every P and Q, everything which is P and Q, is Q.'
'For every P, every P is P.'
'For every x, P, and Q, if every P is Q and x is a P, then x is Q.'

(2) Those which, like 'Every bald man is a man' or 'Every man is a man', are substitution-instances of statements in category (1), i.e., the results of substituting constants like 'bald' and 'man' for the variables in ways defined by rules of substitution in texts of mathematical logic. (3) Truths which I shall describe here as *like* 'Every vixen is a female fox' and 'Every man is an animal'—the point being that, while they are called analytic, they are not merely

13 See my "The Analytic and the Synthetic: An Untenable Dualism" in *John Dewey: Philosopher of Science and Freedom*, S. Hook, ed. (New York: Dial Press, 1950); reprinted in Linsky, *Semantics and the Philosophy of Language*. Also my "A Finitistic Approach to Philosophical Theses," *Philosophical Review*, vol. 60 (1951). See also Quine, "Two Dogmas of Empiricism," *Philosophical Review*, vol. 60 (1951); reprinted with minor revisions in his *From A Logical Point of View*.

the results of putting constants for variables in a truth of kind (1). And finally, (4) mathematical truths like '$7 + 5 = 12$'.

Having made this initial fourfold distinction, it is now useful to observe that (1) and (2) are sufficiently close to each other and sufficiently different from both (3) and (4) in a certain respect to warrant a grand twofold distinction between a class made up of all truths in (1) and (2), to be called 'truths of formal logic', and a class of truths which, while called analytic by many philosophers, are *not* truths of formal logic in the same sense. For purposes of easy reference in what follows, let us call the first group 'I' and the second 'II'. It should be observed that (1) and (2) have in common the fact that they are both formal; (1) obviously so and (2) as the result of our regarding substitution as an operation which preserves formality. The nonlogical constants, some logicians are inclined to say, appear in a nonessential way in truths of kind (2), so that we see the truth of 'Every man is a man' by seeing that it is a substitution-instance of the form 'Every P is P'. Truths in group (1) are what Frege called "general logical laws" in the passage quoted earlier in this chapter, and truths in group (2) are sufficiently like them to be bundled together with them in category I. The truths which make up category II are those whose analyticity has been most seriously questioned by philosophers; as we know, the truths of arithmetic as a whole have caused most worry in this connection. According to more recent and more linguistically oriented formulations of the problem of analyticity, truths in class (3) are analytic because they are the results of putting synonyms of empirical predicates for synonyms in a truth of class I. Thus 'Every vixen is a female fox' is shown to be analytic by showing that 'For every P, every P is P' is a truth of formal logic, that substitution yields 'Every vixen is a vixen', and that replacement of the second occurrence of 'vixen' by its synonym 'female fox' gives the statement 'Every vixen is a female fox'; this test establishes its analyticity. In Frege's words, we have followed the truth right back to primitive truths and have come upon only general logical laws and definitions. The analyticity of '$7 + 5 = 12$' is to be established in the same way. Truths of arithmetic are also regarded as the results of moving from truths in formal logic by means of the definitions proposed in *Principia Mathematica*. Although the process is much more complicated than it is in the case of 'Every vixen is a female fox', it is essentially similar if logicians of the so-called logistic school are right. This is the link that binds truths of (3) and (4) into category II.

These distinctions give rise to a number of problems that are best kept separate. (a) *Can we make the notion of general logical law clearer?* Notice how this can be construed as a relatively trivial problem, if we answer it by defining a 'general logical law' as a true statement in which only variables and logical constants figure essentially. In this respect it is like defining a general biological law as a true statement in which only biological constants and those of presupposed disciplines appear essentially; all we do is to divide 'logical' and 'true', define 'logical' ostensively, and let 'true' fend for itself. Actually *this* problem concerning the notion of general logical law is not a very interesting one when formulated in this way, and those who try to convert it into one by searching for a *criterion* of 'logical constant' waste their time. Such a question is interesting only to those who think we can find criteria for disciplinary names like 'logical' and 'biological' which are based on usage. Now we turn to the far more interesting questions: (b) *Are general logical laws analytic?* (c) *Are general logical laws a priori?* and (d) *Can we clarify the notion of synonymy involved in the definition of the analyticity of statements in group II above?*

6. *Are all logical truths analytic?*

If we assume the accomplishment of the Frege-Russell-White-head program, we assume that we have reached something like the goal Frege describes in the passage quoted earlier. But the Russell of 1912, in spite of being armed with *Principia Mathematica,* did not think he was in a position to say that all of the truths of logic are analytic. He operated with the definition of an analytic statement as one whose "opposite would be self-contradictory", and from his examples one would suppose that he was prepared to call only some of the "general logical laws" analytic, namely, 'For every P, every P is P,' 'For every P and Q, every P and Q is Q', 'For every P and Q, every P and Q is P'. At any rate, these, or rather substitution-instances of them, are his only examples, so that one might almost say that according to Russell in the *Problems of Philosophy* an analytic statement is a statement which *is* one of the above statements or a substitution-instance of one of them or a consequence of them and their substitution-instances. Naturally, such a conception of analyticity would hardly be wide enough to allow Russell to conclude that *Principia Mathematica* refuted Kant, since that would depend on the premise that no logical proposition is synthetic. This premise Russell was evidently not prepared to accept in the *Problems of Philosophy,* so that since he held that the truths of arithmetic were a priori and since he could not show them to be analytic by deduction from *Principia Mathematica* and since he had no other way of answering Kant, he concluded that '$7 + 5 = 12$' is synthetic a priori. If one asks 'How did he know they were a priori?' the answer is very brief—he supposed that he could establish them as true without appealing to experience but rather by examining a connection between universals other than containment in the sense explained earlier.

Russell's *Introduction to Mathematical Philosophy* introduces a new twist in the views he held before he had the benefit of Wittgenstein's *Tractatus,* for while Russell in the *Introduction* reiterates his conviction that the traditional notion of analyticity is too narrow, he no longer resorts to the kantian solution of a synthetic a priori but searches for a definition of analyticity which will be wide enough to embrace the recalcitrant truths of logic. In referring to the older notion of analyticity, according to which a statement is analytic if its contradictory is self-contradictory, he says: "This mode of statement, however, is not satisfactory. The law of contradiction is merely one among logical propositions; it has no special preëminence; and the proof that the contradictory of some proposition is self-contradictory is likely to require other principles of deduction besides the law of contradiction. Nevertheless, the characteristic of logical propositions that we are in search of is the one which was felt, and intended to be defined, by those who said that it consisted in deducibility from the law of contradiction."[14] This characteristic he calls 'tautology'. Of it he says: "I do not know how to define 'tautology.' It would be easy to offer a definition which might seem satisfactory for a while; but I know of none that I feel to be satisfactory, in spite of feeling

[14] *Introduction to Mathematical Philosophy*, p. 203.

thoroughly familiar with the characteristic of which a definition is wanted. At this point, . . . , for the moment, we reach the frontier of knowledge on our backward journey into the logical foundations of mathematics."[15] But not without someone to guide us, for during World War I the key to analyticity passed into the expert hands of Wittgenstein: "The importance of 'tautology' for a definition of mathematics was pointed out to me by my former pupil Ludwig Wittgenstein, who was working on the problem. I do not know whether he has solved it, or even whether he is alive or dead."[16]

Today we know that, while Wittgenstein was alive and did succeed in giving an account of the notion of tautology, the account he gave is not sufficient for characterizing all of the logical truths we need in the course of deducing mathematics from logic. Wittgenstein's definition of 'tautology' was successfully applicable only to the narrow class of truths which comprise the calculus of propositions, and hence was insufficient for Russell's purpose. We know, therefore, that the effort that begins with the traditional notion of analyticity that Russell rejects ends with Wittgenstein's conception of analyticity as tautology, incapable of moving as far as some would have it move. Indeed, Russell himself expressed doubts about its outcome when he said in the *Introduction to Mathematical Philosophy* that the characteristic of tautology "obviously does not belong to the assertion that the number of individuals in the universe is n, whatever number n may be."[17] Such an assertion was made in the case of his axiom of infinity, and another was required (regretfully, he implied) for the truth of logical schemata like '$(\exists x)$ $(Fx$ or $\sim Fx)$' and 'If (x) Fx, then $(\exists x)$ Fx'.[18]

I know of no successful effort to build a logic which (a) sets forth its general laws, (b) shows them to be analytic in a way that somehow circumvents the fact that we cannot produce a criterion of the kind that Wittgenstein produced for the calculus of propositions, (c) shows them to be sufficient for the deduction of all a priori knowledge, and (d) seriously meets the demand of showing

15 *Ibid.*, p. 205.
16 *Idem*, note 1.
17 *Ibid.*, p. 203.
18 *Idem*, note 1.

that all so-called a priori truths are analytic in this way. That such demands are not extravagant is demonstrated by the fact that anti-kantians who proposed to refute Kant accepted some such challenge. Surely they would have agreed that they could not claim to have *shown* in the manner proposed by Frege that all a priori truths are analytic unless they deduced them from statements which are analytic in some clear sense. And if such a challenge is not accepted, I know of no other way in which a philosopher might try to show that all a priori statements are analytic and still be discussing the question raised by his opponents. It is, of course, possible that the problem is itself badly stated and that we would do well to reformulate it so that these embarrassing questions cannot be asked. But such an illuminating change of the subject has not been produced either.

There are those who are willing to abandon as hopeless the effort to define 'analytic' as applied to all logical truth, but who nevertheless accept the innocuous characterization of a logical truth as one which is true and which contains only variables and logical constants essentially. This would characterize the truths of category I (spoken of in Section 5) in an acceptable way, but it would avoid the epistemological question "How do you know they're true?" rather than solve it. It would have the same philosophical standing as a corresponding definition of chemical truth would have, or as a corresponding definition of French truth would have. In the last case as in the others, we are less tempted to ask "How do you know it's French?" than we are to ask "How do you know it's true?" Even if one were satisfied with such an epistemologically neutral definition of logical truth, one would have difficulty in defining truths of category II, e.g., those comprising the nonmathematical part of category II, like 'Every vixen is a fox'. Such a truth is now called analytic because it is deducible from a logical truth by putting synonyms for synonyms. Granting that one has understood what a logical truth is, one must now understand what the operation of putting synonyms for synonyms is, and here we have a difficulty from which, one would suppose, there is no easy "escape" like that which the notion of logical truth provides in the case of category I. This is the area on which I should like to concentrate in the next chaper.

CHAPTER VIII

The Analytic and the Synthetic

1. *The analytic and the a priori*

In discussing the term 'analytic', we should constantly keep in mind the fact that one of its main functions *in philosophy* is to help solve the problem of a priori knowledge, for it is the key term in the statement 'All and only a priori true statements are analytic'. We shall begin by construing this as a *thesis* in philosophy, meaning one for which arguments may be given, just as arguments may be given for the related thesis 'All true mathematical statements can be deduced from logical truths'. It is only by construing it as an arguable thesis (at least at the beginning of our efforts) that we can understand why so many philosophers have tried to support it and why others have in good faith tried to produce counter-examples. The fact that opponents of the thesis try to produce counter-examples suggests that *they* do not think of the predicate 'is an a priori true statement' as *synonymous* with the predicate 'is an analytic statement', and to them it seems much more absurd that those who defend the thesis should maintain that it is analytic than that they should hold that it is true. In a curious way the very formulation of the issue can lead philosophers to use words whose meaning is at issue, for once we ask whether 'a priori' is *synonymous* with 'analytic' we might also be led to ask whether the statement 'All and only a priori true statements are analytic' is itself a priori and analytic. What this shows is the enormous temptation philosophers have to use *something like* the expressions 'a priori knowledge' and 'analytic statement'.

We learn the jargon from our teachers and go on using it compulsively. And even though the man in the street doesn't use it, some philosophers don't doubt that they can make it comprehensible to him merely by showing its connection with words that he *does* use. He understands the words 'look', 'smell', 'listen', 'touch', and 'taste', and so we first persuade him that the word 'experience' is connected with these words by pointing out that if we need to get to know something by looking or smelling or listening or touching or tasting, we need to get to know it by experience, and since these are commonly called sensory activities we qualify the word 'experience' by the word 'sensory' (not worrying too much about whether we thereby suggest that there might be another kind of experience). We then advise the common man (and therefore a part of ourselves) that a statement which is a posteriori true is one whose truth we must get to know by sensory experience. After *that,* what is more natural, even apart from whether we can find examples of it, than to introduce a predicate denoting statements whose truth we don't need to learn in this way, namely the predicate 'a priori'? The procedure merely requires us to accept as understandable a predicate which is the negate of one that we have already understood. We have begun by defining one sort of *getting -to-know* by reference to sensory experience, just as we might define one sort of biped by reference to the possession of feathers. And as the latter procedure makes it easy to construct the predicate 'non-feathered biped', so the predicate 'a posteriori' suggests 'non–a posteriori'. Thus we can persuade ourselves of the reasonableness of introducing the *predicate* 'a priori' even without knowing whether there are a priori statements. Think how much more plausible the procedure is made by actually producing statements traditionally cited as a priori.

We introduce the notion of analyticity by exploiting rudimentary semantics, whereas our conception of the a priori rests on the ordinary man's rudimentary epistemology. It is as easy to take off from the common man's use of the word 'meaning' as it is to take off from his use of the word 'see'. We persuade him without too much trouble that some words have the same meaning as others, e.g., 'vixen' as 'female fox', 'brother' as 'male sibling', and then call attention to a peculiarity of certain statements in which these pairs of synonyms appear, e.g., 'All vixens are female foxes' and 'All brothers are male siblings'; namely the fact that while they are true, our learning their truth requires no more than learning that certain words are synonymous, and does not require any sensory examination of the physical objects denoted by those words.

Let us suppose now that instruction in the use of 'a priori' was given on Monday and that instruction in the use of 'analytic' is given on Tuesday. On Wednesday we ask our common man, our bright child, or our student, 'Are all and only a priori statements analytic?' Now clearly he won't respond as some philosophers do by saying, 'Yes, because we *mean* by an a priori statement one which is analytic'. He has not yet been corrupted. Since both terms 'a priori' and 'analytic' are new to him, he can only rely on the explanations of them given by his instructor, and these surely don't warrant the conclusion that all and only a priori statements are analytic. He might be *tempted* to say this because he knows that an a priori truth is one which he can establish without sensory observation of physical objects, and because he knows that an analytic statement is one whose truth is established merely by examining the meanings of terms or by examining the terms. But at most this knowledge justifies him in saying that all analytic statements are a priori, and not in saying the converse.

2. *Platonism and positivism*

Here is where the advocate of the synthetic a priori has his big opportunity. Even if he admits that we can certify the truth of statements like 'Every cube has twelve edges' without looking at cubes, because we can examine instead the predicates 'cube' and 'has twelve edges' or their meanings, this is not the end of his story. What remains is his contention that the *relation* between (1) these meanings or (2) these terms is not always what the positivist supposes it to be, if we may so label the defender of the view that all and only a priori true statements are analytic. The anti-positivist, or defender of the view that there are synthetic a priori statements, may be a platonist or an anti-platonist, depending upon whether he regards meanings or linguistic expressions as fundamental. Platonism and positivism cut across each other to produce four possible positions.

(a) *Platonistic positivism.* A platonist who is a positivist says that our conviction that a statement is a priori is always based on the identity of meanings. Thus in the case of showing that 'Every vixen is a female fox' is analytic, he begins with the logical truth 'Every P is P', substitutes the word 'vixen' to get 'Every vixen is a vixen', and then says that *the meaning which* 'vixen' *has is identical with the meaning which 'female fox' has,* thereby permitting him to derive 'Every vixen is a female fox' by methods that justify calling it analytic.

(b) *Platonistic anti-positivism.* A platonist who believes in the synthetic a priori may well accept the positivist's interpretation of *this* example, but will then point to illustrations like 'Every cube has twelve edges', *which he maintains is a priori,* and point out that it cannot be derived from logical truths in the manner of 'Every vixen is a female fox', just because we cannot produce a true statement of identity of meanings that will justify the counterpart to the last step in the other case. The situation here is best compared with that of 'Every vixen is a fox' (as opposed to 'Every vixen is a female fox'). Here we show analyticity (according to the platonist's view) by beginning with the logical truth 'Everything which is a P and a Q, is a Q', deriving by substitution 'Everything which is a female and is a fox, is a fox', saying that the meaning which 'is a vixen' has is identical with the meaning which 'is a female and is a fox' has, and concluding that we have derived 'Every vixen is a fox' by methods that justify calling it analytic. But a defender of the synthetic a priori who is a platonist will say of the case 'Every cube has twelve edges' and of others like it that they cannot be derived in this way merely because nothing like the above statement of identity of meanings is defensible in this case.

In the remaining two cases, (c) and (d), both parties—positivist and anti-positivist—are anti-platonists insofar as they both eschew reference to meanings and speak only of linguistic expressions being *synonymous.* Where the positivistic platonist says, 'The meaning which 'vixen' has is identical with the meaning which 'female fox' has', the positivistic anti-platonist (c) says austerely, ' 'Vixen' is synonymous with 'female fox' '. But (d) the anti-positivistic anti-platonist who defends the synthetic a priori has something to say even in metalinguistics. He *now* says that the positivist cannot produce the requisite true statement of *synonymy* in the case of 'Every cube has twelve edges'.

The fact that the opposition between positivist and anti-positivist breaks out in both cases suggests that the fundamental difficulty in the dispute is to be located not only in ontology but also in what Quine has called ideology.[1] That is to say, even when we jump up to the metalinguistic level and talk about predicates being synonymous rather than about meanings being identical, we meet another philosophical problem, for those who disagree with us on the fundamental question 'Are all and only a priori statements analytic?' still have a way of communicating their difficulties.[2] The century or so of conflict between positivist and anti-positivist on this point is indicative not so much of the fact that clear words are being applied differently, but rather of the obscurity which surrounds both the notion of identity of meanings and that of synonymy as between expressions. For this reason the thesis 'All and only a priori statements are analytic' *and* its contradictory are obscure, whether disputed by platonists or anti-platonists. It should be noted therefore that the doctrine of the synthetic a priori cannot profit by the criticism leveled against positivism on this point, for advocates of the synthetic a priori are just as dependent upon the phrases 'is identical with' as applied to meanings and 'is synonymous with' as applied to predicates as positivists are. It should also be noted that our use of the term 'a priori' is not necessarily affected by our critique of analyticity. What *is* affected are two conflicting theses in which the phrase 'a priori' appears. If the use of 'a priori' is to be criticized, it must be examined in its own right. A critique of analyticity may deprive us of one traditional method of *accounting* for a priori knowledge, so that we might be led either to accept this kind of knowledge as a brute fact, or to account for it in some other way, or perhaps to conclude that the predicate 'a priori' is also obscure. But we must not first identify the a priori and the analytic, then attack the analytic, and then conclude that the a priori has also been demolished. That would be the most flagrant use of the doctrine of guilt by association. The a priori is a separate matter.

3. *Analyticity and natural language*

The critical step on which we have focused is that from a statement like 'Every vixen is a vixen' to 'Every vixen is a female fox'.

---

[1] *From A Logical Point of View*, p. 131.

[2] See my "Ontological Clarity and Semantic Obscurity," *Journal of Philosophy* (1951), 48:373–380.

It is a step in which we must preserve analyticity. For if 'Every vixen is a vixen' is analtic, then what we want to justify is the move whereby we deduce 'Every vixen is a female fox' and then say that it too is analytic. It is plain that certain other moves won't accomplish the trick. This is best illustrated in the case of the similar-appearing move from 'Every man is a man' to 'Every man is a featherless biped', where we know only that 'man' and 'featherless biped' have the same denotation. This move does not preserve analyticity and hence does not assure us of the analyticity of the statement derived in this way from 'Every man is a man'. What we are obliged to do, therefore, is to distinguish a move based on mere coextensiveness of predicates from one which will show the resulting statement analytic.

In the history of recent philosophy there have been many different efforts at defining the notion of analyticity, and we cannot examine all of them in documenting the contention that the approach by way of synonymy and identity of meanings is obscure, so we confine ourselves to a few outstanding ones. In confining ourselves to those which make essential use of expressions like 'synonymous' and 'is the same meaning as', we restrict ourselves to a view peculiar to one wing of analytic philosophy, namely, that which ascribes analyticity to sentences of ordinary language or unformalized science. This means, in effect, that we are not at the moment considering what might be called a conventionalistic approach to the problem, nor the views of those philosophers who hold that one should apply the word 'analytic' only to sentences in so-called artificial languages for which so-called rules have been constructed and stated explicitly. With *these* philosophers we will be concerned in the next chapter. In this chapter attention is given to those who (rightly in my opinion) recognize that the notion of analyticity was introduced in order to account for the a priori character of some statements in natural languages, or at any rate of statements that were not then parts of any constructed system or artificial language. Those who *refuse* to say whether sentences in ordinary language are analytic or not (possibly because they share our doubts about synonymy and identity of meanings), sometimes hold that the question of the analyticity of a statement must be transferred to an artificial language whose rules are given explicitly. This and kindred views are *not* under consideration in this chapter.

4. *The view that identity of meaning is more fundamental than synonymy*

The view that we establish the synonymy of expressions (and therefore analyticity) by going behind language, so to speak, or digging under it to meanings whose identity we must see, is closely related, as is evident, to the views of Russell and Frege, who advanced it in one form or another before the emergence of a more linguistic point of view. Most recently it has been defended elaborately and acutely by C. I. Lewis in his *Analysis of Knowledge and Valuation,* where it is explicitly contrasted with the view that linguistic considerations are more basic. What Lewis appears to hold is that expressions of meanings are synonymous because these meanings are related in a certain way, and what he opposes is the reversal of this picture—the tendency to say that the meanings are identical because the expressions are synonymous. According to views like those of Lewis and the early Russell, meanings are extralinguistic entities, and the fact that words which express or connote them are synonymous is dependent on objective relations between meanings, much as the coextensiveness of the words 'man' and 'featherless biped' is dependent on facts of nature. Just as one is inclined to say that the statement 'The Eiffel Tower is taller than Memorial Hall' is true *because* the Eiffel Tower *is* taller than Memorial Hall, and not inclined to say that the Eiffel Tower is taller than Memorial Hall because the statement that one is taller is true, so some philosophers are more inclined to say that two expressions are synonymous because the meanings they express are identical. But the difference in the two illustrations serves to bring out the difficulties in this platonistic approach to synonymy. Most of us are inclined to say that we know how to go about testing whether and convincing others that the Eiffel Tower *is* taller than Memorial Hall, while some of us find it extremely difficult to do the analogous thing in the case of meanings.

Furthermore, there is a relation between the synonymy-statement and the statement of identity of meanings which makes us uncomfortable about being informed that the first is true *because* the second is true. The point is that even if there be meanings which are distinct from the words that connote them, it is difficult to see how useful the hypothesis that they exist is for the purpose at hand. For either (a) the relation which must hold between meanings in order to *ground* a statement of synonymy is so difficult to detect that anyone who has doubts about whether two expressions are synonymous will not be likely to have those doubts removed by an examination of meanings, or (b) asserting its existence will merely duplicate what is to be explained. So far as I know, there never has been a clear statement of what identity of meanings amounts to which could help the cause we are criticizing. I recognize, of course, that failure to define a term is not of itself sufficient to dismiss the term as obscure, but some undefined terms are more obscure than others.

At this point I can imagine someone arguing that in my very statement that the word is obscure or in my declaration 'I do not understand it clearly', I adopt a mode of speech which is as vulnerable by my own standards as I suppose the partisans of identity of meaning are by my standards. But such a dialectician would misconstrue the nature of my criticism. Of course, at some points in philosophical discussion I will say that I don't understand or that I don't find something clear because, as will be evident from later chapters, I refuse to resort to some "criterion" of significance which can be used as a club on others. But in criticizing the notion of identity of meanings I am not put in the same situation as those I am criticizing, just because I am not relying solely on what has been called the "no spikka Engleesh"–move. I assume that the task of philosophy is in part that of clarification and that a philosopher who directs us to examine meanings after we've shown some anxiety about whether two expressions are synonymous does not really help us.

It is worth a digression to point out that we are now considering a doctrine which we have met before, when it was supplied with an allegedly deductive proof, but this time its defense is not deductive. We assume that the advocates of meanings whose views are *now* under consideration *don't* maintain that the existence of meanings *follows* from the fact that some statements are a priori, or from the fact that we understand certain expressions, or from the fact that certain expressions are synonymous. In this case, we assume, the defense is conducted much as a defense of the existence of molecules would be conducted, that is to say, by an argument which says that in postulating meanings we explain certain linguistic facts or phenomena which would otherwise go unexplained. Such philosophers do not hold that all we *mean* by saying that 'vixen' and 'female fox' are synonymous is that one expresses a meaning, the other expresses a meaning, these meanings are identical, and *therefore* meanings exist. What they begin with, it must be insisted, are certain epistemological *facts,* the fact that we sometimes understand linguistic expressions, that there is a priori knowledge, that we understand certain expressions in the same way; these are the epistemological data which are to be accounted for by the "hypothesis" that meanings exist and are related in certain ways. In order to concentrate on such a defense of meanings we must brush aside the *deductive* defense and the view that 'There are meanings' is analytic. For they get in the way of a showdown with the strongest argument for meanings. If we meet *that* we will have been meeting the thesis on its strongest and most sensible ground, though it is ultimately indefensible.

By way of contrast let us recall some of the arguments for molecules as they are reported in *The Evolution of Physics* by Einstein and Infeld. One of the physical facts that the molecular theorist begins with is that of Brownian movements. Brown, a botanist, was working with grains of pollen, that is "particles or granules of unusually large size varying from one four-thousandth to about [one] five-thousandth of an inch in length". He reported that there was unceasing agitation of the granules when suspended in water and visible through the microscope. "How is this motion to be explained?" ask Einstein and Infeld.

"Looking at water through even our most powerful microscopes we cannot see molecules and their motion as pictured by the kinetic theory of matter. It must be concluded that if the theory of water as a congregation of particles is correct, the size of the particles must be beyond the limit of visibility of the best microscopes. Let us nevertheless stick to the theory and assume that it represents a consistent picture of reality. The Brownian particles visible through a microscope are bombarded by the smaller ones composing the water itself. The Brownian movement exists if the bombarded particles are sufficiently small. It exists because this bombardment is not uniform from all sides and cannot be averaged out, owing to its irregular and haphazard character. The observed motion is thus the result of the unobservable one. The behavior of the big particles reflects in some way that of the molecules, constituting, so to speak, a magnification so high that it becomes visible through the microscope. The irregular and haphazard character of the path of the Brownian particles reflects a similar irregularity in the path of the smaller particles which constitute matter."[3]

Here the motion of one body is said to be explained or accounted for by referring to the motion of another one, and presumably this explanation cannot be ridiculed by reciting Molière. Why? Because we do not understand Molière's physician to say that the drug has within it an entity that produces sleep in the way that the water has within *it* entities (molecules) that produce the motion of grains of pollen. We feel therefore that when someone says that a drug has the dormitive virtue he is probably saying in a picturesque way that the drug usually or always puts people to sleep. For this reason, when we ask *why* the drug usually or always puts people to sleep, and are told that this is because it possesses the dormitive virtue, we laugh, as we do when we are told that the candidate lost the election because he didn't get enough votes. In spite of the difference between this example and that of the hypothesis that meanings and their relations explain or account for synonymy, a priori knowing, and understanding, they are also very much alike. To be told that you can understand a predicate *because* it has a meaning is useless precisely to the extent to which this explanation is different from the molecular explanation of Brownian movements and similar to that of Molière's physician. We want, of course, to account for the relation of synonymy, to test and to establish its presence, but we refuse to accept hypotheses which either repeat what is to be explained or introduce things for which there is no independent support.

[3] Albert Einstein and Leopold Infeld, *The Evolution of Physics* (New York: Simon and Schuster, 1938), pp. 64–65.

It must be pointed out that advocates of the view we are criticizing do not suppose that these meanings are *images*. Frege goes to great pains to emphasize that. The platonic tradition is that they are neither mental nor physical. One is led to think, therefore, that they are entities which are introduced as explanatory in an *ad hoc* way. If the notions of understanding and a priori knowledge demand explanation, we can say that the theory of meanings is no clearer than the data which it is supposed to illuminate. It is sometimes said that scientists treat hypotheses about unobservable entities charitably even when they are not wholly satisfied with them, on the ground that some theory is better than no theory at all. But the theory of meanings does not seem to be defensible on these grounds precisely because of its otiose character. When we abandon it we do not feel that we are left incapable of predicting or explaining anything that could have been predicted or explained with its help.

There are those who would reply that this misconceives the aim of philosophical speculation and that we wrongly apply scientific standards to theories or theses that are not intended to solve the kind of problems to which such standards apply. But what *is* the purpose of ontology, then? Do philosophers suppose that they can defend the existence of entities like meanings in any other way? If they cannot, then we must realize that very often no account and no analysis is preferable to one that doesn't really advance our power to illuminate or explain. That is precisely the situation in which an epistemologist who appeals to meanings finds himself. He seems to be able to understand certain words; he seems to make statements whose truth can be established in an a priori way, but he can't provide an account of understanding or a priori knowledge which is clearer than they are to begin with. Under the circumstances, one is inclined to say what Newton once said under similar circumstances, "Hypotheses non fingo".

5. *The ascent to language*

We have up to now considered only the view that one must dig beneath the surface of language to meanings in order to get a satisfactory account of synonymy. The difficulties we have pointed out and others have led some philosophers to suppose that the

problem ought to be approached differently. As a result we have
a tradition of approaching this question *without* moving to another realm of entities like that of meanings, a tradition that tries
to clarify analyticity and synonymy even while it abandons the
effort to establish and test statements of synonymy in an avowedly
non-intensional way. Such a course not only involves an abandonment of the effort to examine the entities which are allegedly connoted by the synonymous terms, but also an abandonment of the
need to examine entities denoted by the synonymous terms. A
philosopher who takes this course not only gives up the effort to
ground synonymy in meanings by saying with Newton, "Hypotheses non fingo", but adds with Laplace, "Je n'ai pas besoin de
cette hypothèse", implying that some more suitable account is available or will be found. There are two variants of this approach that
deserve examination.

(a) One may be described as the view that analytic statements
are those whose denials are self-contradictory.[4] At first blush it
appears to bypass not only meanings but also synonymy in its approach to analyticity. To discover whether a statement like 'All
men are rational animals' is analytic, it says, we don't have to discover whether it is the result of putting synonyms for synonyms in
a logical truth; we need only show that the contradictory of 'All
men are rational animals' is self-contradictory. If it is, we can then
conclude simultaneously that 'All men are rational animals' is
analytic and that 'man' and 'rational animal' are synonymous. But
is the denial of our allegedly analytic statement, namely, 'It is not
the case that all men are rational animals', a *self*-contradiction?
Certainly a purely syntactical approach to the notion of self-contradictoriness does not reveal a sentence resembling '*p* and not-*p*'
in shape nor one resembling 'Some *P* is not *P*'. And even if we
transform the allegedly self-contradictory statement into 'Some
men are not rational animals', we do not get a self-contradiction in
syntactical form. And if it is said that this last statement is seen to
be self-contradictory once we remember the sense in which 'man'
and 'rational animal' are being used, we must point out that this
appeal to the *senses* (i.e., the connotations) of 'man' and 'rational

---

[4] This entire section is a revised version of a passage in my "The Analytic and
the Synthetic" in *John Dewey: Philosopher of Science and Freedom*, S. Hook, ed.;
reprinted in Linsky, *Semantics and the Philosophy of Language*.

animal' and their relations is precisely what this criterion is pledged to avoid. It will not have bypassed "platonic intermediaries" if it doesn't. Will the proponent of this point of view then say that the statement is seen to be self-contradictory when we remember that 'man' and 'rational animal' are synonymous? But then he will not have bypassed synonymy, and his definition of 'analytic' will be none other than the following: An analytic statement is one whose contradictory is the result of putting synonyms for synonyms in a logical falsehood (a logical falsehood like 'Some men are not men' being the contradictory of a logical truth). Thus he will have gotten nowhere slowly, for instead of bypassing the notion of synonymy effectively he will have entered it surreptitiously, and far from having left the notions of analyticity and synonymy for the haven of self-contradictoriness, he will be right back where he started. So that, if we were thinking that we could avoid the dictum 'An analytic statement is the result of putting synonyms for synonyms in a logical truth' and the need to clarify 'synonym', we have been sorely disappointed; we have been led up the garden path, back to synonymy itself.

(b) *"If we were presented with something which wasn't a rational animal, we would not call it a man."* Such language is often used by philosophers who are anxious to clarify the notion of analyticity as applied to statements in ordinary language. In order to test its effectiveness in distinguishing analytic statements *with an eye on the thesis that all and only a priori true statements are analytic,* let us try it on the statement 'All men are featherless bipeds', which by hypothesis is not analytic. In doing so we shall also be trying it on the terms 'men' and 'featherless biped', which are by hypothesis not synonymous. How would those who use this criterion of analyticity and synonymy show that this statement is not analytic and that these terms are not synonymous, in spite of the fact that the statement is true and that the terms do have the same *de*notation?

Surely if we are presented with any one of the actual things that exist in the universe which we know is not a biped, we will not call it a man, and surely if we are presented with another which we know is not featherless, we will not call it a man either. We withhold the term 'man' from those things which we know to be either nonbipeds or nonfeatherless. It won't help to be told that there *might be* a man who is not a featherless biped while there couldn't be a man who is not a rational animal, for this rests the nonsynonymy of 'man' and 'featherless biped' on the fact that "there is a possible but non-actual entity that does satisfy one but not the other predicate", as Nelson Goodman points out.[5] But to admit unactualized possibles is as antithetical to our present program as admitting meanings.

The fact that we *do* withhold the term 'man' from things of which the predicates 'nonfeatherless' and 'nonbiped' are true, as well as from those of which the predicates 'nonrational' and 'nonanimal' are true, is the most serious obstacle in the way of the kind of criterion we are considering. It focuses our attention on the critical statement 'We would not call it a man' or 'We would withhold the term 'man' ', and hence on the pattern of term-withholding that is supposed to underlie synonymy as opposed to that which is associated with a belief in mere coextensiveness of predicates.

Suppose we come to a tribe which has the following words in its vocabulary plus certain logical constants: 'man', 'rational', 'animal', 'featherless', and 'biped'. We are told in advance by anthropologists that 'man' is synonymous with 'rational animal' in that tribe's language, whereas 'featherless biped' is merely coextensive with it. We wish to check the report of the anthropologists that 'man' is synonymous with 'rational animal' in that tribe's language, whereas 'featherless biped' is merely coextensive with it. How do we go about it? In the spirit of the proposed criterion we must show that anything which was not called a rational animal would not be called a man by the people in question. So we show them coconuts, trees, automobiles, palm trees, and ask after each "Man?" We get no for an answer in all cases. They will not repute these things to be men. We must now show that there is a difference in their attitudes toward 'rational animal' and 'featherless biped' in relation to 'man'. We originally showed them things which were not rational animals. But these very things are not featherless bipeds either, and so the negative responses of the natives might just as well be offered as an argument for the synonymy of 'man' and 'featherless biped' as for the theory that 'man' is synonymous with 'rational animal'. It would appear that such crude behavior-

---

[5] "On Likeness of Meaning," *Analysis*, vol. 10 (1949); reprinted in a revised form in Linsky. See p. 68 of the latter.

ism will not avail. They don't call nonfeatherless bipeds men just as they don't call nonrational animals men. The criterion proposed will not allow us to draw the distinction as we wish to draw it, for one of the conditions put upon the proposed criterion is that it help us sharply distinguish between the coextensiveness and the synonymy of predicates, and it has failed this test.

6. *What has been shown and what hasn't*

We should be perfectly clear about what has been attempted and accomplished in this chapter, lest it be confused with things that cannot be defended or with still other things that must be defended on different grounds. We have considered the notion of analyticity as applied to sentences in ordinary language containing extra-logical predicates like the traditional 'man', 'rational animal', etc., in an effort to show that two kinds of approaches to the problem of synonymy and analyticity are defective. One appeals to extra-linguistic entities and their relations, another eschews such reference but is also defective. From this alone one cannot conclude that the notions of analyticity and synonymy are hopelessly obscure. But we must remember that the concept of analyticity is not always applied to ordinary sentences with a great deal of assurance, so that the failures of the "criteria" we have considered cannot be dismissed as we might dismiss a housewife's failure to define 'cockroach' or 'fly'. She uses these words quite confidently as matters stand now, and if she hesitated to call a fly a fly and then swat it, she might well be regarded as excessively anxious or excessively tender. But surely this is not the case with 'analytic' and 'synonymous' as used by some philosophers. Philosophers who exploit *these* words hunt much larger game. We have examined their weapons by methods which are not foreign to their own and our conclusion is somewhat negative. If one makes such criticisms, one can hardly go on to say with absolute confidence that *no* clarification of the notion of analyticity in a natural language is possible. But if a clear explanation is not forthcoming from those who defend the thesis 'All and only a priori statements are analytic', we may well conclude that the thesis is as vague as one of its key terms. And, as we have already seen, this should not give comfort to those who say that there is a *synthetic* a priori, for they are just as vulnerable as their opponents.

CHAPTER IX

Artificial Rescue Efforts

1. 'Analytic' is a philosopher's word

In dealing with the notion of analyticity via that of synonymy, we have been supposing that clarifying both of them is a necessary adjunct to an evaluation of the philosophical thesis 'All and only a priori statements are analytic'. We began by assuming that a philosopher who defends such a thesis is obliged to examine the language of people objectively in order to see whether certain statements in that language are analytic. To this end he must see whether certain statements are logically true and whether certain expressions are synonymous, and therefore his job appears to be just as *descriptive* as that of any student of language. Just as a linguist might wish to count the number of letters, syllables, or sounds in a given sentence, or just as anyone might be interested in whether a given sentence ends in a word that rhymes with one that another ends with, so the philosopher we have in mind is interested in finding out whether all members of a certain class of statements are analytic—whatever that means. To this extent we assumed that he was trying to discover an objective property of a sentence just as the others tried to discover objective rhyming relations and objective numbers of letters, etc. But, alas, we have concluded that the word 'analytic' is not sufficiently clear to justify confident descriptive and "objective" use.

One writer on the subject has remarked on the fact that some critics of the notion of analyticity may very well have forbidden the use of all the fuel the definition of analyticity may need.[1] He correctly observes that some philosophers will not accept the terms 'analytic', 'possible', 'necessary', 'self-contradictory', 'synonymous', 'meaning', and others unless at least one of this group of terms is defined exclusively by reference to terms outside of this group.

---

[1] Benson Mates, "Analytic Sentences," *Philosophical Review,* vol. 60 (1951).

And then he comments, "It may easily happen that the conditions of adequacy for a definition are so strong that no adequate definition is possible. As will be remembered, Tristram Shandy's father found it practically impossible to explain the subtler parts of metaphysics to Uncle Toby, who could only understand military terminology."[2] This is a very discerning observation, but one is tempted to reply that it does more to discredit the whole circle in which the term 'analytic' travels than it does to condemn the narrowness of that term's critics. Moreover, it is somewhat ironic that the parochialism of Uncle Toby should be cited in defense of a point of view which is most actively defended in our time by logical positivists, for positivists, of all philosophers, might be charged with the rigidity of Uncle Toby.

The language of those who speak of analyticity and its partners resembles the language of those who describe the activities of that other nefarious circle: the modalities. Those who hope to make *necessity* virtuous by recalling its association with *possibility* waste their time, for he who has difficulty with *necessity* to the point of seeking a philosophical explanation will not be satisfied with *possibility*. If the night follows us without surcease we may begin to suspect that we are in a valley of permanent darkness, and that maybe 'analytic' and its mates are beyond our powers of illumination. What we want is some way of breaking through this small circle of obscurity into the light of day, some escape from the night in which all the cows are black. The sad fact is that most of the terms usually offered in the explanation of 'analytic' *are* of little help to the man who is genuinely perplexed about the problem of identifying analytic statements. It is absurd to pretend that there is a great deal of consensus on how to use the term and that the philosophical task is merely a matter of defining a term which we know how to use perfectly well. Terms like 'analytic' and 'meaning' in that special use which is necessary for the theorist of the a priori are not like those terms which a common moorean man might apply with utter confidence even in the absence of a criterion, analysis, definition, or whatever it is that philosophers seek. 'Analytic' and 'synonymous' are *philosophers'* words, introduced in order to solve a difficult philosophical problem, and while they should be treated with all the sympathy that the difficulty of the

2 *Ibid.*, p. 529.

problem demands, it must be remembered that they are swords of criticism and hence obliged to be sharper than most, particularly when they are brandished so fiercely.

2. *Conventionalism, synonymy, and platonism*

In the previous chapter we dealt with two approaches to analyticity via synonymy, which are both opposed to an approach that we may call conventionalistic in a sense that will subsequently become clearer. It is instructive to note that the views we considered, along with a variety of conventionalism that we shall consider in a moment, constitute a sequence. Of these, conventionalism is least "deep"; the view that 'synonymous' is an undefined but clear descriptive predicate is a little deeper; and the view that we must look to underlying platonic meanings in order to justify our statements of synonymy (and hence our definitions) is last and most "penetrating" of all. Such a picture of the sequence is most likely to be drawn by those who adopt the third approach, and they are likely to think of going deeply as an advantage. Their point is that we can only justify defining 'man' as 'rational animal' and hence calling 'All men are rational animals' analytic by pointing out that 'man' is synonymous with 'rational animal', and that we can only justify the statement that 'man' is synonymous with 'rational animal' by seeing that the meanings of these terms are identical.

One can think of a parallel in a different case, but a case that reveals the similarity between a cartesian theory of mind and a platonic theory of meaning. Suppose we were obliged to decide on a replacement of a certain professor, Mr. *A*. Suppose we decide that he is to be replaced by Mr. *B*. This is the free act that corresponds to the defining activity already mentioned (even to the point of involving replacement!). The counterparts of those who appeal to synonymy in the above situation are those who now say that we can only justify our decision by knowing that Mr. *B* is at least as able as Mr. *A*. And those who correspond to the partisans of meanings in the case of analyticity are those who urge that knowing that Mr. *B* is at least as able as Mr. *A* requires knowing that *the mind* of Mr. *B* (this corresponds to *the meaning* of 'man') is not inferior to *the mind* of Mr. *A* (this corresponds to *the meaning* of 'rational animal').

Of course, the partisans of meanings say, we are free to define terms as we choose, just as we are free to replace professors as we choose, but there is a logic of *correctly* defining terms, just as there is a logic of *properly* replacing professors, and the ultimate relation to which the first logic drives us is the identity of meanings, just as the second drives to the superiority of minds. And just as the reference to cartesian minds doesn't improve our capacity to replace professors, so the reference to platonic meanings doesn't improve our capacity to replace words.

3. *Conventionalism, nominal definitions, and semantical rules*

Faced with the otiose character of platonism and the ontologically respectable but obscure ideology of what might be called *synonymism,* some philosophers who strive to defend the analyticity of all and only a priori statements have resorted to a variety of *conventionalism.* Such conventionalism may take two forms: first an older one whose stock phrase is 'nominal definition', and then a more recent one which talks the language of *semantical rules.*

In spite of the fact that most philosophers who have tried to deal seriously with the problem of the a priori recognize that they are faced with statements made in an unformalized language whose a priori truth is to be explained, some conventionalists have persisted in holding that the analyticity of these a priori statements is somehow connected with an arbitrary definition, i.e., a convention. According to *these* conventionalists, if one is asked why one feels justified in saying that 'Every brother is a male sibling' is analytic, one should reply that it can be deduced from the logical truth 'Every brother is a brother' with the help of a nominal or conventional definition of 'brother' as 'male sibling'. Such a view is often advanced (most pointlessly) by conventionalists who, when faced with the standard examples supplied by those who believe in the synthetic a priori, say that one *might* define the word 'cube' in such a way as to make C. H. Langford's perplexing example 'Every cube has twelve edges' analytic.[3] But the question is: How is the word used in fact? And where no actual conventions have been made, where no actual definitions have been given, it seems silly

[3] Langford, "The Notion of Analysis in Moore's Philosophy" in *Philosophy of G. E. Moore,* P. A. Schilpp, ed. (Evanston, Ill.: Northwestern University Press, 1942).

to say that the fact that a certain convention *might* be made guarantees the correctness of the critical step in establishing analyticity.

Even the partisan of the synthetic a priori knows that a philosopher might rig up a definition or "rule" which could "account" for the troublesome statements, so that it seems hard to suppose that crude conventionalists really understand or take seriously the position of their opponents. Now as I have already indicated, my criticism of the notion of analyticity does not imply an acceptance of the doctrine of the synthetic a priori, but it does involve convergence with it in a way that deserves elaboration, especially for those who think of the synthetic a priori as a tool of terrible people and who are likely to think of any charitable comment on it as evidence of the blackest philosophical reaction. Proponents of the synthetic a priori have given voice to uneasiness about the doctrine that all and only a priori statements are analytic, but they have gone too far. Understandably, the partisans of the synthetic a priori fail to see that their opponents have clearly shown that all and only a priori statements are analytic. Here I agree with supporters of the synthetic a priori because I believe that the notion of analyticity has not been clarified. Therefore I might summarize my attitude toward theorists of the all-analytic a priori in the words "They shouldn't say that". Those who believe in the synthetic a priori agree, but then they go too far in the other direction by crying, "They should say the contradictory". Needless to add, the synthetic a priorists shouldn't say *that*—and for the same reason. And, interestingly enough, while the synthetic a priorists usually agree that some of the a priori statements called analytic by the philosophers they oppose are rightly called analytic, I am afraid that I must dispute even that. All of this shows the complexity of the doctrinal relations involved and should ward off the tendency to amalgamate different doctrines because of their joint disagreement with a third—a tendency which is, sadly enough, present in philosophy as well as politics.

4. *The social contract, the linguistic contract,
   and performatory phrases*

A reasonable amount of free association brings to light an illuminating political counterpart to conventionalism in the theory

of the a priori: the theory of the social contract. The theorist of the
social contract is usually anxious to show that a certain course of
action is right—let us say rebellion, as in the case of Locke—and in
order to do so cites the "fact" that there was a contract at some
point in time whereby one party was to get something from the
other in exchange for a consideration. When it has been pointed
out that such a contract was never in fact made, some theorists of
the contract have been as unconcerned as a conventionalist when
he is told that a definition of the kind he postulates has never been
made. But what else does the contract theorist do when faced with
doubts about the historicity of the contract? He says that the contract is a *fiction*. And what does the conventionalist in the theory
of the a priori say? In effect, he too says that the definition is a
fiction because he maintains that we can account for the analyticity
of the statement under consideration by treating it *as if* it were the
result of rewriting a logical truth with the help of a definitional
rule of replacement. Such a reply makes clear that theorists of the
all-analytic a priori can't always account for analyticity by pointing
to an actual definition because frequently there is none, just as the
theorists of social contract cannot successfully justify the statement
that rebellion is right by pointing to an actual contract. At best,
the theorist of the social contract can maintain that *if* a contract
had been made, then a certain course of action *would be* right,
and the conventionalistic theorist of analyticity can maintain that
if there had been a definition, then a certain statement would be
analytic. I say "at best", but the best in this case is none too good,
for we want to know what is involved in making a definition or a
convention of the requisite kind.

For this it won't help to pursue the similarity between the
political theorist and the theorist of analyticity any further, because differences start to emerge that are likely to obstruct understanding of our problem. For example, a theorist of the social contract is not likely to do what his counterpart in semantics can do
and has done. First of all, the political theorist doesn't withdraw
the moral judgment he originally tried to justify by appeal to the
nonexistent contract, but the semantic conventionalist may refuse
to call sentences analytic if a linguistic contract has not been made.
Our linguistic conventionalists are able to do and say things that

are not usually open to the poor political conventionalists who cannot arrange to make a social contract now. The linguistic conventionalists may start building artificial languages with the help of so-called semantical rules and, what is equally important, they may then say that a statement is *never* to be called analytic unless it has already been codified in a language whose rules have been laid down. But in that case they have cut themselves off irrevocably from the view that their word 'analytic' "explains" the a priori-ness of statements that stimulated the original theory of the all-analytic a priori. They can no longer say that they have discovered that sentences which are described as a priori by traditional philosophers are analytic, for according to their view there is no such thing as the objective analyticity of sentences in ordinary or scientific use.

This view of 'analytic' is the counterpart of the empiricist theory of meaning to which some positivists have been reduced. Just as they are forced to give up the search for a criterion of meaningful or of an a posteriori sentence which would describe the class of sentences independently specified as a posteriori, so proponents of the corresponding approach to 'analytic' are forced to give up the analogous descriptive effort in the case of the a priori. And just as the positivist theorist of meaning now says that we ought to *call* certain sentences empirically meaningful, so the positivist theorist of the a priori can only say that we ought to *call* certain sentences analytic. We shall see in a moment that this *is* the upshot of certain theories of analyticity and therefore that 'analytic', like 'meaningful' and 'postulate', ceases to be a "descriptive" predicate but is sometimes applied to sentences in what J. L. Austin has called performatory phrases.[4]

Austin is mainly concerned with the peculiarities of the sentence 'I know', which, he thinks, behaves like 'I promise', and I am saying that 'This is a postulate' as initially announced by a logician who is constructing a system also behaves like 'I promise'. The point is that saying 'I promise' *is* promising; it is not a case of describing myself (as saying 'He promises' is a case of describing

---

[4] Austin, "Other Minds," *Proceedings of the Aristotelian Society*, supplementary vol. 20 (1946); reprinted in A. G. N. Flew, *Logic and Language: Second Series* (Oxford: Blackwell, 1953). See pp. 142–147 of the latter.

him). Now Austin is mainly concerned with sentences (like 'I know' and 'I promise') which are in the first person singular, and in the present indicative tense, whereas 'This is a postulate' is not. Nevertheless, I think 'This is a postulate' functions in a similar way in the context I have mentioned. We do not use it to say something about a sentence, as saying that it contains so many words would be a matter of saying something about a sentence. Of course, there are other uses of 'This is a postulate' which are not performatory. For example, when another person, who has become familiar with the system that I have built, says that a statement which I have "made" a postulate is a postulate, *he* uses the sentence 'This is a postulate' descriptively. But that is beside the point at the moment. 'This is a postulate' in the mouth of someone who describes a feature of my system is used in a manner which is different from the manner in which I use it when I'm building the system. When he says 'This is a postulate', he is describing a state of affairs which is the result of what I *do* when *I* say 'This is a postulate', very much as his statement that I have made a promise (which he couches in the third person by saying 'He has promised') is different from my promising, which I do by saying 'I promise'. Now just as a postulate in a given system is a sentence of which the logician or mathematician says 'This is a postulate', just as a meaningful expression is one about which a positivist says 'This is meaningful', so an analytic statement in a given language is one over which the ritualistic 'This is analytic' may be pronounced. What we must question, then, is the general advisability of such ritual rather than the truth or descriptive meaning of the sentences with which it is performed. And when I say "general advisability", I mean the advisability of introducing this kind of linguistic ritual into philosophy. The ritual of promising has a clear social function and is not likely to be questioned by any one. But the ritual of dubbing some sentences 'analytic' in a performatory manner must be examined in great detail just because there is reason to think that it is a worthless and meaningless ritual, meaningless not merely in the sense of not describing anything clearly, for in that sense of 'meaningless' 'I promise' is meaningless too, but rather in the sense of 'useless'. To this question we shall return later on. Right now we must examine what I have called the second kind of conventionalism, the kind that introduces the notion of semantical rule as a foundation for analyticity.

5. *Semantical rules: a way out?*

Conventionalism of the kind that depends on the notion of semantical rule usually begins with the construction of an artificial language. In order to construct a language we must present *rules*. Among these rules there may be those which say that such and such statements are the analytic statements of language L_0. For example, the following is a rule of language L_0 that I have in mind right now: 'All and only men are rational animals' is analytic in L_0. Now let us try to imagine a situation in which such a rule might be of some use to someone. A student leafs through a book entitled L_0 and written by a follower of Professor Carnap. The student comes across the statement 'All and only men are rational animals' somewhere in the middle. His socratic teacher (also a follower of Professor Carnap) asks him, "Is this an analytic statement?" The student cannot answer. He mumbles, "I don't know." The socratic teacher tries to help him in a mean sort of way; he asks him "Well, then, is it synthetic?" The boy is still dazed, and so the teacher must set him right—unsocratically. He tells the boy that whenever anyone asks him whether a statement is analytic he should always snap back, "In what language?" So, whenever he opens up a book like L_0 and is asked whether a given statement in it is analytic, he can assume that the question means, "Is it analytic-in-L_0?" But to answer this he need only consult the rules of L_0, which are conveniently stated at the beginning. The boy is then persuaded in a very progressive way to turn to those important opening pages and there he sees on page 2 the sentence (in very bold, black type):

> RULE I: 'All and only men are rational animals' is analytic in L_0.

The student now asks a simple question of momentous proportions: "But what does the rule mean?" About *this* question there appears to be some doubt in the minds of those who dispute about Carnap's views. Some, like Quine, appear to think that it's a reasonable question that is never answered,[5] while others are horrified at the thought of anyone asking it. Philosophers of the latter persuasion sometimes claim that the word 'analytic' is an "age-old" word for which an "explication" is now being presented. But what is that "explication" if it consists in nothing but a list of sentences after each of which an arbitrary sort of star is stuck, namely 'is analytic-in-L_0'? Every philosopher will admit that the student who finds the unstarred sentence in the middle of the book is given a perfectly good criterion for finding out whether it is analytic by being told that he should look up the section on rules and find out whether that sentence is starred, i.e., called analytic-in-L_0. But some insist that our inability to answer the boy who asks for clarification of the rule is fatal. For all the information we can give to a student who asks us what we mean by saying that a given sentence is analytic-in-L_0, is that it is one of those statements of which it is said at the beginning, "These and only these are analytic-in-L_0". Moreover, as Quine has pointed out, this does not define the general notion of being analytic for any unspecified artificial language L.[6] To be analytic in L_0 is to be a statement of which it is said that it is analytic in L_0; to be analytic in L_1 is to be a statement of which it is said that it is analytic in L_1, and so on.

It is obvious how philosophers who adopt this semantically regulative view of analyticity try to meet the criticisms of those who happen not to agree with their doctrine that all and only a priori statements are analytic. They can simply take any statement S that is alleged to be a priori synthetic and build a language L_2 for it which contains the rule 'S is analytic in L_2'. Having constructed the language in this way, they can hardly understand a man who says that this sentence S which they have labeled 'analytic-in-L_2' is really synthetic. For after all, *they* have built the language L_2 with their own hands; they should know what is or what is not analytic within it.

In assigning this view of 'analytic-in-L_0' to conventionalists, we are aware of the fact that there are other versions of the same tendency, according to which statements are not made analytic-in-L_0 by being called analytic-in-L_0. For example, there is the alternative

---

[5] See Quine, *From A Logical Point of View*, ch. 2, sec. 4.
[6] *Idem.*

approach which is examined by Quine and found wanting for reasons that deserve careful scrutiny. He says:

"Let us then turn to a second form of semantical rule, which says not that such and such statements are analytic but simply that such and such statements are included among the truths. Such a rule is not subject to the criticism of containing the un-understood word 'analytic;' and we may grant for the sake of argument that there is no difficulty over the broader term 'true.' A semantical rule of this second type, a rule of truth, is not supposed to specify all the truths of the language; it merely stipulates, recursively or otherwise, a certain multitude of statements which, along with others unspecified, are to count as true. Such a rule may be conceded to be quite clear. Derivatively, afterward, analyticity can be demarcated thus: a statement is analytic if it is (not merely true but) true according to the semantical rule.

"Still there is really no progress. Instead of appealing to an unexplained word 'analytic,' we are now appealing to an unexplained phrase 'semantical rule.' Not every true statement which says that the statements of some class are true can count as a semantical rule—otherwise *all* truths would be "analytic" in the sense of being true according to semantical rules. Semantical rules are distinguishable, apparently, only by the fact of appearing on a page under the heading 'Semantical Rules'; and this heading is itself then meaningless."[7]

The situation in which we find ourselves on the subject of analyticity is the following. If we adopt the view that 'S is analytic' is a descriptive sentence that can be established by seeing whether S, a sentence in a natural language, is the result of putting synonyms for synonyms in a logical truth, we run into all the difficulties we have pointed out in a previous chapter. If we hold instead that 'analytic' is best applied to sentences in artificial languages in a performatory manner, we see certain difficulties in clarifying 'analytic-in-L_0'.

6. *A parallel in the philosophy of law*

We are reminded of a similar situation in the philosophy of law. Suppose we want to discover a general characteristic of all

[7] *Ibid.*, p. 34.

sentences which are legal statutes—independently of their being promulgated by a sovereign body. Are we likely to find one? Can we say that there is any property of all sentences which makes them statutes, and which legislative bodies must discover before they enact these sentences as statutes? Is there some quality which inheres in statutory sentences and on which legislators report before they make them officially into statutes? No, and in the same way there is no inherent quality of analyticity in a sentence which a logical legislator can discover before stamping it 'analytic'. And if we conclude that making a sentence a statute consists in calling it a statute under appropriate circumstances, we see the difficulty in *defining* 'statute in C' where 'C' is a variable ranging over nations or sovereign bodies. For if we take a deliberately simplified view of a statute of England as one of which the appropriate sovereign body says in a performatory way, 'This is a statute of England', and if we take a corresponding view of a statute of France, we develop an illuminating analogy with the relativistic view of 'analytic'—even to the point of making it very difficult to produce a *definition* of 'statute in C' where 'C' ranges over nations. For we know that different sovereign bodies in different countries say very different things during the legislative ceremony, just as a wedding ceremony usually concludes with words which are irreplaceable and peculiar to the religion or country in question.

The question naturally arises: Do we now have the solution of the problem of 'analytic'? Is the sentence 'This is analytic' in the mouth of a logician constructing a specific artificial language performatory and hence unsusceptible to "analysis" or contextual definition in a way that would yield a general criterion of 'analytic'? We are tempted to say that this is the most plausible interpretation that can be given to the relativistic, artificial approach to 'analytic', but while it helps us understand the approach we may still query the wisdom of assigning 'analytic' in this performatory way. That is to say, we may ask about the wisdom and usefulness of this descriptively meaningless ritual. For after all, we the philosophers perform it and if all the philosophers of the world were to give up the ritual it would die. What reason is there for perpetuating it? We know that there is good reason for perpetuating the analogous ritual of law, but is there equally good reason for perpetuating the ritualistic talk of positivistic semantics?

One way to begin answering this general question is by asking ourselves two more specific questions as applied to a given case of 'analytic'-making. Suppose, for example, that we are faced with the responsibility of making 'All and only men are rational animals' analytic. First we ask the question: What characteristic of this sentence justifies our pronouncing it analytic in the way that a minister pronounces a couple man and wife? And next: What do we signify by calling it analytic rather than synthetic? In the case of calling something a statute or marrying people, all sorts of factual reasons or characteristics of the statute and the people are offered, and it is all too clear what is signified when we declare something a statute or pronounce a couple man and wife. But do we have comparable answers to these two questions in the case of 'analytic'? Moreover, what is gained by making an invidious distinction between two classes of accepted sentences: the analytic and the synthetic?

To achieve a better understanding of these questions and to answer them, I will turn to a consideration of certain kindred problems in ethics. There are at least two respects in which calling sentences analytic and calling them meaningful in a performatory way are analogous with the situation in ethics. For one thing, the mere fact that 'This is analytic' in the mouth of a logical legislator is performatory suggests that it is a sentence resembling 'This is right' in not being "descriptive"; for another, if we raise the question whether a given sentence *ought* to be called or made analytic we are raising a question that is even more obviously like a moral question. Moreover, if we inquire into the process of reasoning that leads us from saying that a sentence or an expression has a certain characteristic to saying that it *ought* to be called meaningful or that it ought to be called analytic, we inquire into a problem very similar to one which so-called ethical analysts have discussed. A proponent of a moral rule will assert, for example, that stealing is wrong, while the parallel in the case of the empiricist theory of meaning is the judgment that only observable predicates or those properly connected with them ought to be called meaningful. If positivist theorists of analyticity were to imitate Hempel's treatment of 'meaningful', they would say that all statements which are known a priori ought to be called analytic, rather than give us the impression that they were asserting a universal, descriptive statement that might be verified by examining so-called a priori statements to see whether they are analytic.

If this is a correct analogy, we see that the decision to call certain statements 'analytic' and to call certain predicates 'meaningful' neither *accounts* for nor analyzes the fact that these particular statements are known a priori to be true, nor does it explain what is meant by saying that these particular predicates are observable. At best the epistemological fact that certain statements are accepted a priori is given as a reason for *marking* them 'analytic', just as the fact that certain expressions are "observable" is given as a reason for marking them 'empirically meaningful'. We see therefore that the more traditional view of the relation between epistemology and semantics has been reversed. Far from being clarified by reference to analyticity and meaning, the notions of a priori and a posteriori appear to be ineliminable components of rules which direct us to honor certain sentences semantically with the titles 'analytic' and 'synthetic'. To what good purpose, if any, we shall ask later.

The legal analogy may be pressed to further advantage by considering the following statement by a distinguished lawyer: "As a lawyer, I know guilt and innocence are legal terms. As such, I would not know whether [a man] were guilty or innocent until he was found one way or the other by a jury."[8] Now I think philosophical words like 'defined' are in a similar category as 'guilty'. That is to say, a term is a defined term just in case it has been treated linguistically in a certain way, just in case it has been written down, followed by a certain sign like the double bar, followed by the so-called definiens, followed by some symbol like 'Df', as in many contemporary logic books. And just as we can give arguments in defense of our having made a certain definition, so a jury must give arguments (to itself) for having "found" a man guilty, which means for having pronounced the word 'guilty' at the proper time. The legal situation presents all of the problems presented by the philosophical situation. The word 'guilty' comes to be used in two different ways, one legal and one not, and yet both of them figure in

[8] Judge Harold R. Medina, quoted in *The Christian Science Monitor*, August 18, 1954 (Boston).

legal decision. The lawyer we have quoted may well think of 'guilty' as meaning 'said by a jury to be guilty', but the jury in its *deliberations* will use the word differently, for they will imagine themselves obliged to settle a question of fact, like "Did he pull the trigger?", that is, to find out whether the man "really is" guilty before they say 'guilty' to the judge in that way that becomes so all-important for the lawyer we have quoted. In *their* mouths at the time the verdict is rendered, the word 'guilty' does not mean 'called 'guilty' by us', even though it may to the lawyer quoted.

A similar situation is presented in baseball. A player is out on one usage just in case the umpire has called him 'out' or jerked his thumb in a certain way. But the umpire who bawls 'Yer out!' presumably bases his bawling on a fact, like the fact that the player has reached first base *after* the ball has been caught by the first baseman with his foot on the bag.

I suggest that some philosophers think that words like 'defined', 'analytic', and 'meaningful' are all like 'out' and 'guilty' in *two* respects. First they suppose, and I think rightly, that being defined is merely a matter of whether someone has said or done the proper things to a word or expression; in effect, that a definitional equivalence is one that has been *said* to be a definitional equivalence, and that being analytic is also a matter of whether someone has performed the proper ritual over a sentence. But then they add—and here is where I think they go wrong—that there are underlying "factual grounds" analogous to the fact that this man did commit the murder or the fact that this man did get to the base after the ball, which underlie or support performatory statements like 'I define so-and-so as such and such'. It is the second contention that is most dubious in the case of logical legislation. The case of an act of definition or an act of postulation is more like the case of the legislature which makes a certain imperative sentence a law or a statute, because in such a case there are *no* facts which bear the same relation to legislation as a man's failure to get to first base before the ball bears to the umpire's calling him 'out'. Indeed, the theory of natural law is inadequate precisely because it imagines that there are such prelegislative facts which force legislators to call certain sentences statutes. And the theory of "real definitions" is, in a sense, the logical counterpart of the doctrine of natural law. It amounts to the thesis that there are certain pre-established synonymies or real definitional facts which antedate the making of "nominal definitions" and which these nominal definitions are supposed to mirror faithfully on pain of being called "*merely* nominal definitions".

Now I do not deny that there are factual *considerations* that have a bearing upon which definitions we should make or which statements we should take as postulates, but I am denying that they are what I shall call exact factual counterparts of the performatory sentences by whose means we make the definitions or postulates, that is to say, the sentences by whose means we do the defining and the postulating. Moreover, I assert that these factual considerations that underlie or support the definitional or postulational decisions we do make support quasi-moral judgments to the effect that those are correct or justified decisions. But unlike many recent philosophers who advocate a related doctrine in ethics proper, I do not think that a special logic is involved here, though my defense of this last view must wait until a later chapter.

It should be clear that I have no objection to the notion that a philosopher makes a certain sentence analytic by calling it that, nor to the view that a philosopher makes a certain expression meaningful by calling it that. That is the easiest and the unobjectionable part of the process. What is objectionable is the fact that very often the "factual considerations" that play such a tremendous role in law, for example, the factual considerations that support our calling a certain sentence a statute, lack counterparts in the case of analyticity and meaningfulness. And what is also objectionable is the fact that this type of activity—analytic-making that transcends definition in the obvious logical sense, and meaningful-making—often lacks anything corresponding to the social purpose of legislation in society. These are no mean objections, for they call into question the ground and the function of two of the most important types of positivistic philosophical activity.

PART III

WHAT SHOULD BE

CHAPTER X

The Naturalistic Fallacy
and the Nature of Goodness

1. *From existence to decision*

The suggestion that some nonethical terms are more closely linked with ethical terms than might be supposed can only be helpful if we have some insight into the way in which ethical terms behave. One rarely finds that the behavior of *any* kind of term is similarly viewed by all philosophers, so that one seldom communicates or is immediately persuasive when one says that a term of one kind behaves like one of another and rather distant kind. One must face the disconcerting fact that for every philosopher who might develop some sense of illumination upon hearing it said that 'analytic' is more like 'good' than it is like 'table', there are several who are dubious or depressed at the thought. The second response is especially characteristic of those analytic philosophers who have avoided ethics as though it were a poor relative in the philosophical family. I am fully aware of this sort of attitude, but not as impressed as some by the successes of other branches of philosophy. And so I turn to ethics for illumination, not so much for direct illumination as for the kind of indirect lighting which comes when one sees that the reasons for our difficulties in defining analyticity and meaningfulness might be very like the reasons for a similar situation in ethics. And since I think that reflection on ethical questions should lead us to recognize that there is something important in the view that 'good' and 'right' are not "descriptive", I begin with a consideration of the most influential source of this view in the twentieth century, the *Principia Ethica* of Moore.

It might be said that far from providing an alternative to platonism and other inadequate theories of existence, necessity, and meaning, Moore's doctrine is the ethical counterpart of the epistemologies we have rejected. For after all, platonistic theorists of understanding and the a priori postulate meanings as entities we grasp when we understand, while Moore postulates nonnatural characteristics as the entities we ascribe to things when we evaluate. Therefore, far from throwing light on the problems we have wrestled with, Moore's view, it might be said, is full of the same kind of darkness and dormitive virtue. If all this were said, I should agree but then add that we who approach Moore's *Principia Ethica* today should be well inoculated against the kind of hypostatizing that produced meanings, sense-data, natural properties, and nonnatural properties as ways of accounting for understanding, perceiving, describing, and evaluating respectively. In the end we shall be forced to reject Moore's account of evaluation but not without having gained insight into some of its peculiarities, peculiarities which are like those involved in the application of 'analytic', 'synonymous', 'clear', and 'meaningful'. The very fact that 'analytic' and 'good' have both driven some philosophers to platonistic extremes and the very fact that both of them have been so resistant to definitional treatment suggest that the cause and cure might be similar in both cases.

The history of analytic ethics in the twentieth century follows a pattern that reflects parallel tendencies in epistemology and metaphysics. For just as philosophers in the age of existence introduce attributes or meanings in order to account for the fact of understanding, so these same philosophers marked out a special kind of attribute—the nonnatural attribute—in a similar effort to account for evaluation. And just as epistemologists of the linguistic age hoped to solve the problem of the a priori and the a posteriori by appealing to notions of analyticity and empirical meaningfulness that would apply to language as ordinarily used, so writers on ethics of this period appealed to the notion of emotive meaning in order to characterize ethical language. But there is a third phase of ethical philosophy in which philosophers have developed doubts about both anti-naturalism and orthodox positivism and which may be called the ethics of decision. In this chapter we shall examine the platonistic, anti-naturalistic ethical views of the early Moore; in the next we shall turn to those of orthodox positivism; and after that we shall begin to consider the problems and issues of the most recent period of ethical philosophy with an eye on the wider issues that are common to ethics and the more general notions of the philosophy of language.

2. *Moore's ethical views and his philosophical method*

Moore's main doctrine as set forth in *Principia Ethica* achieved enormous influence, in part because it was the most powerfully defended ethical theory in the history of analytic philosophy. Stated briefly, it is the view that goodness is a simple, nonnatural attribute. While the early Russell was concerned to show that there are such things as attributes, Moore's main contribution to the theory of attributes as universals consisted in emphasizing three divisions within the genus: one between so-called natural attributes and nonnatural attributes, another between simple and complex attributes, and a third between intrinsic and nonintrinsic attributes. Just as Russell's supposition that attributes exist was the result of his view that they are the things we grasp when we understand general terms, so Moore's supposition that nonnatural attributes exist was the result of *his* view that we *as*cribe a peculiar kind of property, a nonnatural property, when we evaluate. In both cases a queer entity is offered in explication or explanation of what is undeniable, namely that we do understand and that we do evaluate. But in Moore's case as in Russell's, a mode of explanation is introduced which is more obscure than that which it is supposed to analyze, account for, or illuminate. Once again an epistemological or metalinguistic fact is wrongly thought to be clarified by an appeal to dubious ontology.

In considering Moore's view we can take advantage of some of the logical and semantical points introduced in earlier chapters, since Moore is one of the most logically and semantically minded theorists in the history of ethics, and his work has had more influence than that of any philosopher in pushing moral philosophy in a semantical direction. It is perhaps the best example of a tendency on the part of analytic philosophers to concentrate on the meanings of terms, except for one ironic twist. While the aim of analytic philosophy as conceived by Moore is to *produce* analyses of the meanings of terms, it was Moore's point in *Principia Ethica* that the meaning or connotation of 'good' is an unusual attribute and incapable of analysis.

It might be added parenthetically that the fate of many other

attributes or concepts is similar in Moore's philosophy. So many
are either unanalyzable or not analyzed that one is bound to suspect that there is something about Moore's conception of his task
that makes it extraordinarily difficult or even impossible of achievement. So often the examples of successful analyses arrived at by
Moore's method are relatively uninteresting ("To be a brother is to
be a male sibling"), and so often when he applied it to more philosophical words like 'good', 'material object', and 'analytic', it was peculiarly prone to stall. Whether for the same reason in all cases is
difficult to say. One is tempted to say that the notion of identity
of meaning involved in Moore's view of analysis was so obscure
that one would never know when a successful analysis had been
achieved, but then we cannot deny that to be a brother *is* to be a
male sibling. One is tempted to say that all the words which resisted moorean analysis were of the same kind, i.e., "normative",
and therefore that all of Moore's unanalyzed and unanalyzable
terms were such for reasons like that involved in the case of 'good',
but this would swell the list of "normative" terms beyond all
reason. One is tempted to say that the search for synonyms is
doomed just because, as Nelson Goodman has argued, no two
terms are ever exactly alike in meaning,[1] and therefore that it is
not surprising that the only successful analyses to which Moore
could point were those of Russell and Frege, who really did not
look for synonyms but only for extensional equivalents. One is
tempted to say all of these things and more in diagnosis of Moore's
long list of unanalyzed and/or unanalyzable terms, and there is
probably a bit of truth in all of them. But since we are not concerned here with the whole of Moore's philosophy, we need not
stop to consider them. Here we are concerned only with Moore's
views on the word 'good' or, as he would prefer to say, on the attribute, property, or characteristic of being good.

Unlike vixenhood, which is both natural and complex, goodness is neither according to Moore. Stated in this way his thesis is
rather straightforward. It requires elucidation and argumentation
but nothing comparable to what has been stirred up by Moore's
use of the phrase 'naturalistic fallacy' to describe what his opponents commit. Philosophers don't mind being contradicted, but

[1] "On Likeness of Meaning" in Linsky, *Semantics and the Philosophy of Language.*

understandable pride forces them to bridle when charged with a *fallacy*. That charge is best understood after a few introductory remarks on Moore's fundamental concern in ethics.

3. *Ethics and analysis*

The fundamental question of ethics from Moore's viewpoint is 'What is good?' Even in electing this as the *fundamental* question, Moore adopted a certain position in the history of ethical controversy, but we are not here interested in the contrast between him and those philosophers who might take as fundamental the question 'What is right conduct?' Since so many ethical philosophers elevate rightness to the position Moore gave to goodness and then claim that rightness is a simple, nonnatural attribute, we can see how both disputants in this quarrel illustrate a *type* of thinking that overarches their differences about the logical order of *rightness* and *goodness*, a type of thinking that asserts and tries to prove the existence of simple nonnatural attributes.

As we have seen, Moore's raising the question 'What is good?' is in a sense a rhetorical device, for we do not get an answer to the question from him. His main point is that we *can't* get an answer to this question if it is construed as philosophers ought to construe it, that is to say, as a request for a definition. In asking 'What is good?' the philosopher is not asking for an example of goodness as he might ask for an example of manhood and expect a specific man's name in reply; nor is he asking the kind of question which might be answered by saying 'Books are good', for this is still not a definition. The first construal of the question merely elicits the name of a single concrete example, like Socrates, while the second elicits a class of examples, like books. Moore is interested in neither of these. Nor is he satisfied with an answer that does better than 'books' in a certain respect, that is to say, one that presents an adjective or noun true of all and only good things, much as 'featherless biped' is said to be true of all and only men. That wouldn't do either because it would fail to express the *connotation* of 'good', much as 'featherless biped' fails to express the connotation of 'man' in spite of covering all the examples. What Moore thinks a philosopher *should* produce in reply is an expression which bears to 'good' the relation that 'rational animal' is sometimes said to bear to 'man' or 'male sibling' to 'brother'—*if he could*. But Moore's chief point is that he *can't* produce this; he *can't* find an expression which will serve in the definiens of 'good' by expressing the connotation of 'good' in the way that 'rational animal' expresses the connotation of 'man', and this inability to do so is the linguistic expression of the simplicity of goodness.

The philosopher's inability to do for 'good' what he is able to do for other words like 'man' or 'brother' or 'vixen' is thought to be a reflection of something deeper. Hence Moore's answer to his own fundamental question is "that good is good and that is the end of the matter". In other words, that which the adjective 'good' expresses or connotes cannot be defined. I use the words 'expresses' and 'connotes' because the words Moore uses may be misunderstood. Moore talks about the word 'good' "standing for" and even "denoting" the "object" or "idea" *good,* but I can interpret him more easily by thinking of the object or idea which moral philosophers *want* to analyze (but which turns out to be unanalyzable according to Moore's view) as *the attribute of being good,* hence as that which is *c*onnoted by the word 'good' in the millian semantics. It is essential, therefore, to realize the degree to which Moore opposed what might be called a linguistic view of philosophical analysis. In *Principia Ethica* he is not trying to give one word's meaning in other words. He says so explicitly. For one thing, he says, if he had wanted to do that he would have considered how people do in fact use the word 'good'. He adds that it would be foolish of course to use the word 'good' for something which it did not usually express, and so he says: "I shall, therefore, use the word in the sense in which I think it is ordinarily used; but at the same time I am not anxious to discuss whether I am right in thinking that it is so used. My business is solely with that object or idea, which I hold, rightly or wrongly, that the word is generally used to stand for. What I want to discover is the nature of that object or idea, and about this I am extremely anxious to arrive at an agreement."[2] Moore is really interested not in the question 'What is good?' but rather in 'What is goodness?' For this reason, it is as

2 *Principia Ethica*, p. 6. Like all students of the naturalistic fallacy, I am indebted to William K. Frankena's important article "The Naturalistic Fallacy," *Mind,* vol. 48 (1939); reprinted in Sellars and Hospers, *Readings in Ethical Theory* (New York: Appleton-Century-Crofts, 1952).

misleading for him to ask, 'What is good?' as it would be to ask, 'What is true?' when one meant to ask, 'What is truth?'

The *analysandum* or the thing to be analyzed in Moore's case is neither the word 'good' nor the class of good things. We have already seen that it is not the verbal expression 'good'; let us now see why it is not the class of good things. First of all Moore says: " 'Good,' . . . if we mean by it that quality which we assert to belong to a thing, when we say that the thing is good, is incapable of any definition, in the most important sense of that word."[3] This I take as unmistakable support for the view that the entity in question is an attribute or a *quality*. But then he distinguishes between this attribute and an entity which he calls "*the* good". *The good*, he says, might be definable. "I suppose it may be granted that 'good' is an adjective," he says. "Well," he continues, " 'the good,' 'that which is good,' must therefore be the substantive to which the adjective 'good' will apply: it must be the whole of that to which the adjective will apply, and the adjective must *always* truly apply to it. But if it is that to which the adjective will apply, it must be something different from that adjective itself; and the whole of that something different, whatever it is, will be our definition of *the* good."[4] Now in spite of certain difficulties produced by this last passage, I suggest that *the* good may be thought of as the class of good things, i.e., as the extension of 'good', and that Moore may be thought to maintain that the class of good things may be identical with the class of, say, things conducive to pleasure, and in this sense we might say that *the class* of good things might be definable. I fail to see any other clear interpretation of "the good" or "the whole" to which the adjective good "applies".

This interpretation is further supported when Moore compares goodness with yellowness and says (in effect) that just as we can't define yellowness by saying that it's the attribute of emitting or reflecting light of 5,893 Ängstrom units, so we can't define goodness analogously. We may find other properties which are possessed by all and only good things, just as we can find that the property of emitting or reflecting light of 5,893 Ängstrom units is possessed by all yellow objects, but that's another matter. Moore grants that

[3] Moore, *Principia,* p. 9.
[4] *Idem.*

these other properties might be named, but goes on to say: "far too many philosophers have thought that when they named those other properties they were actually defining good; that these properties, in fact, were not simply 'other,' but absolutely and entirely the same with goodness. This view I propose to call the 'naturalistic fallacy' and of it I shall now endeavor to dispose."[5]

4. *The naturalistic fallacy*

According to one interpretation of Moore's words, we commit the naturalistic fallacy in passing from the statement that the class of good things is identical with the class of things conducive to pleasure to the statement that the attribute of being good is identical with the attribute of being conducive to pleasure. But this fallacy, which we may call '(M)', is merely a special case of the mistake of inferring that attributes are identical from the fact that corresponding classes are identical. It is therefore a mistake which is not peculiar to ethics, for it is one recognized by most philosophers who distinguish between classes and attributes. As we have seen, two classes can be identical even when the corresponding attributes are distinct; the class of featherless bipeds is identical with the class of men while the attribute of being a featherless biped is not identical with the attribute of being a man, and though we are told on good authority that the class of creatures having hearts is identical with the class of creatures having kidneys, no one would maintain that the attribute of having a kidney is identical with the attribute of having a heart.

It should be repeated that mistake (M) is a mistake *in inference,* having nothing to do with the fact that the terms in question are ethical or not. One can make it no matter what terms or kinds of terms appear in putative premise or conclusion. And if one restricts one's self to saying that only errors in inference are fallacies, then the *mere assertion* that goodness is identical with, say, the attribute of being conducive to pleasure is no more a fallacy than is the assertion that the attribute of having a kidney is identical with the attribute of having a heart. Both may be *false* assertions, but it is not customary to say that anyone who asserts a false proposition is committing a fallacy in making that assertion. The most

[5] *Ibid.,* p. 10.

we are likely to say is that if a man has made a false assertion of the identity of attributes like some of those mentioned, then he should not be tempted to support it with an argument that would be fallacious in the manner indicated.

It is only by keeping clearly in mind the fact that these are different kinds of mistakes with which Moore charges his opponents, and by disentangling the charges, that we can come to understand something of the controversy that followed the appearance of his book. Let us examine (M), the inferential kind of mistake, a little further. In other parts of his book Moore lists fallacious inferences that are similar to the one discussed above in a very important respect; he generalizes the mistake even beyond that of inferring the identity of attributes from the corresponding identity of classes. Thus he considers the case of a man who would conclude from the statement 'I am having the sensation of pleasure' the statement 'I am the same thing as having pleasure'. But if this is an example of the same fallacy for Moore, we must broaden our description of the fallacious inference. We cannot describe *this* as a mistake of kind (M), simply because the conclusion here, though an identity-statement, is not a statement of the identity of *attributes,* and the premise is not a statement of the identity of classes. There are times when Moore illustrates the fallacy he has in mind by citing someone who infers the statement 'I am the same as pleased' from 'I am pleased', and here we may describe the fallacy as that of moving from an assertion of predication to a corresponding assertion of identity, parallel to concluding that Socrates is the same as the property of being a man from the fact that he is a man. But if we ask ourselves what the mistake in (M) has in common with *this* mistake, one can only say that both fallacious inferences are inferences in which an identity statement is wrongly inferred from some other statement that might be thought of as entailing that identity statement.

It is important to bear in mind that the *basic,* non-inferential mistake for Moore is that of confusing one entity with another. And this is the most important charge aimed at a philosopher who says (a) *that goodness is identical with being conducive to pleasure.* But since Moore recognizes that there might be some other proposition which the philosopher *might* think of as implying (a), like (b) *that the class of good things is identical with the class of things conducive to pleasure,* Moore warns against committing the fallacy of *inferring* (a) from (b).

It must be insisted, however, that sometimes Moore speaks of the naturalistic fallacy as the fallacy of inferring statements like (a) from statements like (b), and sometimes he speaks of it as the fallacy of identifying things like goodness with things other than itself. Now these are closely related mistakes from a logical point of view but they are distinct, for a man might confuse goodness with being conducive to pleasure without giving any reason at all. Such a man would be identifying two discernibles according to Moore, and therefore committing a fallacy in one of Moore's senses of the word 'fallacy', but he would not be committing a fallacy of inference like that schematized in (M) above.

5. *The same fallacy outside of ethics*

As we have seen, the mistake of identifying discernibles, like the mistake of inferring false identity-statements from premises that don't imply these identity statements, is very general and applies to cases other than those in which ethical terms or so-called natural predicates are involved. Moore puts this point most clearly in the following passage, in which he explains the relevance of the word 'naturalistic'.

"If I were to imagine that when I said 'I am pleased,' I meant that I was exactly the same thing as 'pleased,' I should not indeed call that a naturalistic fallacy, although it would be the same fallacy as I have called naturalistic with reference to Ethics. The reason of this is obvious enough. When a man confuses two natural objects with one another, defining the one by the other, if for instance he confuses himself, who is one natural object, with 'pleased' or with 'pleasure' which are others, then there is no reason to call the fallacy naturalistic. But if he confuses 'good,' which is not in the same sense a natural object, with any natural object whatever, then there is a reason for calling that a naturalistic fallacy; its being made with regard to 'good' marks it as something quite specific, and this specific mistake deserves a name because it is so common. As for the reasons why good is not to be considered a natural object, they may be reserved for discussion in another place. But, for the present, it is sufficient to notice this: Even if it were a natural object, that would not alter the nature of the fallacy nor diminish its importance one whit. All that I have said about it would remain quite equally true: only the name which I have called it would not be so appropriate as I think it is."[6]

All of this makes the general outline of Moore's position on the naturalistic fallacy clear. Goodness cannot be identified with any natural characteristic. The naturalistic fallacy in its inferential form consists in making mistake (M) schematized earlier; the naturalistic fallacy in its non-inferential form consists in identifying goodness with a natural quality. Therefore the non-inferential form of the naturalistic fallacy consists in confusing a nonnatural object with a natural object. But there are other species of the same confusion, namely, confusing one natural object with another natural object, and confusing one nonnatural object with another nonnatural object. Each such confusion, of course, might be arrived at by specious reasoning of the kind outlined in (M), but Moore prefers to concentrate on that kind and to label the inferential fallacy involved the "naturalistic fallacy", under conditions indicated in the last quotation from *Principia Ethica*.

6. *The simplicity of goodness*

Turning now from the comparatively obvious point that (M) is a mistake, and that distinct things are not to be confused, we must examine what is another one of Moore's most important contentions: that goodness is simple. The contention that goodness is simple performs a function very much like some of the other statements about platonic entities we have already examined. That is to say, it is intended as some sort of explanation of a metalinguistic fact: the fact that Moore could not define the word 'good' to his own satisfaction. The simplicity of goodness is supposed to explain a human failure. And yet plainly in one sense one can always define *the word* 'good'. One can always say, 'I define the word 'good' as short for 'conducive to pleasure' ', or what not. The situation here is quite similar to that involved in the case of

[6] *Ibid.*, pp. 13–14.

'analytic' as described in a previous chapter. Construed in one way, definition is partly a process of uttering the words 'is defined as' or 'is a definition' at the right time and in the right place, and being undefined or primitive is a state in which terms find themselves when this linguistic process has not been performed. Being unmarried is a similar state.

The introduction of the notion *indefinable,* which allegedly transcends the question of what linguistic decisions have been made, impels philosophers to speak of simple attributes. If we identify the definability of an expression with our power to *call* it definitionally equivalent to some other expression, then clearly no expression is indefinable so long as our powers of speech hold out. But it is plain that definability is not construed in this way by those who think as Moore did. They think of being definable as something that might better be called 'correctly definable', for they tend to say that whereas we can always write '*Df*' beside certain equivalences, as in 'Man = Featherless Biped *Df*', not all such definitions are *correct* definitions, because a correct definition is one in which the definiens at least has the same connotation as the definiendum. Understood in this way, the thesis that the word 'good' is indefinable amounts to the thesis that no man can *correctly* say that he has defined the word 'good'. Reason: 'Good' is synonymous with no logically complex predicate. Reason for *this:* The word 'good' expresses the attribute *goodness,* which is simple. But now the question arises: Can we know that an attribute is simple in a way that really explains our failure to find a "correct" definition? In other words, if we have not been able to turn up a definitional equivalent for a word which is synonymous with that word by presystematic standards, does the "discovery" that the word expresses a simple attribute really explain our failure? I don't think so. I think that the effort to account for the indefinability of linguistic expressions by reference to the simplicity of meanings is on a par with the effort to account for the understandability of a term by saying that it has a meaning, and with the effort to say that being true by virtue of relations between meanings accounts for being a priori. Once again, an ontological or semantic explanation is offered which is of no use whatsoever.

Both here and in the case of those who advise us to construct definitions of 'analytic' that reflect analyticities in ordinary discourse, philosophers operate with the same stereotype or model. They think that the maker of analytic statements and definitions must somehow mirror analyticities and synonymies which hold in ordinary discourse, and then these are in turn thought to be the reflections of deeper relations between meanings. This is expressed in one of Moore's more important statements, one in which he explicitly reveals the closeness between the notions of indefinability and analyticity and implicitly reveals his inability to clarify the word 'simple' as applied to attributes in a purely nonlinguistic way.

"If I am asked 'What is good?' my answer is that good is good and that is the end of the matter. Or if I am asked, 'How is good to be defined?' my answer is that it cannot be defined, and that is all I have to say about it. But disappointing as these answers may appear, they are of the very last importance. To readers who are familiar with philosophic terminology, I can express their importance by saying that they amount to this: That propositions about the good are all of them synthetic and never analytic; and that is plainly no trivial matter. And the same thing may be expressed more popularly, by saying that, if I am right, then nobody can foist upon us such an axiom as that 'Pleasure is the only good' or that 'The good is the desired' on the pretence that this is 'the very meaning of the word.' " [7]

Recalling my interpretation of "the good" as the class of good things and hence of "the desired" as the class of desired things, we may take the last sentence of this passage as implying *not* that the statement 'The class of good things is identical with the class of desired things' is *false* but rather that it is not analytic. And Moore's point, generalized, is that *no* statement of class-identity *of this sort* is analytic. He expresses his point by saying that all propositions about the good are synthetic, without realizing, or perhaps because he doesn't believe—it doesn't matter—that 'The good is the good' (or 'The class of good things is identical with the class of good things') is about the good and analytic. But this lapse, if lapse it is, is not important; for that matter, Moore didn't have in mind the more general, tricky complaint that since the good is the class of

[7] *Ibid.,* pp. 6–7.

good things, we can produce an analytic proposition about *the good* by substituting 'the class of good things' for the variables in any theorem of the algebra of classes. What he had in mind were the nonformal identities involved in traditional definition, and he was saying, as I interpret him, that no statement of the form 'The good is the ____', where the blank is replaced by a logically complex predicate not containing 'good', is analytic. 'The class of vixens is identical with the class of female foxes', or alternatively in Moore-like language, 'The vixen is the female fox', *is* analytic, and so we may say that 'vixen' *is* definable from this viewpoint because 'female fox' is a logically complex expression. But according to Moore, the analogous things are just not true of *goodness*, the good, and 'good'.

What I wish to bring out by this is the fact that the substitution of so-called philosophic terminology like 'analytic' and 'synthetic' does not really clarify Moore's statement that the word 'good' is indefinable, nor, and this is more important, does it somehow eliminate *his* need to appeal to the notion of simplicity as applied to attributes. The very fact that 'The good is the good' is analytic (which Moore didn't seem to realize) makes it impossible for Moore to distinguish 'good' from other predicates by saying that *no* proposition about *the good* is analytic. And if his point should be reformulated by saying that no proposition about the good which contains a grammatically complex predicate in place of the blank in 'The good is the ____' is analytic, we should have to remember that according to Moore's view the important thing is not grammatical complexity but rather something that might be called logical complexity, which applies to attributes rather than to linguistic expressions.

Moreover, Moore cannot seriously appeal to Bishop Butler's aphorism: "Everything is what it is, and not another thing." For the attribute of being a brother is what it is and not another thing, and yet the statement 'The attribute of being a brother is identical with the attribute of being a male sibling' is presumably true. Unfortunately Moore does sometimes speak as though he could seriously use Butler at this point, but that is probably the result of his own conviction that all of the complex attributes he can think of are such that their names when put for the blank in 'Goodness is identical with _____' yield false statements. The fact is that once Moore has abandoned the purely factual, metalinguistic way of stating the thesis, namely ' 'Good' has no complex synonyms', he is in danger of oscillating between the extreme of Butlerian triviality and that of absurdity. Thus the formulation 'No attribute which is other than goodness is identical with goodness' is trivial, for something analogous is true of *all* attributes; while the formulation 'No attribute is identical with goodness' is absurd because goodness is identical with goodness. A formulation (in the "material mode") which avoids this is 'No complex attribute is identical with goodness', but this is hardly an advance on 'Goodness is not complex', which, in turn, hardly merits the title of being a clarification of 'Goodness is simple'. In the end, therefore, our efforts *to clarify* what Moore means by saying that goodness is simple—whether they abandon the material mode for the formal mode or not—seem inadequate to convey his point. In the end Moore seems forced to attribute simplicity to attributes in an absolute, nonlinguistic way, which simplicity he offers as the explanation of our inability to define the term 'good'. It would appear that we must *see* that goodness is simple, just as we must *see* that certain things are good. Not only is goodness simple but simplicity is too! Simple is simple and that is the end of the matter.

This upshot should not be surprising to us. For after all, our reflections in previous chapters have led us to despair about attempted clarifications of 'analytic', 'meaningful', etc., and, as we shall see, 'simple' is very much in their company. The philosopher who asks us to look at meanings in order to see that they are identical and in this way see why there is a priori knowledge usually supplies no criterion for the identity of meanings; the physician who asks us to *see* that opium has the dormitive virtue usually gives no criterion for detecting whether anything has the dormitive virtue; and the philosopher who invites us to see the simplicity of attributes in order to understand why certain expressions are indefinable is equally uncommunicative.

7. *The attempt at proving the indefinability of goodness*

To inveigh against appealing to the simplicity of attributes is not to deny that some terms are *un*defined. And if applied to *terms* rather than attributes, the word 'simple' is merely another way of saying 'not defined in the system'. But it is absurd to ask of a given undefined term what there is about it that makes it undefined other than the fact that it is called such. Saying 'This is undefined' at the beginning is performatory in Austin's sense, and much like 'I take this as undefined'. We may go on to dispute the wisdom of calling a term undefined and thereby making it undefined, but that is like disputing the wisdom of a minister's refusing to marry a certain couple.

In maintaining that Moore does not really give any analysis of the notion of simplicity as applied to attributes, we must face the fact that he tries to *prove* that goodness is simple. It is very rare to find proofs in philosophy where undefined terms are involved, and for this reason we have reason to be suspicious of his proof.

The *locus classicus* of his argument is in Section 13 of *Principia Ethica*. There Moore tries to show that there are only two alternative views to the one he maintains and that both of these are false. The two alternatives to the view (1) that goodness is simple are (2) that goodness is not simple and (3) that the word 'good' means nothing at all. Stated in other terms, the three exclusive and exhaustive alternatives contemplated by Moore are (1) that the predicate, i.e., the linguistic expression 'good', cannot be defined even though it connotes an attribute; (2) that the predicate 'good' *can* be defined (and a fortiori does connote an attribute); (3) that the predicate 'good' is without meaning, i.e., connotes no attribute (nor for that matter, any sense at all). I now turn to his refutation of (2) and (3) whereby he hopes to establish (1), the only remaining possibility.

The possibilities are stated by Moore in such a way as to cause confusion after some of our millian and fregean formulations, so we must explain and comment on Moore's terminology in order to avoid more difficulty than is necessary. For example, Moore says: "If it is not the case that 'good' *denotes* [my italics] something simple and indefinable, only two alternatives are possible: either it is a complex, a given whole, about the correct analysis of which there may be disagreement; or else it means nothing at all."[8] Therefore we must remind ourselves of our decision to speak of

[8] *Ibid.*, p. 15.

the quality or attribute under discussion as what is *con*noted by the linguistic expression 'good' and not as that which is *de*noted by it. If we were to select any one entity as that which is *de*noted by the adjective 'good', it should be the class of good things or *the good*.

Also, we must constantly keep Moore's use of the word 'whole' in mind. It may help unravel the motives underlying statements that might otherwise seem woollier than they are. We should recognize that a whole for Moore is something that has parts and is complex, and that therefore some word connected with it is definable; while an entity that is not a whole is partless and simple, and the word associated with *it* is indefinable. So far as one can make out, Moore construes *the good* as a whole. But then if we are right in construing the good as the class of all good things, we might be forced to regard classes as heaps and to think of their members as *parts* of them. The difficulties in this view are considerable, so perhaps it is wiser to construe the class of good things as a whole whose "parts" are classes into which it may be decomposed by discovering the boolean operations involved. Thus the class of fathers would contain as parts the class of males and the class of parents, and the boolean operation here would be class multiplication.

This gives a clue as to how we might construe Moore's statement that some *attributes,* namely the complex ones, are wholes, while others (the simple ones) are not. Surely attributes cannot be thought of as heaps, and therefore their complexity is probably like the complexity of classes when classes are not construed as heaps. The complexity of an attribute would then be the complexity it has relative to the attributes of which it is, so to speak, *logically* composed. The attribute of being a brother is logically (not spatially) composed of the attribute of being a male and the attribute of being a sibling, where the mode of composition is the operation of conjunction of attributes. (While all cases of analysis of attributes which follow the classic pattern of definition by *genus* and *differentia* or something like it will use conjunction, this is not necessary, of course.)

Having agreed that the complexity of an attribute or its wholeness is not a spatial matter, we may see the speciousness of the invidious distinction that Moore makes between 'good' and 'horse'.

This will serve as another clarifying observation preparatory to our consideration of Moore's rejection of alternatives (2) and (3) mentioned above. In defining 'horse', Moore says:

"We may mean that a certain object, which we all of us know, is composed in a certain manner: that it has four legs, a head, a heart, a liver, etc., etc., all of them arranged in definite relations to one another. It is in this sense that I deny good to be definable. I say that it is not composed of any parts, which we can substitute for it in our minds when we are thinking of it. We might think just as clearly and correctly about a horse, if we thought of all its parts and their arrangement instead of thinking of the whole: we could, I say, think how a horse differed from a donkey just as well, just as truly, in this way, as now we do, only not so easily; but there is nothing whatsoever which we could so substitute for good; and that is what I mean, when I say that good is indefinable." [9]

Now, what is *the whole* or the complex entity which *might* be invidiously compared with the simple attribute of being good, as a result of this discussion of the definability of the word 'horse'? One would have thought that it was *the attribute of being a horse* rather than anything as concrete as Bucephalus. And what is the complexity other than the *logical complexity* of this attribute that might distinguish it from goodness? To be a horse is to be an animal having four legs, a head, a heart, a liver, a tail, all arranged in a certain manner. Unfortunately the example is confusing because there are two kinds of complexity illustrated here that must be kept separate. First, the important kind of complexity which I have called the logical complexity of the attribute of being a horse, and second, the essentially irrelevant common spatial complexity of all concrete horses. The fact is that the sense in which *horsehood* is a complex attribute is also the sense in which certain properties of numbers are complex, and yet the complexity of, say, the property of being odd is no function of a supposed internal *spatial* arrangement of individual numbers like 1, 3, 5, 7, etc.; numbers have no spatial parts. Moreover, it might happen to be true that every good, concrete thing did possess one common structural arrangement without thereby affecting Moore's thesis, for the at-

[9] *Ibid.*, p. 8.

tribute of having that structural arrangement might not be identical with the attribute of being good. I conclude that Moore's example of 'horse' is an unfortunate one just because it obscures the character of the complexity (and hence of the simplicity) of attributes dealt with in Moore's ethical theory.

8. *The attempt examined further*

With all of this out of the way we may now return to the alternatives (2) and (3) that Moore is obliged to refute in order to substantiate his thesis that goodness is logically simple. Against (2), or the view that 'good' can be defined, Moore argues that "whatever definition be offered, it may be always asked, with significance, of the complex so defined, whether it is itself good."[10] Before proceeding any further we must mark a difficulty in this statement. Supposing, as we have, that the complex in question is an attribute like being conducive to pleasure, we may now ask what it means to say that that attribute, whether simple or complex, *is* good. Is this connected with asking (a), whether a certain abstract entity *possesses* goodness? Is it therefore like asking of *being conducive to pleasure* whether it *is* an attribute? Or is it tantamount to (b), asking of the attribute of being conducive to pleasure whether *it is identical with* goodness?

Without turning to Moore's actual example in support of his contention, it might be well to consider these two possibilities abstractly, as it were. First (a). If Moore is right, the proof of the indefinability of 'good' is the fact that whenever a definition of 'good' is offered, we may take the attribute expressed or connoted by the definiens, e.g., being conducive to pleasure, and now ask with significance "Is this attribute good?" The implication is that in the case of a definable word like 'vixen', we cannot significantly ask this or an analogous question of the attribute connoted by 'female fox', namely the attribute of being a female fox. But it seems obvious to me that *if we can ever ask such a question with significance,* we can ask it with equal significance in both of these cases. I conclude, therefore, that (a) will not accomplish what Moore wants it to accomplish, namely, a proof of the indefinability of 'good'.

Now let us consider alternative (b). Here the indefinability of

[10] *Ibid.*, p. 15.

'good' is supposed to hinge on the fact that we can always ask *with significance* of any proposed *analysans* like *being conducive to pleasure,* not whether it *is* good, but whether it is *identical* with goodness. But then, in order to distinguish sharply between the unanalyzable goodness and, say, the analyzable vixenhood, Moore must say that we can *never* ask with significance of the complex attribute of being a female fox whether it is identical with the attribute of being a vixen. And yet if it could not be *asked* with significance whether being a vixen is identical with being a female fox, it could never be *asserted* with significance; and if it could never be asserted with significance, Moore's whole analytical enterprise would consist in asserting insignificant statements. One must conclude from this that Moore could not have proven the simplicity of goodness to his own satisfaction by either of the two versions of the argument we have just considered, and one cannot think of a third interpretation that does his argument more justice or puts it in a better light.

9. *Is goodness a nonnatural attribute?*

It remains to show that Moore did not *prove* the nonnaturalness of goodness. In his reply to C. D. Broad in *The Philosophy of G. E. Moore,* Moore admits that his previously published statements on naturalness had been obscure, and he tries to throw more light on them, thus making that reply plus two pages in *Principia Ethica* and his essay "The Conception of Intrinsic Value"[11] the chief sources of his published views on this subject. We must make the most of these straws, as the point is central to analytic ethics in the twentieth century.

Of his views in *Principia Ethica,* Moore himself says: "I agree . . . that in *Principia* I did not give any tenable explanation of what I meant by saying that 'good' was not a natural property."[12] Nevertheless, his views on the notion of natural property in that book, as well as the reasons for his change of attitude toward them, are sufficiently interesting to warrant a brief examination, particularly in a study in which it is maintained that an understanding of the historical background of contemporary problems can be illuminat-

---

[11] Moore, *Philosophical Studies* (New York: Harcourt, Brace, 1922), pp. 253–275.
[12] "A Reply to My Critics," *Philosophy of G. E. Moore,* Schilpp, ed., p. 582.

ing. It reveals, among other things, the extent to which Moore's early views were dominated by an extreme platonism, in a sense more extreme than that of Russell in the *Problems of Philosophy*.

By "nature" Moore said he meant that which is the subject of the natural sciences and also of psychology. Nature includes all that has existed, does exist, or will exist in time, and therefore a stone would be a natural object, our minds are natural objects, our thoughts are natural objects. When we deal with entities of this kind, says Moore, we have little difficulty in defining what we mean by 'natural'. "But when we begin to consider the properties of objects, then I fear the problem is more difficult. Which among the properties of natural objects are natural properties and which are not?" And now I quote Moore's answer in full:

"Can we imagine 'good' as existing *by itself* in time, and not merely as a property of some natural object? For myself, I cannot so imagine it, whereas with the greater number of properties of objects—those which I call the natural properties—their existence does seem to me to be independent of the existence of those objects. They are, in fact, rather parts of which the object is made up than mere predicates which attach to it. If they were all taken away, no object would be left, not even a bare substance: *for they are in themselves substantial* [my italics] and give to the object all the substance that it has. But this is not so with good."[13]

Concerning this passage I wish to remark, first of all, that in holding that some *properties* are substantial, Moore not only departs from the view on universals advanced by Mill and discussed in Chapter IV above, but also from that of Russell in the *Problems of Philosophy* and from those more recently expressed by Ryle. Moore holds in *Principia* that some attributes are "substantial", whereas it was Mill's view that none are. Mill says:

"Attributes are never called Beings; nor are feelings. A being is that which excites feelings, and which possesses attributes. The soul is called a Being; God and angels are called Beings; but if we were to say, extension, colour, wisdom, virtue, are beings, we should perhaps be suspected of thinking with some of the ancients,

13 *Principia Ethica*, p. 41.

that the cardinal virtues are animals; or, at the least, of holding
with the Platonic school the doctrine of self-existent Ideas, or with
the followers of Epicurus that of Sensible Forms . . . We should be
supposed, in short, to believe that Attributes are Substances."[14]

And in *Principia Ethica* Moore holds (in opposition to Russell in
the *Problems*) that *the sense* in which *some* universals exist is precisely the sense in which physical objects exist. No distinction is
made between different senses of the word 'exist' when it is applied
to concrete entities and attributes, and therefore the multivocalism
of Ryle is not adopted. Finally, it should be said that whereas it is
possible to distinguish Moore's views on the simplicity of goodness
from his views on its nonnaturalness, as we have throughout this
chapter, at least some of his difficult statements on simplicity are
illuminated (though not justified) by his reflections on nonnaturalness. I have in mind his discussion of the sense in which "a horse"
is complex. We now see that it was his view that natural properties
are substantial which permitted him to say that a concrete horse is
made up of natural qualities *as parts*.

In 1942 Moore virtually surrendered the entire passage on the
definition of "natural properties" in the *Principia* of 1903.

"I implied in *Principia,* p. 41, that the difference between those
properties of natural objects which I called 'natural,' and 'good'
which I declared *not* to be natural, was that all natural properties
could exist in time *by themselves,* whereas the property which was
that particular sense of the word 'good' with which I was concerned,
could *not.* Mr. Broad says he does not believe that those properties
of natural objects which I called 'natural,' e.g., the property of
being brown or that of being round, in the sense in which a penny
may be brown and round, could exist in time all by themselves,
i.e. without being, at any time at which they did exist, properties
of some natural object which also existed at that time and possessed them. I entirely agree with Mr. Broad as to this. I not only
don't believe that such properties could exist in time by themselves; I feel perfectly sure that they could not. This suggestion
which I made in *Principia* seems to me now to be utterly silly and
preposterous. And I also agree with Mr. Broad that it is wrong to

14 Mill, *A System of Logic,* p. 31.

say, as I did say, of the natural properties of a thing that 'they are rather *parts* of which the thing is made up than mere predicates which attach to it'." [15]

Because of Moore's dim view of his treatment of natural properties in *Principia Ethica,* we must turn to his paper "The Conception of Intrinsic Value" and to *The Philosophy of G. E. Moore* for further light. Both of these make clear that he regarded goodness not only as a simple, nonnatural property but also as an *intrinsic* one. They also shed further light on his notion of a natural characteristic.

10. *Goodness as an intrinsic, non-descriptive attribute*

Moore begins his paper on intrinsic value by saying that he will try to define more precisely the most important question at issue when it is disputed with regard to any value-property as to whether it is or is not a "subjective" property. And after pointing out by means of illustrations what he understands subjectivists to maintain, he tries to show that their most serious opponents are not those philosophers who contend for objectivism in the sense of maintaining merely that a value-property like goodness is not subjective, but those who maintain something stronger, namely, that goodness is *intrinsic* in a sense to be explained in the next paragraph. A subjectivist in esthetics—a closely allied subject—will maintain that "any statement of the form 'This is beautiful' merely expresses a psychological assertion to the effect that some particular individual or class of individuals either actually has, or would, under certain circumstances, have, a certain kind of mental attitude towards the thing in question".[16] But, Moore points out, in the case of goodness and beauty most philosophers who oppose subjectivism do not do so merely out of a desire to establish the non-subjective character of these attributes, but out of a desire to do that and more. The more consists in holding that these properties are intrinsic as well as objective. The reason why the battle lines haven't been clearly marked on this point, Moore says, is that almost all of the opponents of the view that goodness is intrinsic hold that it is subjective. In other words, the view that goodness is

[15] *Philosophy of G. E. Moore*, pp. 581–582.
[16] *Philosophical Studies*, p. 254.

both objective and nonintrinsic is held by very few people. But the fact that it is a possible view is illustrated by certain positions in ethics called "evolutionary". If a philosopher holds that "what is meant by saying that one type of human being A is 'better' than another type B, is merely that the course of evolution tends to increase the numbers of type A and to decrease those of type B",[17] he is holding that the relation of being better than is objective in the sense of not depending on mental attitudes of people; but he is, nevertheless, not maintaining that goodness is intrinsic as Moore does.

For Moore a property is intrinsic to whatever possesses it just in case the possession of it depends on the intrinsic nature of the thing which does possess it. Thus according to his view yellowness bears a relation R_1 to a yellow sense-datum which is such that whether the datum possesses yellowness depends exclusively on the intrinsic nature of that datum; and analogously goodness bears a relation R_2 to a good thing which is such that whether the good thing possesses it depends exclusively on the intrinsic nature of that good thing. However, there is a respect in which the relations R_1 and R_2 are *dis*similar, and the dissimilarity is conveyed by the following abstract example. Suppose you had a sense-datum which possessed both the attribute of being yellow and the attribute of being beautiful, then although its yellowness and beauty would both be such that whether the datum possessed them depended exclusively on the intrinsic nature of the datum, someone who said that the datum was yellow would be *describing* it while someone who said that it was beautiful would not be describing it. This distinction between yellowness and beauty is most important.

When Moore says that whether a datum possesses a certain property depends exclusively on the intrinsic nature of the datum, he implicitly denies that the datum's possession of yellowness depends on the causal constitution of the universe; he holds that if the datum were yellow it would be yellow in any universe, no matter what the causal laws of that universe. Moreover he asserts that any datum which is exactly like this one would also be yellow, whatever the constitution of the universe. "Suppose you take a particular patch of colour, which is yellow. We can, I think, say with

17 *Ibid.*, pp. 255–256.

certainty that any patch exactly like that one, *would* be yellow, even if it existed in a Universe in which causal laws were quite different from what they are in this one. We can say that any such patch *must* be yellow, quite unconditionally, whatever the circumstances, and whatever the causal laws. And it is in a sense similar to this, in respect of the fact that it is neither empirical nor causal, that I mean the 'must' to be understood, when I say that if a kind of value is to be 'intrinsic,' then, supposing a given thing possesses it in a certain degree, anything exactly like that thing *must* possess it in exactly the same degree. To say, of 'beauty' or 'goodness' that they are 'intrinsic' is only, therefore, to say that this thing which is obviously true of 'yellowness' and 'blueness' and 'redness' is true of them." [18]

It must be added that Moore understands the phrase 'is exactly alike' and the equivalent phrase 'is of the same intrinsic nature' in such a way that two things which are numerically different may nevertheless be exactly alike and of the same intrinsic nature. This is one reason why he cannot identify the 'must' as a logical 'must'. In speaking of it he says:

"But what precisely is meant by this unconditional 'must,' I must confess I don't know. The obvious thing to suggest is that it is the logical 'must,' which certainly is unconditional in just this sense: the kind of necessity, which we assert to hold, for instance, when we say that whatever is a right-angled triangle *must* be a triangle, or that whatever is yellow *must* be either yellow or blue. But I must say I cannot see that all unconditional necessity is of this nature. I do not see how it can be deduced from any logical law that, if a given patch of colour be yellow, then any patch which were exactly like the first would be yellow too. And similarly in our case of 'intrinsic' value, though I think it is true that beauty, for instance, is 'intrinsic,' I do not see how it can be deduced from any logical law, that if A is beautiful, anything that were exactly like A would be beautiful too, in exactly the same degree." [19]

We have now shown how Moore's conception of depending exclusively on the intrinsic nature of a thing leads him to invoke a

[18] *Ibid.*, pp. 268–269.
[19] *Ibid.*, pp. 271–272.

conception of "unconditional" necessity that is admittedly obscure; indeed, just as obscure as the notion of analyticity involved in Moore's theory of the simplicity of goodness. We may now consider the method whereby Moore tries to distinguish nonnatural intrinsic properties like goodness and beauty from those which are natural, like yellowness as applied to a sense-datum. At the end of his essay "The Conception of Intrinsic Value", Moore says that he can only "vaguely express" the kind of difference he senses between natural intrinsic properties and nonnatural intrinsic properties, by saying that the former "*describe* the intrinsic nature of what possesses them in a sense in which predicates of value [nonnatural intrinsic properties] never do".[20] And it is this lead that he continues to follow in his most recent reflections on the subject. He says that there is a sense of the word 'describe'—only one of the senses in which it is ordinarily used, he adds—"such that, in ascribing to a thing a property which is not a natural intrinsic property, you are not describing it *at all,* whereas, if you ascribe to a thing a natural intrinsic property, you always are describing it *to some extent,* though of course the description may be very vague and very far from complete".[21] We are told nothing more about the word "describe" in this connection, and although Moore does not provide a word for the activity that stands to nonnatural attributes as describing does to natural ones, one obvious candidate is 'evaluation'.

11. *Conclusions*

After this long examination of Moore's ethical doctrines, it might be desirable to summarize some of the results that bear on the main concerns of this book.

(a) *On simplicity.* First of all, the examination helps round out in a purely historical way the ontology of pre-positivistic platonism. Earlier we observed that one of the chief elements in that philosophy was its view that the mental activity called understanding is one in which we grasp meanings conceived as nonmental, nonphysical entities. Now, Moore's reflections in ethics add a number of distinctions within the class of attributes or meanings of general terms. Some of them are said to be simple and some of them com-

---

[20] *Ibid.,* p. 274.
[21] *Philosophy of G. E. Moore,* p. 590.

plex. And while in the course of his effort to say what he means by calling an attribute simple (in this case *goodness*), Moore adverts to the notion of analyticity, I do not think that this should obscure the fact that *he* did not think of the simplicity of goodness as a merely linguistic matter, as one might suppose by concentrating on one of his formulations and on the fact that analyticity is a property of verbal expressions. That is to say, I have tried to show that *in the end* the simplicity of goodness, for Moore, does not rest on the fact that no sentence of the form 'Good is ———', where the expression put for the blank does not contain 'good', is analytic, but rather on his supposed detection of the simple attribute of simplicity in goodness. But had Moore been more thoroughly linguistic in his emphasis and framed his thesis by exclusive reference to the metalinguistic notions of 'analytic' and 'definition', he would have been able to maintain no more than this: that in the ordinary ethical usage of 'good', he finds nothing that would justify our defining 'good' and much to justify the opposite course. In other words, once we abandon Moore's platonistic notion that we can look at a property like goodness with the mind's eye and *see* whether it possesses the property of simplicity, his metaphysical descriptivism, if I may call it that, cannot be transformed into a metalinguistic descriptivism. He should not, in my opinion, then reformulate his point by saying that the predicate 'good' is not synonymous with any complex predicate, chiefly because the word 'synonymous' is subject to all of the difficulties previously discussed.

What, then, is an alternative way of communicating Moore's thesis, on the assumption that it or something like it is communicable? I think the outline of an answer is this.

Although definability or indefinability is prima facie a question of whether or not something *can* be done, there is another way of looking at the matter which suggests that the 'able' ending of 'definable' is more like the ending of the word 'desirable' than is usually recognized. If we consider first the words 'defined' and 'undefined', we see that they may sometimes be used descriptively, insofar as we can say that if you want to know whether a term is defined or undefined, you look at the stipulations of the person who is building the system. If he says (in a performatory way), 'I define an ellipse as the locus of a point that moves so that the sum of its undirected distances from two fixed points is equal to a constant', then you may say (descriptively) that the term 'ellipse' *is* defined in his system. If he says, as he might, 'I take the term 'point' as undefined', then you may say (descriptively) that the term 'point' is undefined. Now, it might happen that a term which is left undefined by a given logician, mathematician, or system-builder is in fact one that *might* be defined in terms of the other undefined terms of the system, in which case this could be called to the attention of the person building the system. An additional definition might then be advocated; someone might say, in effect, 'In your system it would be well to define so-and-so as such-and-such'. But if this is advised, grounds must be offered for the advice, and they may be offered in a sentence which is descriptive or factual by comparison with the sentence with which one does the defining ('I define so-and-so as such-and-such') and by comparison with the sentence in which one asserts the advisability of the defining ('It would be well to define so-and-so as such-and-such'). Some philosophers have held that the synonymy of the term defined and its defining phrase in ordinary language is the necessary and sufficient condition for the propriety of a definition; others have said that identity of extension is enough; still others, like Nelson Goodman, have proposed an even weaker condition as a basis for promulgating definitions of philosophical interest. The important point, however, is the fact that 'definable as' may mean something like 'justifiably or advisably defined as', if it is viewed in this light.

If, by contrast, we think of 'definable as' as meaning 'can be defined as' (or worse, as meaning 'must be defined as'), we are liable to forget that we *can* define a term in any way we choose, and we are liable to identify definability in a certain way with conditions that are more properly construed as *grounds* that are offered in justification of defining terms in that way. Now under certain conditions, being definable as such-and-such *may* be identified with conditions that might otherwise be viewed as grounds for defining a term as such-and-such, notably in metamathematics, where identity of extension may be the only consideration that weighs with the investigator, and where the definability of one expression in terms of another may therefore be treated simply as a matter of whether they have identical extension or denotation. But this is not the only view of the matter that may be taken, and moreover its concentration on what is the case, rather than on what is justifiably done, is certainly not sufficient for answering the question 'Why should I build a system in which a, b, and c, are taken as undefined terms?' That is a question for a philosopher of philosophically minded mathematician (much as the critique of ends in ethics is a question for a philosopher). And what I urge in contrast to Moore is that the selection of certain terms as primitive cannot be satisfactorily based by a philosopher on the metaphysical "fact" that these terms express or connote simple attributes. A clearer kind of justification is needed, one which is fundamental in epistemology and the philosophy of language.

Now I don't mean to say that this kind of justification is the same as that which is involved in the case of moral decisions in the usual sense, but it is very close. What I am saying is that to debate the defin*ability* of term 't' is to debate the advisability or justice or propriety (which word of that ilk to use will become of great moment to us later) of saying at some point 'I define 't' as short for 'r O s' '. The parallel between 'I define' and 'I promise' has been observed by Austin in this connection, and therefore the parallel I propose between definability and what might be called "promisability" should be evident. In the latter case we would ask ourselves, "Should I say 'I promise to do such-and-such'?" In the former, "Should I say 'I define so-and-so as such-and-such'?" Both questions are related in turn to questions like 'Should I *do* such-and-such?' where the doing is less verbal.

Now, in converting definability into a quasi-ethical question about whether we should *say* certain things on certain occasions, I have not said how such quasi-ethical questions are or should be settled. To that problem I shall turn later. But here I want only to record the conversion and to remark on the fact that I have, ironically enough, converted the apparently descriptive question of simplicity or definability of an ethical term into a quasi-ethical question which is not reducible to a metaphysical question about the properties or relations of attributes "out there". In doing so I not only illustrate one of the central theses of this book but also face the difficult task of analyzing the nature of these quasi-ethical decisions which concern the linguistic philosopher and epistemologist. That I will try to do in a later chapter.

(b) *On nonnaturalness.* In the later pages of the chapter we saw that Moore added two other distinctions within the class of attributes or meanings of general terms. First, the distinction between an attribute which is intrinsic to a thing and an attribute which is not. This is of interest to us mainly for historical reasons, for it shows once again how important the notion of necessity— whether analytic or not—is in the philosophy of Moore. Just as he repairs to the idea of analyticity in trying to define the simplicity of goodness, so he must appeal to a nonlogical, nonanalytic species of necessity in calling it an intrinsic property.

Far more important for our purposes, however, is Moore's distinction between two kinds of intrinsic properties. In some cases he calls the intrinsic property which we grasp *natural,* because it is one that we ascribe in the course of describing a thing's intrinsic nature; in some cases he calls it *nonnatural,* because it is one that we ascribe in the course of *evaluating* a thing. It is also important to observe that Moore rejects his earlier, more metaphysical characterization of natural properties as "silly and preposterous" and replaces it by a characterization in which he makes reference to the activity of *describing.* For this reason, the ontology of intensional platonism is portrayable by reference to three kinds of activity: an attribute is what we grasp when we understand a general term; a natural attribute is what we ascribe to something when we describe it; a nonnatural attribute is what we ascribe to something when we evaluate it.

Moore's revision of his characterization of nonnatural attributes completes a certain tendency in twentieth-century analytic philosophy and prepares the way for another. In saying that a natural attribute is one that is ascribed in the course of a description, in saying that a nonnatural attribute is one that is ascribed in the course of an evaluation, in saying that an attribute is what we grasp in the course of understanding, a philosopher implies that we all have some kind of common-sense familiarity with understanding, description, and evaluation and that these are, in a sense, the fundamental data of philosophy. In his latest phase Moore implies that describing is, after all, a more clearly understood activity than the notion of naturalness which he defines in terms of it. I suggest, therefore, that the belief that we *improve* our situation by asserting the existence of entities like nonnatural attributes is misguided.

I suggest that the postulation of attributes, natural or otherwise, simple or otherwise, in no way clarifies these mental or linguistic activities, and I have already tried to show that their existence is not logically implied by the fact that we engage in these activities.

Under the circumstances, a philosopher may take one of two courses. One is to deny heroically and foolishly that understanding, description, and evaluation take place and that they are distinguishable human activities. If correct, this denial would dissolve any epistemological "proof" of the existence of meanings, natural attributes, and nonnatural attributes, and it would remove the need for postulating them as the things we grasp in the course of understanding, description, and evaluation. But it would also be absurd. Another alternative is to accept the fact that we do sometimes understand, describe, and evaluate, but that the existence of queer entities is not demanded by nor does it illuminate these important human activities. In this book I adopt the second course, and I point out that the need or desirability of asserting the existence of nonnatural characteristics is eliminated once we refuse to postulate the existence of *any* characteristics. As soon as we give up the view that understanding requires universals, or that the assertion of singular statements involves us in ascribing a property, then there is no need to treat description and evaluation as species of the ascription of properties. A man who understands a term is one who uses it in a certain way; a man who describes an object applies general terms to it in a certain way; a man who evaluates an object applies general terms in another way; a man who defines a term does certain things with that term; a man who does not define a term but understands it uses it another way. This is the outline of another way of philosophizing about these mental activities. I espouse it, of course, with the realization that we must say something more about these activities, but in the conviction that we had even better do without any further philosophical "analyses" of them than accept unilluminating, occult ontological explanations of them.

Finally, I should like to say that our examination of Moore's ethical views has not contributed directly to the solution of the epistemological problems we brought to this chapter. Instead, it has shown that Moore's notions of naturalness and simplicity are themselves in need of a similar kind of clarification. But it has also confirmed the belief that some of the fundamental problems of philosophy arise in connection with human activities like understanding, evaluation, defining, knowing without recourse to experience, and describing. And it has helped us see that far from being perfect tools for philosophizing about ethical terms, they are themselves in need of illumination. In the following chapter we will examine certain positivistic efforts to make up some of the deficiencies in Moore's treatment of ethical terms while salvaging some of his insights. We shall be forced to reject some of these devices, but it should be said that the program of this book is very similar, and, indeed, that one of the chief problems of philosophy is to give an account of the differences and connections between description and evaluation without resorting to attributes—natural or nonnatural, simple or complex, intrinsic or extrinsic.

CHAPTER XI

Semantics and Ethical Discourse

1. *Moore and the ethics of logical positivism*

Moore's ethical views have had enormous impact on analytically minded philosophers, even on positivists and empiricists who can not tolerate nonnatural qualities. Indeed, the most typical tendencies in positivistic ethics grow out of acceptance of a positivistic theory of knowledge and a sympathy with certain of Moore's ethical doctrines. On the one hand certain positivists say that all knowledge may be conveyed in statements which are either analytic or synthetic, and on the other they accept Moore's conclusion that 'good' is not a descriptive predicate. And if 'good' is not a descriptive predicate, it follows that so-called ethical sentences in which it figures in an essential way are not descriptive either. But if they are not descriptive sentences they cannot be synthetic for a positivist, since he equates the descriptive and the synthetic. Moreover, if they cannot be deduced from the truths of formal logic by putting synonyms for synonyms, they are not analytic, and it is presumed that they are not self-contradictory because they cannot be derived from the contradictories of logical truths by this same process. How, then, shall we classify ethical sentences?

Moore's attempt to provide a place for them is regarded with deep suspicion by positivists because he is willing to say that in ethical judgment we ascribe a nonnatural quality to things. But his doctrine on this point is treated in a manner distinctly different from that in which the positivists treat the comparable doctrine of the synthetic a priori. The positivist says that there *is* no example of a synthetic a priori proposition and that all alleged examples of its kind are mistakenly categorized by kantians, since the examples they offer are either a posteriori (and hence not a priori) or analytic (and hence not synthetic). But ethical sentences are tougher cus-

tomers and not easily fitted into the positivistic framework of ana-
lytic-or-synthetic, and it takes an ethical naturalist to handle them
as roughly as positivists handle the synthetic a priori. Nevertheless,
the positivist must deal with ethical sentences in some way. If he
cannot join them to the system of knowledge he must beat them
into recognizable shape.

In this chapter and the next we shall consider three components of the positivist effort to distinguish between description and
evaluation, without appealing to Moore's distinction between natural and nonnatural qualities. (a) One is a logico-semantical effort
to distinguish between the entire class of so-called ethical sentences
and the entire class of empirically meaningful sentences. It is not
only reminiscent of Moore's argument but, as we shall see, its proponents have difficulty in avoiding something like a distinction
between natural and nonnatural qualities. It is much too crypto-
moorean. (b) A second is the distinction between cognitive meaning and emotive meaning which emerges in a mellower period of
positivistic reflection. 'Cognitive meaning' and 'emotive meaning'
are explained in a way that makes us wonder whether some equally
mysterious descendant of Moore's distinction between natural and
nonnatural qualities hasn't been retained. It too is crypto-moorean
and, furthermore, its version of the indefinability of 'good' is
dominated by a questionable theory of emotive meaning. (c) Of
all three components of what may be called the orthodox positivistic view of ethics, the distinction between disagreement in belief and disagreement in attitude is most suggestive and illuminating in spite of being blackened by the carbon of misleading
semantics. When this is scraped off the lamp shines much more
brightly and helps us arrive at a solution of some of the key problems of ethics and the philosophy of language. It is not surprising
that a distinction between the psychological notions of *belief* and
attitude should be helpful in the treatment of description and
evaluation. We will turn to this distinction in the next chapter
and deal with points (a) and (b) in this one.

2. *Three positivist tenets on ethical naturalism*

In spite of their rejection of Moore's method, certain supporters of a positivist approach to ethics are in one respect exces-

sively and inconsistently tied to Moore's outlook. When Moore rejected naturalism he did not conclude that sentences containing the word 'good' were meaningless. For him they continued to express propositions, to have meanings, because the predicate 'good' continued to be meaningful, to express an attribute (though of a peculiar sort). Thinking in this way, he spoke of ethical statements as true and also of connotation of the term 'good'. But the whole purpose of *some* positivistic rejections of ethical naturalism is to show that if ethical sentences are not empirically meaningful they have no meaning at all. Because Moore was a platonist he not only could speak of predicates having meanings but also could single out some of these as nonnatural meanings, as it were. But even when a positivist continues to be a platonist and to talk about empirical or descriptive sentences *having* meaning and descriptive predicates *having* meaning, he rarely agrees with Moore in saying that ethical predicates and sentences *have* (nonnatural) meaning. That is precisely what the positivist—platonistic or otherwise—wishes to deny, and that is why the following formulation of a positivistic rejection of ethical naturalism is a poor vehicle for satisfying that wish: "In our language, sentences which contain normative ethical symbols are not equivalent to sentences which express psychological propositions, or indeed empirical propositions of any kind."[1] This is too crypto-moorean for a positivist, as we shall see.

This statement is really the third in a (possibly redundant) conjunction of statements often defended by positivists who by doing so contradict other things they believe: (a) No ethical sentence is analytic; (b) no ethical sentence is synthetic (i.e., empirically meaningful); and (c) no ethical sentence is logically equivalent to an empirical sentence. It should be observed that on most positivistic accounts the last statement makes implicit use of the notion of analyticity, since, for most positivists, saying that two sentences are or are not logically equivalent amounts to saying that the biconditional (or the 'if and only if'-sentence) joining them is or is not analytic. For this reason (c) might be replaced by (c'): No biconditional joining an ethical sentence with an empirically meaningful or synthetic sentence is analytic.

[1] Ayer, *Language, Truth, and Logic*, p. 105.

3. *The concentration on ordinary language*

Before any attempt to show the crypto-mooreanism and hence the inconsistency of this positivistic formulation, it is important to stress the fact that most ethical positivists formulate their theses so that they apply to sentences in ordinary language. Far from resorting to the view that an analytic sentence is merely one that we *call* analytic, or to the view that a meaningful sentence is one that we *call* meaningful in a constructed language, emotive theorists give the impression that their view would suffer through such an interpretation. For some of them, like A. J. Ayer, do not deny "that it is possible to invent a language in which all ethical symbols are definable in non-ethical terms, or even that it is desirable to invent such a language and adopt it in place of our own; what we are denying is that the suggested reduction of ethical to non-ethical statements is consistent with the conventions of our actual language. That is, we reject utilitarianism and subjectivism, not as proposals to replace our existing ethical notions by new ones, but as analyses of our existing ethical notions."[2] There are indeed those among the emotivists who pride themselves on their feeling for ordinary language and on the fact that their conclusions are the results of their sensitive understanding of what they sometimes call the living context in which language is written and spoken. Such philosophers find it extremely difficult to accept artificial approaches to the notion of analyticity, approaches whereby they may only apply the term 'analytic' to, or withhold it from, sentences in a language whose rules are explicitly formulated, a language in which the analytic sentences are made analytic by the fact that they are called analytic or by the fact that certain formulae are called definitions. They should find it equally difficult to hold that meaningful expressions become meaningful by virtue of being terms which are labeled meaningful. The positivist in ethics usually adopts a more descriptive version of 'analytic' and 'meaningful', in that they are used by him to *describe* sentences in ordinary language. Therefore he cannot easily support his attack on ethical naturalism by a move comparable to the rational reconstructionist's elimination of metaphysical sentences, that is to say, by *seeing to it*

[2] *Idem.*

that the terms 'right' and 'good' do not turn up in the vocabulary of "the empiricist language". The positivist in ethics is much more blunt, much more assertive, and therefore more vulnerable. His thesis that no sentence which contains "normative ethical symbols" is logically equivalent to an empirically meaningful sentence therefore becomes the residuary legatee of most of the difficulties to which we have been calling attention in this book: notably the problem of clearly defining 'logically equivalent' (and hence 'analytic') as applied to sentences in ordinary language, and the problem of similarly defining 'empirically meaningful' as applied to sentences in ordinary language.

4. *A logical difficulty in the positivist criticism of naturalism*

With these preliminaries in mind we may now turn to more specific difficulties in the tripartite attack on ethical naturalism presented in Section 2 above, in an effort to show that even if one were to grant certain ethical positivists their dubious notions of analyticity and meaningfulness, they would have to meet other difficulties. We may begin with the last thesis, (c′): No biconditional joining an ethical sentence with an empirically meaningful (synthetic) sentence is analytic, and formulate a puzzle connected with it. Let us suppose that sentence 'N' is a proposed naturalistic translation of some ethical sentence 'E', in which case the positivist, in attacking the naturalist, says that 'E if and only if N' is not analytic. But if he says merely that the biconditional is not analytic and doesn't add that it is meaningless, some might suppose him to say that it is still true or false. And if 'E if and only if N' is true or false, we should be able at least to assign truth-values to the components 'E' and 'N'. But if a positivist believes (as some do) that no ethical sentence has cognitive meaning, and this we take as implying that such sentences are incapable of having truth or falsity applied to them in the way demanded by elementary truth-functional logic, then since 'E' lacks meaning we should never be able to form a meaningful biconditional out of 'E' and 'N' and hence never be able to assert the analyticity or non-analyticity of 'E if and only if N'. In short, the very position that some positivists wish to defend seems incapable of formulation in the manner in which they have formulated it.

Under these circumstances one would expect supporters of this inconsistently formulated view to *re*formulate it, for plainly if ethical sentences aren't logically equivalent to empirically meaningful statements they are not logically equivalent to them in the way that chairs and tables aren't equivalent to empirical statements. That is to say, they aren't even *candidates* for being logically equivalent to empirical sentences in the way in which something that is true-or-false is a candidate. This point may be brought out by contrasting the thesis of an anti-behaviorist in psychology with an anti-naturalistic positivist. An anti-behaviorist will say something like 'There are psychological sentences which are not logically equivalent to behavioristic sentences'. To substantiate this let us suppose that he produces one such sentence 'P' about which he says that no behavioristic sentence 'B_1', 'B_2', . . . 'B_n' is logically equivalent to it. If this generalization is tantamount to saying that 'P if and only if B_1', 'P if and only if B_2', . . . 'P if and only if B_n' are none of them analytic, then at least these biconditionals are meaningful, i.e., true-or-false. And if they are meaningful, then their components are too, so that 'P' must be meaningful if the very thesis of the anti-behaviorist is to be formulable. In this sense psychological sentences *are* candidates and *capable* of being elected to logical equivalence with behavioristic sentences even if they aren't equivalent to them, while the corresponding sentences in the case of ethical anti-naturalism must be deprived of the very kind of meaning which they must have if the thesis of anti-naturalism is to have any sense. It follows that the positivistic variety of ethical anti-naturalism which we have been examining not only cannot be formulated when its proponents use the dubious notions of analyticity and synonymy but, as we shall see, is best formulated without their aid. The ethical anti-naturalist whose view we have been examining wants to eat the meaning of ethical sentences and have it too. For him, ethical sentences must be meaningless enough to be nonsynonymous with "empirically meaningful sentences", but meaningful enough to be components of biconditionals. How far is this from Moore's anti-naturalism? If the sentences are meaningful enough to form components of meaningful biconditionals, they might well be regarded as having the sort of meaning Moore assigned to them when he called them sentences with which we ascribe nonnatural attributes. This is what I mean by crypto-mooreanism.

The predicament we have been describing is a product of the fact that the positivist wants to construct a gulf between scientific sentences and ethical sentences that will be great, but not quite so great as the gulf between scientific sentences on the one hand and tables and chairs on the other, and this traps him into giving ethical sentences the meaning that he wishes to deny them. There can be no doubt that part of the difficulty arises from the positivist's (laudable) anxiety to say that, different as they might be from scientific sentences, ethical sentences are more like scientific sentences in a certain respect than either of them are like nonsentences. To this fact all of us must hold on for dear life, if only because we understand ethical sentences and scientific sentences in the same sense of 'understand' or in two senses which are closer to each other than either is to the sense in which carpenters "understand" furniture. It is this or something like it that leads Moore to say that ethical sentences express propositions and that ethical predicates connote nonnatural attributes.

The puzzled positivist must reformulate his point without lapsing into mooreanism or into the difficulties attendant upon his own inconsistent formulation. And how shall he do it? Can he do it by saying simply that ethical sentences are (a) not analytic and (b) not synthetic, and thereby deleting the puzzling part (c') of the thesis in Section 2? No, because this produces a similar puzzle. If he says merely that ethical sentences are not analytic, he implies that they are synthetic or self-contradictory, which he doesn't want to imply; if he says merely that they are not synthetic he implies that they are analytic or self-contradictory, which he shouldn't either. What he *wants* to say is that they are not the sorts of things to which either 'analytic' or 'synthetic' applies, in order to suggest that one should never ask, 'Is it analytic or synthetic?' about an ethical sentence, any more than one should ask this of a table or a chair. *But this he can accomplish simply by saying that they are not the sorts of things to which 'true' or 'false' should be applied, thereby removing any need to use the dubious notions of analyticity or syntheticity in the formulation of his thesis.* It should be observed that a more old-fashioned philosopher, who is likely to speak of propositions or the meanings of sentences to begin with, has a relatively easy time *formulating* the thesis of the positivist (even though he is likely to disagree with it). For him it is simply the view that ethical sentences express no propositions, and the positivist we have discussed *could* say just that even though he accompanies it with a contextual definition of this notion of *expressing a proposition* according to which a sentence expresses a proposition or has meaning if and only if it satisfies the "empiricist criterion of meaning". If a positivist should boldly say that ethical sentences express no propositions, i.e., are not the sorts of things to which we should apply 'true' or 'false', he is not likely to fall into any of the puzzles mentioned, for the statement that certain sentences are not of the sort to which we should apply 'true' or 'false' is not inconsistent. Indeed it is not an ordinary factual statement but is rather normative, so that once again the positivist is obliged to formulate his position in legislative rather than in assertive terms, even the positivist who *thinks* his thesis on ethics is a descriptive thesis about ordinary language. In this respect it corresponds to the proposal that we should call a priori sentences analytic and sentences appropriately related to observable predicates empirically meaningful.

The boldest (and in a sense the clearest) positivistic rejection of ethical naturalism is quite different from Moore's, while the point of view we have been criticizing is still surreptitiously dominated by his outlook. Moore's anti-naturalism, because it allows ethical sentences to express propositions and knowledge, to *have* meaning even though they can never have the *same* meaning as any descriptive statement, is much more like the thesis that biology is not reducible to physics than it is like the posivitist's anti-naturalism. For the anti-physicalist does not deny that biological sentences have meaning; he merely says that none of them has the same meaning as any physical statement.

Interestingly enough, Russell has taken both sorts of anti-naturalistic positions in his long lifetime and has formulated them with characteristic brevity. The first, the moorean variety, he expressed in a trenchant statement which he made in 1910 while writing under the influence of *Principia Ethica:* "The object of ethics . . . is to discover true propositions about virtuous and vicious conduct, and . . . these are just as much a part of truth as true propositions about oxygen or the multiplication table. The aim is, not practice, but propositions about practice; and propositions about practice are not themselves practical, any more than propositions about gases are gaseous. One might as well maintain that botany is vegetable or zoology animal. Thus the study of ethics is not something outside science and coordinate with it: it is merely one among sciences."[3] The other was defended by Russell twenty-five years later when he said: "Questions to to 'values'—that is to say, as to what is good or bad on its own account, independently of its effects—lie outside the domain of science, as the defenders of religion emphatically assert. I think that in this they are right, but I draw the further conclusion, which they do not draw, that questions as to 'values' lie wholly outside the domain of knowledge."[4]

5. *Enter emotive meaning*

We have already called attention to the fact that a philosopher who decides that ethical sentences are different from scientific sentences because we *should not* apply the terms 'true' or 'false' to the former is obliged to remember that tables and chairs fall into this same negatively defined category. The terms 'true' and 'false' should not be applied to them, and yet they are very different from ethical sentences in other respects. This is where the notion of emotive meaning enters into certain positivistic treatments of the problem of ethics: as part of an effort to show that while ethical sentences are very different from scientific sentences in lacking "cognitive meaning" or "descriptive meaning", still ethical sentences have something called "emotive meaning" which distinguishes them from blocks and stones and senseless things. Among those who introduce the notion of emotive meaning there are at least two kinds of philosophers: (1) those who think that ethical sentences lack cognitive meaning, and therefore have nothing but emotive meaning; (2) those who think that ethical sentences possess emotive meaning in addition to cognitive meaning and that

---

[3] "The Elements of Ethics," reprinted in Sellars and Hospers, *Readings in Ethical Theory*, p. 1.
[4] *Religion and Science* (New York: Henry Holt, 1935), p. 230.

the possession of such emotive meaning is what serves to identify them as simultaneously ethical *and* scientific. According to this second view, which is now the more common of the two and which we will consider at length, there are two uses of 'scientific': (a) the broad and generic use according to which to be scientific is to have descriptive meaning and *possibly* emotive meaning, and (b) the narrower use according to which to be scientific is to be descriptive but definitely *not* emotive. According to the view of philosophers in group (2), ethical sentences may very well be scientific in sense (a) but not in sense (b), for according to this view ethical sentences are *predominantly* emotive. We are asked by the second kind of philosopher to imagine a spectrum of sentences all the way from the infrared of a pure exclamation which possesses emotive meaning only, passing through the region of poetry where emotive meaning predominates but in which a bit of cognitive meaning rears its head, into the region of ethics which is heady while it's hearty, on to the region of science where emotive meaning gradually declines until we reach the point of purely cognitive-empirical expression, the ultraviolet of physical language perhaps. Thus we run the gamut from 'Hurrah!' through the lyrics of Yeats, on to *The Wasteland* perhaps, into 'This is good', 'Stealing is wrong', slowly into *Das Kapital* and the *Interpretation of Dreams,* and finally into the emotive zero of '$E = mc^2$'.

The distinction between descriptive and emotive meaning has been viewed as a device for shoring the better fragments of three supposedly ruined ethical theories: naturalism, the anti-naturalism of Moore, and certain violently positivistic views. It tries to satisfy naturalism by admitting that ethical sentences *may* have cognitive meaning; it tries to explain Moore's inability to provide a satisfactory synonym for 'good' by calling attention to the fact that 'good' has no emotive synonyms; it agrees with the positivist in avoiding nonnatural qualities. In some ways, therefore, it tries to accomplish the neatest trick of fifty years of ethical controversy. Beginning with what Stevenson calls a "working model" of ethical disagreement,[5] it pictures two people arguing as follows:

A: This is good.
B: No, it is bad.

[5] C. L. Stevenson, *Ethics and Language* (New Haven: Yale University Press, 1944).

and reformulates their argument in the following manner:

A: I approve of this; do so as well.

B: No, I disapprove of it; do so as well.

In this working model each man's statement is divided into a declarative and an imperative part (which are misleadingly called conjuncts) and the point is made that whereas the declarative part of A's statement expresses an empirical belief, namely that A does approve of the thing in question, the imperative part does nothing of the kind. If called upon to support the declarative part of the sentence, A will reiterate or call for an examination of himself; if called upon to support the imperative part, he will do something very different. Upon the exchange as modeled here, Stevenson comments: "The declarative parts of the remarks show that the men have opposed attitudes, one approving and the other disapproving. The imperative parts show that each man is suggesting that the other redirect his attitudes."[6] But later he apologizes for this because of the bareness of its descriptive component and its failure to capture the rich, thick, live essence of ethical discourse and controversy. This, he thinks, can be accomplished only by proper attention to emotive meaning. The point is that while the imperative component in the above model is what is used in self-consciously *ordering* the other party to change his attitudes, a more refined analysis would point to the emotive meaning of '*x* is good' as accomplishing the same result by *suggestion*. The total psychological effect of saying '*x* is good' is the effect which is produced, not by the inadequate 'I approve of *x;* do so as well' but rather, one might say, by taking the imperative component, pulverizing it, and sprinkling the resulting powder on 'I approve of *x*' so that it now glows with emotive meaning and bathes *x* in a reflected glory. The glow will induce all sorts of responses to *x* that can't be induced by the bare imperative. Indeed, as we shall see, emotive meaning is defined as the sign's disposition to induce these emotive effects. Therefore, while the descriptive meaning of '*x* is good' might be rendered by a bare descriptive sentence like 'I approve of *x*' or others, no such unclothed translation of the descriptive component will have the persuasive effect of '*x* is good' precisely because the former won't glow in the same way—in fact can *never*

6 *Ibid.,* p. 22.

glow in the same way because, Stevenson holds, there are no emotive synonyms. Thus he says that any effort at defining 'good' will
resemble Webster's definition of 'nigger' as 'Negro—now usually
contemptuous', where the emotive meaning is *characterized* rather
than given or expressed by the accompanying stage whisper.

In certain respects, the distinction between cognitive and emotive meaning may be viewed as a product of the conviction that
there are two uses of 'understand' which were not distinguished
by Moore. For while Moore doesn't say so in so many words, he
may be interpreted as having said first: that descriptive predicates
and evaluative predicates are both understood in the same sense
of 'understand' and both have meaning in the same sense, and
second: that the fact that all descriptive predicates have natural
attributes as their meanings, while all evaluative predicates have
nonnatural attributes as their meanings, implies the need for a
distinction between two species of meanings, natural and nonnatural. And these two species of meanings, it might be suggested,
are the ancestors of the distinction between cognitive and emotive
meaning. It is possible, of course, that some advocates of the notion
of emotive meaning might object to the implication of guilt by
ancestry. The category of emotive meaning, they might argue, was
introduced as a philosophically respectable replacement for what
I have called nonnatural meaning, and therefore it is misleading to
link them both in this way. Moreover, it might be pointed out
by *some* that while the cognitive meaning (sense or connotation) of a predicate is usually identified with an attribute and
hence with an abstract entity, the emotive meaning of an expression is much more psychological in character; hence it is wrong
to speak of both of them as species of one genus, as wrong as it
might be to classify a man's head and the shape of his head as belonging to him in the same sense of 'belong'. And so on this view
we understand the cognitive meaning of an expression in one sense
of 'understand' and the emotive meaning in another.

This merely reveals a split in the camp of those who would distinguish between descriptive meaning and cognitive meaning. For,
by contrast to the first group who distinguish different senses of
'understand' and different senses of 'meaning', there are some who
insist that descriptive meanings and emotive meanings *are* species

of a single genus and who are not fazed by the contention that descriptive meanings and emotive meanings are different in kind. Philosophers in this second group psychologize *both* descriptive *and* emotive meaning in their effort to bring them under one genus. This one-genus version of the distinction between descriptive and emotive meaning has been most systematically expounded, and so we turn to it for light.[7] However, the earlier historical remarks about the connection between natural versus nonnatural meaning and about this psychological distinction between descriptive and emotive meaning might produce a confusion which ought to be headed off at once. The moorean distinction between natural and nonnatural meaning is a distinction within the class of connotations of predicates. But the more psychological distinction, as we shall see in a moment, is a distinction between two subclasses of a class of entities that do not stand to predicates as connotations or denotations do. Those who make it, strain to avoid the view that meaning is "reference" (without making clear whether this "reference" is connotation or denotation), since, as it is put, "we shall want to say that some words (such as 'alas') have no referent, but do have a kind of meaning."[8] The aim of such a point of view may be formulated as follows. Philosophers who defend it want to make statements of the form 'The expression *x* has a meaning *y* and *y* is emotive' and also statements of the form 'The expression *x* has a meaning *z* and *z* is cognitive', in which the word 'meaning' will be used in the same way. Given this aim they rightly shy away from identifying meaning with connotation *or* denotation, since it would be extremely difficult to formulate a distinction between cognitive and emotive *connotations* in Mill's sense or a distinction between cognitive and emotive *denotations*.

There is nothing wrong with the effort to give a psychological account of meaning, but the way in which some philosophers go about it is distinguished by a peculiar blend of psychologism and platonism, one might say. More often those who wish to approach meaning psychologically are anti-platonic and anxious to define the expression 'is synonymous with' psychologically, in order to avoid the hypostasis suggested by the term 'has the same meaning as'.

---

[7] I have in mind Stevenson's analysis in *Ethics and Language*.
[8] *Ibid.*, p. 42.

This explicitly anti-platonic approach is deliberately bent on eliminating expressions like 'the meaning' or 'the same meaning', deliberately bent on avoiding an explanation of synonymy by reference to "platonic intermediaries". Beginning with synonymy, proponents of this approach want a psychological criterion for it, so that they may escape its ontologically charged ancestor, *having the same meaning*. But those who adopt what I have called a blend of psychologism and platonism do not adopt this second approach because they want to say things like 'The cognitive meaning of 'good' is so-and-so' and 'The emotive meaning of 'good' is such-and-such', where both 'so-and-so' and 'such-and-such' will normally be replaced by the names of nonlinguistic entities that are neither connotations nor denotations of the term 'good'.

It is this interest in providing *the meaning* of a given expression that launches some of them into highly elaborate and ultimately obscure analyses of these two species of meaning, according to which the descriptive meaning of the term is its *disposition* to produce *cognitive* responses which are fixed by linguistic rules, and its emotive meaning its *disposition* to produce emotive responses of a certain kind. Although those who support this view of meanings as dispositions are conscious of the dangers of "hypostatizing" them, their explanations seem to fly in the face of their own caution. For how will they translate sentences of the form 'x has y as its meaning', especially after inveighing against "hypostatizing" dispositions? Will they say, 'x has y as its emotive meaning if and only if under conditions $C_1, C_2, \ldots C_n$, x is followed by emotive response y', and something similar in the case of cognitive meaning? But what will they put for 'y' in both definitions? Surely not the names of dispositions if they fear hypostasis. And yet if dispositions are not the range of this variable, these philosophers will not have followed the program of identifying meanings with dispositions. If instead they say something like, 'x has y as its emotive meaning if and only if x has a disposition y to affect its hearers so that under conditions $C_1, C_2, \ldots C_n$, x produces tears, groans, and deep uneasiness', they plainly "hypostatize" dispositions, unless they can eliminate the reference to dispositions in the definiens. Apart then from the vagueness of 'cognitive' and 'emotive', they seem saddled with ontological difficulties that make us suspect crypto-mooreanism once again. What are these dispositions? And how different is an emotive meaning (disposition) from a non-natural meaning (attribute)?

Presupposing the existence of dispositions is one of the lesser difficulties in the view under consideration. If asked what the cognitive meaning of a specific sign is, an advocate of this view must reply, in effect, that it is the sign's capacity to stimulate "cognitive responses" in its hearers. But *what* cognitive responses? He can't answer with highly general terms like 'thinking', 'supposing', 'presuming', and so on. Too many signs would come to have the same meaning. Take the sentence 'The Eiffel Tower is over 100 feet high', which all of us understand. What is *the* disposition to respond cognitively which is fixed by linguistic rules, and which is *the* cognitive meaning of this sentence? What cognitive responses do the linguistic rules say that I should have when I hear this sentence? Can the psychological theorist present them without saying that they consist in part of my "thinking" the logical consequences of this sentence, so to speak, and will he be able to explain this notion of logical consequence without appealing to the notion of sameness of cognitive meaning he is trying to explain?

Furthermore, *can* it be demonstrated on this theory that no linguistic expression will have the same emotive meaning as any other? It must be remembered that this is an extremely important part of the emotive theory of ethics, as it aims to provide a non-moorean defense of Moore's thesis of indefinability, by asserting that 'good' cannot have its emotive meaning communicated by any other word or phrase. Can this difference between descriptive and emotive meaning be brought out by means of definitions of cognitive and emotive meaning like those proposed? I doubt it. For as soon as one tries to present *the* cognitive meaning of an expression along the psychological lines suggested, one finds it extremely difficult to see that terms have even *descriptive* synonyms. Those who defend this point of view can make sure that there are pairs of descriptive synonyms but no pairs of emotive synonyms only by doing two things: first, by introducing into the definition of 'cognitive meaning' the notion of *rules* that prescribe proper cognitive responses to a sign, but which don't prescribe them so minutely as to make it impossible for two signs to have the same cognitive meaning; and second, by eliminating the notion of regulated response from the definition of the emotive meaning of a sign. For this reason the cognitive meaning of a sign is conceived rather tidily as something that two different signs *can* share, while the emotive meaning is allowed to sprawl wildly and romantically, to the point where any given sign has its own *peculiar feel, color, nuance, shading,* and *individuality.*

But this neglects the element of convention or rule in emotional response to language. If a man were to grin every time we said, 'God dammit!' we might suppose that he didn't understand us, that he didn't know "the emotive meaning" of the expression. But in that case our conception of its emotive meaning would be determined by some idea of how people *should* respond emotionally to a given sign, and not simply by *every* emotional response that is in fact produced by the sign. Therefore, the connection between exclamation and emotional response is also governed by rule to a certain degree, and if we could specify some minimum amount of regulated emotive response to a given expression, we might be able to fix its emotive meaning in a way that would not rule out emotive synonyms. One feels therefore that the distinction between cognitive and emotive synonymy as outlined (and its proponents confine themselves to outlines too) does not effectively support the thesis that 'good' is indefinable. And for this reason it does not provide a view of 'good' which will capture Moore's intent without using Moore's own language and metaphysics.

One also feels that in spite of an apparent desire to avoid certain semantical notions in distinguishing between cognitive and emotive meaning, proponents of this view are in fact wedded to them. For on what grounds can we say that "the linguistic rules of English" count, for example, *thinking* that Socrates is an animal as a "correct" cognitive response to the sentence 'Socrates is a man', while they do *not* rule out *laughing* uproariously as an incorrect response to what is commonly thought to be a sad exclamation? Since the notion of cognitive meaning depends on there being rules governing the cognitive response to signs, where a cognitive response can be a case of thinking something, it must be remembered that these rules are supposed to take us from linguistic to non-linguistic phenomena, from signs to responses. These rules are not conceived as they are in logical systems, that is, as rules that conduct us from statements to statements. Presumably the rules say that if you are presented with such-and-such a sign you ought to respond in a certain way, and if they are so conceived, there is nothing to prevent us from saying that emotive responses are "regulated" just as cognitive responses are. But if we say this, it becomes difficult to hold that there are pairs of cognitive synonyms but no pairs of emotive synonyms. Alternatively, if we identify the cognitive meaning of an expression with its regulated response, we might broaden the notion of a "correct cognitive response" to the point where it would be hard to say that signs have exact descriptive or cognitive synonyms. But once again, in doing this we can hardly preserve the contrasts that emotive theorists are bent on preserving.

In conclusion, we are confirmed once more in our suspicion that most philosophical talk about meaning is obscure, whether it be platonistic or psychological. And while we are ill advised to build a theory of ethical discourse by appealing to the distinction between natural and nonnatural meanings as Moore does, it seems equally ill advised to do so by appealing either to a highly debatable distinction between cognitive and emotive meanings conceived as dispositions, or to poor old analyticity. Therefore we turn to the less semantical and less platonistic distinction between disagreement in belief and disagreement in attitude, in anticipation of more insight than we have gotten from intensional or psychological semantics. We shall be rewarded here, however, only after dispelling some of the remnants of intensional semantics.

CHAPTER XII

Belief, Performance, and Justification

1. *Belief and attitude*

Because our previous reflections have raised grave doubts about the notions of meaning—both cognitive and emotive—we turn with a sense of relief to a part of the positivistic approach to ethics which is less analytical in the conventional sense, less dominated by the quest for meanings. Of course we are not wholly free of the need to discuss the related notion of analyticity, for its influence is extremely pervasive, so pervasive that we shall be obliged to show its irrelevance to a point in the theory of the relation between attitude and belief.

In directing our attention to the relation between attitude and belief, we come closer to one of the main goals of this study, since we have already seen how much of philosophy consists in making legislative decisions and justifying them. Although these legislative acts are not statements, we may ask whether there is nevertheless a kind of rational support that we can bring to bear in defense of them. For this reason the relation between belief and attitude is extremely important for a consideration of ethics itself and for the problems to whose brink we have been led in other parts of the work. It commands the attention of a moral philosopher who is interested in the relation between "fact" on the one hand and actions like loving, approving, hating, and stealing; it also commands the attention of those who are interested in more "cognitive" linguistic activity like defining, adopting sentences as postulates, accepting terms as undefined, and affirmation. From now on, therefore, we shall not be interested in whether all ethical discourse glows over its object and hence induces attitudes, but rather with the relations between these attitudes and beliefs about the object. For after all, independently of whether the emotive theory is correct in assigning such a central role to emotive meaning, we do have attitudes, and we are sometimes called upon to justify them and sometimes anxious to persuade other people to share them. In the course of such justification and persuasion, we sometimes cite beliefs and knowledge and thereby make it reasonable to ask about the pattern of such argument. We will begin our consideration of these questions by examining the views of C. L. Stevenson. Because he is preoccupied with the problem of ethical *argument* and debate, Stevenson is concerned with the relations between agreement in belief and agreement in attitude, between disagreement in belief and disagreement in attitude.

2. *Disagreement in belief and disagreement in attitude*

Scientific disagreements, according to Stevenson, are relatively easy to characterize. "In such cases one man believes that *p* is the answer, and another that not-*p*, or some proposition incompatible with *p*, is the answer; and in the course of discussion each tries to give some manner of proof for his view, or revise it in the light of further information."[1] It is important to remember that on this formulation we agree and disagree about values of '*p*'. For the moment we needn't worry about the status of these values of the variable '*p*'. If we are worried about the resulting platonism we may, as we shall in a moment, talk about accepting sentences, since in one manner of speaking an answer is an utterance, and it is about answers that our two people disagree in Stevenson's formulation.

According to Stevenson's views, a discussion between *X* and *Y* can terminate so that *X* and *Y* both agree on sentence *S* or disagree (or neither agree nor disagree, that is to say, *not* agree). How does agreement come about in scientific discussion? It comes about when *X* presents for *Y*'s consideration (or conversely) other sentences *T*, *U*. etc., which *Y* or *X* accept and which stand in a certain relation to *S*, the sentence at issue. Notice, then, that scientific discussion is a process in which we "get" other people to accept a certain sentence, but the getting takes a special form. It is what some people call "rational" because it takes the form of presenting other sentences which stand in what may be a relation of logical

[1] *Ethics and Language,* p. 2.

implication, for example, to that which we get others to believe. Now it is conceivable that we might, and very frequently we do, cause other people to agree with us by doing all sorts of other things, but that is not of interest to Stevenson in this context. He is interested in a special kind of influence, the kind which logicians (inductive and deductive) describe and systematize, not the kinds described by rhetoricians, hypnotists, and druggists. He is not interested in *any* method of bringing people to agree in belief with us, but more specifically in how we get people to share our belief by so-called logical and rational means.

Stevenson says further that "Two men will be said to disagree in attitude when they have opposed attitudes to the same object— one approving of it, for instance, and the other disapproving of it —and when at least one of them has a motive for altering or calling into question the attitude of the other."[2] Notice the word 'object'. It is used by Stevenson in such a way as to make it non-sensical or improper or ungrammatical to think of a proposition or a sentence as such an object. Actually, Stevenson's definition of disagreement in attitude is not as precise as his definition of disagreement in belief, if only because the range of the variable here is not as clear as that of 'p', in spite of the difficulties associated with the values of p and propositional platonism. It would appear that these objects are non-propositional and non-sentential, but *what* they are positively is always difficult to find out in ethical literature, and even Stevenson, who is comparatively fastidious on such matters, is no exception. The Glenwood Restaurant, Jones, a million *thises*, ends and means—all of them make up the converse domain of Stevenson's attitudinal relations, but sentences or propositions do not. This last fact is intimately connected with the fact that belief is not here construed as an attitude, though Stevenson has some interesting asides to make on this omission. If I disagree with you about S in that I accept it and you reject it, Stevenson does not regard our disagreement as a disagreement in attitude about S. But if I like *paté de foie gras* and you dislike it, we disagree in attitude about *paté*.

Now all of this, in spite of any inclinations that one might have to think that accepting a sentence is having an attitude toward

[2] *Ibid.*, p. 3.

that sentence, leads up to an important point. And it is wholly irrelevant to *that* point for a critic to keep saying, 'Yes, but accepting a sentence is also having an attitude toward it', as if that controverted Stevenson's main point, which is, as I understand it, that two people can agree completely in their beliefs about *a given object* and yet disagree in attitude toward *that object*. If a series of statements about O are presented to both parties, even though they make no incompatible statements about O they may have opposed attitudes toward O. The general point of which this is an example would emerge more clearly if we were to insist that both the definition of disagreement in belief and the definition of disagreement in attitude contain a reference to an object O as the center of disagreement, and thereby make the definiens in each case a three-termed relational predicate somewhat as follows:

(A) X and Y disagree in belief about O just in case X and Y accept incompatible sentences about O.

(B) X and Y disagree in attitude about O just in case X and Y have opposing attitudes toward O.

We can see from this that even if we regard accepting a sentence as having at attitude toward that sentence, we cannot dispute Stevenson's main distinction on that ground. For let us grant that accepting sentence S_1 about O amounts to "approving" of S_1, and that disagreeing with a person who accepts S_1 amounts to accepting a sentence S_2 about O that is incompatible with S_1 and therefore amounts to "approving" of S_2. Nevertheless, the fact that I "approve" of sentence S_1 about O and that you "disapprove" of this sentence (which means that we disagree in belief about O) is perfectly compatible with the fact that both of us approve of O itself (which means that we agree in attitude about O). Therefore, Stevenson's most important point survives.

3. *A useful specification*

If one were making an extensive study of these two kinds of disagreement, one might develop alternative interpretations of them, since one might construe disagreement in belief as relative to a certain topic, or one might construe it in an absolute way. In ordinary language we can say that X and Y disagree (in belief) about the weight of O while they agree (in belief) in its length, in which case we cannot flatly say that they agree or disagree in belief about O. But for various reasons it seems desirable to use the absolute sense here. If X and Y disagree about the weight of O, we shall say that they disagree in belief about O. We may imagine ourselves uniting into one vast conjunction all of the sentences about O which X accepts, then doing something similar for all the sentences about O which Y accepts, and then asking whether these two long sentences are incompatible. (Whether we should also compare the sentences they don't accept or the sentences they reject is a neat question.)

Similarly, we might say that people can have a pair of opposing attitudes toward an object at the same time that they have another pair of converging attitudes. Here we might as well construe the relation absolutely by saying that X and Y disagree in attitude just in case they have *any* opposing attitudes toward O (whether or not they also have converging attitudes toward it). (It is an interesting psychological question whether we can sum up their total attitudes, but we need not consider it here.)

Now that we have made all these qualifications we must ask how Stevenson conceives of the relation between these two types of disagreement. He appears to hold that neither of the sentential functions[3] (a) 'X and Y disagree in belief about O' or (b) 'X and Y disagree in attitude about O' implies the other or the other's contradictory. This means simply that two people who disagree in belief about O *might* at the same time have opposed attitudes toward O, also that two people who disagree in attitude toward O might not agree in belief about it. In Stevenson's language, "The relationship between the two sorts of disagreement, whenever it occurs, is always factual, never logical."[4] And for a philosopher whose other views are as positivistic as Stevenson's, this probably implies that statements like (1) 'If Jones and Smith disagree in belief about this restaurant, then Jones and Smith disagree in attitude about it' and (2) 'If Jones and Smith disagree in belief about this restaurant, then Jones and Smith *don't* disagree in attitude about it' are neither of them "analytic".

---

[3] See Ch. v, sec. 2 above for an explanation of this term.
[4] *Ethics and Language,* p. 6.

4. *Some relations between the two kinds of disagreement*

Once again it will be our task to show that the notion of analyticity or the notion of "logical relation" is not necessary in the formulation of the point that Stevenson wants to make, and that in a certain way it is confusing to formulate the point with their help.

I will begin somewhat obliquely. Let us apply the phrase 'disagree in propensity toward O' to people X and Y just in case X pushes O and Y pulls O whenever they are close to O. Let us suppose that Jones and Smith disagree in propensity toward O. Now clearly Jones and Smith might also disagree in belief about O: Jones might think it was two feet long and Smith might think it was not two feet long. Some philosopher might then announce that the sentential function 'X and Y disagree in belief about O' does not logically imply 'X and Y disagree in propensity toward O' or its contradictory. If we were satisfied with the notion of analyticity, we might not be suspicious. Moreover, we might ring all the changes on this theme that Stevenson rings on his. Their agreeing in belief about O would not imply logically that they agreed in propensity toward O (or that they didn't); their agreeing in propensity toward O would not logically imply agreement in belief about O, etc., etc., and naturally neither kind of agreement would entail or be entailed by either kind of disagreement. But this is all beside the important point. Even if the notion of analyticity were not so obscure as to arouse our suspicions whenever it is used, the point involved here should be made without any use of it or the notion of entailment, since what is involved is the fact that a pushing or a pulling is not the sort of thing that can be derived from *any* sentence by deductive or inductive means (a platonist would say that they are not the sorts of things that can be supported logically by a proposition, without altering the substance of the point). And this is merely another way of saying that they are not the sorts of things to which we should apply the words 'true' or 'false'. Once again we see that the positivistic or near-positivistic effort to create a gulf between science and ethics is best carried out without the use of analyticity.

This situation is extremely similar to the one considered in the early parts of the last chapter, since Stevenson's implicit use of 'analytic' is, like Ayer's, beside the main point, which *should be* that neither propositions nor sentences are attitudes. It has nothing to do with the supposed non-analyticity of the two conditionals that join sentential functions (a) and (b) in the previous section, and is therefore made more clearly if we dispense with the machinery of *disagreement* in belief and *disagreement* in attitude, and just concentrate on the difference between a declarative sentence and an attitude. If X, who has described O as well as he can, should ask himself, "Am I logically bound to like O?" it is plain that his answer should be that likings, so to speak, don't follow from sentences or propositions.

No sensible philosopher can deny *this*. Any failure on the part of descriptive sentences, reasons, or beliefs to support an *attitude* by not implying it deductively or inductively is due to the non-declarative, non-sentential, or non-propositional nature of a feeling or attitude. In this respect it is like the chair we so conveniently used in making a similar point in the last chapter. We don't affirm attitudes; we have them. We don't affirm chairs either; we sit on them. And for this reason it might be less misleading to say that, in general, attitudes like chairs are neither logically implied nor not logically implied by statements expressing beliefs.

5. *Performance and justification*

It might be thought that the situation changes radically if we construe that which is to be justified not as the bare having of an attitude but as the voicing of it. But this is not true, since even the sentence 'I approve of this' is sometimes used so that it is neither implied nor not implied by factual or descriptive sentences. When 'I approve of O' figures in ethical argument, I suggest that it functions neither as an account of an episode that is going on "within me" at the moment of approval nor as a description of one of my traits or "dispositions". Nor does it function as a statement about O. It is very close to being performatory in just the sense in which 'I promise' is performatory and in the sense in which the logical legislator's 'I define' is performatory. When I say, 'I approve of this', I put my stamp of approval on something, and this is a free act for which I can be criticized and which I can be called upon to defend. For this reason even the *sentence* 'I approve of this' is neither implied nor not implied by factual sentences that express beliefs. When *I* say, 'I approve of *O*', I am not always describing *O* (though when I say, 'He approves of *O*', I am), and therefore a sentence of the form 'I approve of *O*' in the first person singular, present indicative tense need not be the sort of thing that can be implied by factual or descriptive statements about *O*. For the same reason no number of factual sentences about an equivalence like 'man = rational animal' can imply or not imply 'I define 'man' as 'rational animal' ' or 'I make it a postulate'.

In moral discourse, when I ask you why you have done something, whether that be a linguistic thing like putting your stamp of approval on something or a nonlinguistic thing like shooting someone, I'm not asking you to produce premises from which your stamping or shooting *follow*, because they, like attitudes, aren't "the sorts of things" that should be said to follow from factual statements. That is why you and I may agree completely "in belief" about something even though I should stamp it 'approved' while you stamp it 'not approved'. (This is no more surprising than the fact that we can both describe an object in the same way even though I should be pulling it and you should be pushing it.) And most important of all, that is why the request for a justification of my approval of something is not a request for a proof of the fact that I *do* approve of something, whether I myself or someone else makes the request of me. When we are asked for a justification of our putting our stamp of approval on something, we are asked to show that it is *right* to approve of that thing, and *this statement* of rightness may be supported by argument. Those philosophers who represent ethical statement by 'I approve of this; you ought to do so too' have actually reversed the correct picture of ethical argument in holding that the first "component", 'I approve of this', is "descriptive" or statemental and hence supportable by adducing empirical statements, while the second is not. If I should say to you, 'I approve of this; you ought to do so too' and you should be minded to dispute with me, would you bother to ask me to *prove* that I approve? Obviously not. You would conclude that I approved from the fact that I had *said* 'I approve'. But you *would* ask me to justify my approval; you *would* ask me to show that it was *right* for me to approve, and in doing so you would be illustrating the fact that the second part of my utterance, namely, 'You ought to do so too', is its arguable part. But whether *it* is supportable by adducing "factual", "descriptive", or "empirical" statements becomes a question that we must consider very carefully, for we cannot treat 'You ought to approve of this' as a performatory utterance.

'You ought to approve of this' is a moral judgment, and we must conclude our discussion of more or less orthodox positivistic views of ethical statements by saying that they have not provided a solution of this problem. Neither the notion of analytic nor the notion of meaning can be effectively used by an ethical positivist who supposes himself to be *describing* ordinary ethical discourse. By a strange twist he is forced to construe some of his own utterances as performatory, expressing them most clearly as 'I call all observable predicates meaningful', 'I call 'all men are animals' analytic', and, most important for ethics, 'I call no sentences containing ethical words true-or-false'. And once he sees this he will have seen that the basic theses of positivism must be queried by asking: 'Are we justified in calling all observable predicates meaningful?' and 'What do we signify or accomplish by calling them meaningful?'; 'Are we justified in calling 'all men are animals' analytic?' and 'What do we signify or accomplish by calling it analytic?'; 'Are we justified in refusing to call sentences containing ethical words true-or-false?' and 'What do we signify or accomplish by this?'. In short, the language of justification once more appears to be more fundamental than one might have supposed, and therefore the problem with which we came to ethics is still with us, but in a clearer form once we recognize that nonnatural qualities and emotive meanings will not help us and that they cloud the issue. The problem of justifying human action and performance as it is discussed in moral philosophy is very similar to the problem of justifying linguistic performances that are central in contemporary semantics. If anything, the discussion of the ethical problem reveals that some of its semantic counterparts are more complex and confused. For after all we do not doubt the *significance* and *usefulness* of saying, 'I promise' and 'I pronounce the patient dead' and 'I pronounce you man and wife'—we are merely interested in the pattern of justifying these linguistic performances. But in the semantic case we even ask what is signified by the newer rituals involved in 'I pronounce this analytic' and 'I pronounce that synthetic'.

6. *Three types of linguistic performance*

We may distinguish at least three ways of using sentences that have figured in the previous discussion. One is for purposes of description, the second is the performatory use, and the third is for purposes of justification or evaluation or criticism of the performance in question. The trio will often appear in a cluster in both ethical and logical situations. In the ethical case it is illustrated by the distinction between (1) saying that as a matter of fact a man is generous, (2) putting one's stamp of approval on him in a performatory way by saying, 'I like him', and (3) saying in a moral way that it is right to like him. In the logical case it is illustrated by the parallel distinction between (1′) saying that there is a great deal of evidence for an equivalence like 'man = rational animal', (2′) saying, 'I define 'man' as 'rational animal' ', and (3′) saying in a quasi-moral way that one is justified in making that rather than some other equivalence one's definition. And what we have seen in this chapter is that it is absurd to expect a sentence like 'I like him' to *follow* from sentences like 'He is generous', so that it is clear why bits of "reasoning" that move from sentences like the latter to sentences like the former are not obviously like scientific explanations or logical arguments. We may say something analogous about the kind of "reasoning" that moves from sayings like those mentioned in (1′) to sayings like those mentioned in (2′). We must add, however, that some philosophers have wrongly concluded that because the process of getting people to stamp with approval those things we have stamped with approval (to agree with us in attitude) is neither inductive nor deductive, we must regard ethical argument as a purely causal process. According to this view, if we prefer to recite to our friend those descriptive sentences which *he* accepts in an effort to get him to say, 'I too approve of O' rather than to use clubs, threats, or drugs, we are merely making moral judgments about the methods of moralists.

As opposed to this, it seems to me that another conclusion is in order. We must grant that the step from one factual premise like 'O is generous' to 'I approve of O' is neither inductive nor deductive, but then add that this proves nothing about ethical reasoning as that is normally conceived. The mark of ethical reasoning is not that it carries us from a stimulating descriptive statement like that mentioned in (1) to a linguistic performance like that mentioned in (2) but rather that it carries us from an informative descriptive statement like that mentioned in (1) to an informative and evaluative statement like that mentioned in (3). This is equally true of what I have called the corresponding logical situation, and therefore the problem is to illuminate the jumps from (1) to (3) and from (1′) to (3′), recognizing that in neither case are we faced with the problem of nudging or drugging people into certain actions but rather with that of *showing* them that such actions are justified. Once we abandon the view that the evaluative statements to be supported are "cognitively meaningless" in some objective sense (as we have), we cannot avoid a careful consideration of this kind of argument. And, as we have seen, if one thinks of the utterance 'They are meaningless' as itself performatory, one must justify *this* performance by means of a process very like the one we must now examine. Such are the ironies of philosophy.

CHAPTER XIII

Ethical Argument

1. *From Moore to Aristotle: Does ethics
   require a special mode of argument?*

The history of ethical theory from Moore to the present may
be viewed as an effort to flee from platonism without being driven
into the arms of what may be called analytic naturalism, or the
view that ethical predicates are synonymous with natural predicates. Even after logical positivists had risen to challenge the platonism of Moore, they continued to cry "Death to utilitarianism!"
They hooted at the theory that ethical predicates express nonnatural qualities, because there was no room for such mysteries in
their philosophy; they held (against naturalists *and* Moore) that
ethical sentences are cognitively meaningless. The radicals were
followed by moderates who conceded that ethical sentences might
have cognitive meaning but that this was not the key to ethical discourse. The moderates focused their attention on emotive meaning, a kind of Christmas cheer generously sprinkled on sentences
like 'I approve of this' in order to produce a shiny ethical judgment. It was said that one can support the descriptive component
of ethical sentences by citing empirical evidence, but that one
could hardly prove a cheer or a glow. At best one can cause others
to cheer and glow in the same way, but this causal process is not
argument in the traditional sense: it is an attempt on my part to
get you to glow where I glow. It is not a matter of supplying premises from which conclusions follow—deductively or inductively—
it is rather a matter of stimulating people to respond agreeably.
Ethical persuasion according to this view, therefore, must always
involve a link which forms neither an inductive nor a deductive
argument, *and hence not an argument at all.*

In this chapter we shall consider a more recent effort, as made, for example, by Stuart Hampshire in a very stimulating essay, to preserve ethics against excessive scientism, an attempt on the part of moralists who hold that reasoning does take place in ethics, that ethical reasoning is not just a matter of stimulating others to adopt your own attitudes, to cheer on your side, or to do as you do, but a real, 'honest'-to-'goodness' rational argument that is neither inductive nor deductive in nature. Once again analytic naturalism is attacked, because the newer moral philosophy holds with Moore and all varieties of logical positivists that ethical sentences cannot be translated into descriptive sentences. Instead we have non-translational bridges of inference that conduct us from factual premises to ethical conclusions, bridges that are neither deductive nor inductive, neither logical nor empirical. The result is a position strongly reminiscent of Pascal's reasoning by heart. Inductive arguments have *their* rules, deductive arguments have theirs, and ethics has a logic logicians never know.[1]

We shall be forced to reject this point of view, even after considering some of the extremely interesting and ingenious arguments in its behalf. Moreover we shall try to show that those who try to defend it by describing ordinary usage fail to defend it successfully, because they fail to see that they are making a proposal or decision and not simply describing our actual linguistic habits.

Broadly speaking, there are two defenses of the theory that ethical reasoning involves a peculiar kind of argument: (a) a view that is reminiscent of one interpretation of Aristotle's doctrine of the practical syllogism, according to which ethical reasoning carries us from premises that are statements to a "conclusion" that is an action rather than a statement; and (b) the view that, while the conclusion of an ethical argument is a statement, it is a statement so different in kind from the premises that a peculiar kind of bridge —a New Yorker might say an interborough bridge—is necessary for safe conduct from one to the other.

2. *What are the premises and conclusions of ethical argument?*

Philosophical talk in ethics often takes over the idioms of other parts of philosophy. If one feels no qualms about the words 'propo-

---

[1] The preceding two paragraphs have been extracted, with revisions, from a review by myself of David Baumgardt's *Bentham and the Ethics of Today* which appeared in *Partisan Review* for July-August 1953. I wish to thank the editors for permission to reprint.

sitions' and 'facts', one will not hesitate to use them in the conventional platonic way. One will talk of sentences expressing propositions, of predicates expressing attributes, and so on. But if one is aware of the dangers of this way of speaking, as one should be, one will feel uneasy about indulging in it. And yet sometimes one must grit one's teeth and hiss with the vulgar (philosophers) in order to communicate with them. Therefore, in this chapter I shall be somewhat uninhibited about speaking dangerously (as I have in earlier parts of this book), not only because many of the issues which come up in connection with ethical arguments are basically irrelevant to questions like "But are there propositions and are there facts and are there attributes?" but also because I hope and believe that the language of hypostasis can be removed in favor of more austere and less platonistic speech. So while there is some danger in saying that we use sentences in order to make statements, because it sounds like 'We use hammers in order to make houses' and because a house is a *thing* which is different from a hammer, the same point may be made more safely by saying that we use sentences in order to state or to engage in stating. The point is that using a sentence in a certain way breathes life into the sentence but that life need not be thought of as a soul inhabiting a body. Fortified by this preface, we may now speak of a sentence, a statement, a judgment, and a belief not as if it were analogous to speaking of a horse, a centaur, a unicorn, and a griffin but rather as if it were analogous to speaking of a horse, riding, ploughing, and cavalry-charging.

We are prompted to speak of sentences, statements, judgments, and beliefs by the following exposition of the view of many post-kantian philosophers by Stuart Hampshire, who opposes that view and who proposes instead the view we are considering in this chapter: "There is an unabridgeable logical gulf between *sentences* which express *statements* of fact and sentences which express *judgments* of value and particularly moral judgments . . . Post-Kantian philosophers . . . have generally agreed in regarding the logical independence of moral and empirical *beliefs* as defining the main problem of ethics."[2] This is the gulf which post-post-kantian ethical argument is supposed to bridge.

There is one thing about this description that makes the gulf

2 "Fallacies in Moral Philosophy," *Mind* (1949), 58:466, my italics.

seem rather queer. It begins by describing a gulf between *state-ments* of fact and *judgments* of value, and then it winds up by describing a gulf between moral *beliefs* and empirical *beliefs*. Now this change in the way of describing the gulf is not merely the result of an effort to achieve stylistic variety, but is rather the semiconscious voicing of a puzzle, for while at first a gulf between things as different as a statement and a judgment does seem to require a bridge from one borough to another, as it were, a gulf between two *beliefs*—even two beliefs which are admittedly as different as an empirical belief and a moral belief—is at worst like a bridge from a residential to a business district of the same borough. So, while much has been made of the new kind of argument being between statement and judgment, and hence much implied about its being a different *kind* of argument, the description of the gulf as one between two kinds of *beliefs* makes us doubt whether a new kind of inference is necessary. So long as we stick with the description in terms of beliefs we can dispense with a radically new kind of inference or argument.

Because some defenders of this new point of view depend heavily on what they regard as the statement-to-judgment pattern of ethical argument, it is of considerable importance to be clear about the difference between statements and judgments. We may say that every sentence that is used to make a statement is also used to record some judgment of the person making the statement. Thus we use the sentence 'The cat is on the mat' in order to make the statement that the cat is on the mat and to record our judgment that he is. But on this usage the moral sentence 'He ought to have given back the book' is also used to make a statement. Therefore it is quite misleading to speak of some sentences expressing statements and of others as expressing moral judgments, as if those sentences which did express statements aren't used to record factual judgments and as if the sentences that are used to record moral judgments aren't used to make statements. Whether the statements made by the use of ethical sentences should be regarded as statements of *fact* is another question that may be examined later. At the moment I wish only to remind readers of the possibility of speaking in this way, and to say that when we use the word 'judgment' in this context it is very difficult to regard the gulf described as one which requires an interborough bridge. For obviously the factual premises of the argument as well as the ethical conclusion *both* record judgments. It is not as if factual sentences did not record judgments while ethical sentences did. The sentence 'Jones promised it to Smith' can be used to make a statement and to record a judgment *about* Jones or, more indirectly, about Jones's action; and similarly 'It was right of Jones to give it to Smith' may be used to make a statement about an action of Jones and to record a judgment about an action of Jones.

This *might* silence the engineers of an interborough bridge were it not for the fact that they say something else. Hampshire, for example, complains about those ethical philosophers who use the expression 'moral judgment' in the sense of *moral judgment about actions* to the exclusion of 'judgment' in what is called the primary sense of 'decision'.[3] This view of judgment as decision is a fundamental component of the view that there *is* a peculiar gulf to be bridged, a gulf between statement of fact and decision. Those who adopt this view blame the post-kantians for supposing the gulf to be unbridgeable but praise the post-post-kantians for designing the right kind of interborough bridge (or tunnel!). Nevertheless, this post-post-kantian point of view merely repeats in a more subtle form the mistake of those who regard statements as premises and an *obvious* nonstatement as the conclusion of ethical argument. Such a position is different from that according to which attitudes are conclusions, but strongly resembles it. By contrast, defenders of the view we are now examining explicitly regard the conclusion of ethical argument as a conscious action, a decision to do something, and hence they are not satisfied with the view that factual beliefs merely *cause* the "ethical conclusion", particularly since they stress the fact that ethical argument must be viewed from the standpoint of an agent who asks himself, "What ought I to do?" and whom they rightly refuse to regard as a man in search of a cause. Nevertheless, they continue to view the termini of ethical argument so as to require a new bridge of inference, precisely because they tend to construe the conclusion of an ethical argument as a nonstatement or a nonbelief while they regard the things with which we do the justifying as statements or beliefs. It is not surpris-

[3] *Ibid.*, p. 469.

ing, therefore, that they should speak of a new variety of inference. Nor would it be surprising if, after saying that our seeing of Jones is a reason for believing that Jones is in town, the same philosophers were to conclude that this too requires a new mode of reasoning, distinguished from inductive and deductive reasoning because its termini are as different from each other as seeing and believing.

In spite of the great similarity between the view that there is a special logic of ethical inference and certain aspects of the emotive theory, there is some need to examine the use of the perplexing word 'decision' by those who say that there is a special logic of moral decision. It must be remembered, however, that while they urge that in ethical argument we argue in defense of *judgments* in the sense of *decisions,* and that this is why deduction is not appropriate, it cannot be said with equal confidence that argument in defense of moral judgment *about* actions is not deductive. For this reason the view that we defend an ethical *statement,* although closer to the truth, is more easily refuted when coupled with the view that a third mode of argument is necessary in ethical justification.

3. *The moral agent as his own moral critic*

In an effort to associate the theory of interborough ethical transit even more closely with Aristotle, Hampshire says that whereas Aristotle is concerned with analyzing the problem of the moral *agent,* the typical contemporary moral philosopher is concerned with analyzing the problem of the moral *critic.* Aristotle, it is said, "describes and analyses the processes of thought, or types of argument, which lead up to the *choice* of one course of action, or way of life, in preference to another, while most contemporary philosophers describe the arguments (or lack of arguments) which lead up to the acceptance or rejection of a moral *judgment about actions.*"[4] But we must distinguish the process of describing the processes of thought which "lead up" to choices from those which are arguments *in behalf of* such choices. If we restrict ourselves to the former, we may find that some people come to the decision *to do x* without ever going through the step of deciding that *x* is

[4] *Ibid.,* p. 467.

the best thing to do. But this is a process which should be distinguished (here as in the case of scientific discovery) from the process of *defense* or argument, which is a relatively owlish activity that may go on even after the choice or the decision *to do x* has been made, which may be carried out in defense of a decision *that* something ought to have been done.

And what are choices? They are associated with what we do when we use sentences like 'I *choose to* give the book to him' and 'I *decided to* give the book to him'. And surely we do speak of arguing in behalf of these choices *to* or decisions *to*. Yet our *defense* of them almost always takes place by way of defending another kind of decision, like the decision *that* giving the book to him is the best thing to do. We are rightly reminded that Aristotle points out that "deciding *that* x is the best thing to do and deciding *to* do x are both distinguishable and separable",[5] but we are also told by Hampshire, who supports the "third argument", that a decision that x is the best thing *to* do is the conclusion of a moral argument. We are told that a moral problem occurs when one is confronted with "a difficult and untrivial situation in which one is in doubt what one ought to do, and then, after full consideration of the issues involved, one arrives at a conclusion. One's conclusion, reached after deliberation, expressed in the sentence '*x* is the best thing to do in these circumstances', is a pure or primary moral judgment (the solution of a practical problem)."[6] But *this is a judgment about an action.* Even though it is *my* judgment, made in an effort to solve *my* problem, I make the judgment with the understanding that someone else might check the steps in my argument. There is no profound difference between this "pure or primary moral judgment" and the judgment of the critic. When arguing in behalf of a belief that x is the best thing to do, one is serving as one's own critic.

If ethical argument were always and necessarily argument from statements to decisions in the sense of decisions *to do x*, without the mediation of decisions that x is the best thing to do, we *might* speak of ethical argument as quite different from other kinds of argument. But we have seen that ethical argument in behalf of the

[5] *Ibid.*, p. 474.
[6] *Ibid.*, p. 469.

decision *to do* x requires the mediation of arguments in behalf of the decision *that* x is the best thing to do. For this reason we turn to the view we called (b) in Section 1, the view that while the conclusion of an ethical argument is a statement, it is a statement so different in kind from the premises that a peculiar kind of inferential bridge is necessary. This leads us to examine arguments in behalf of decisions that something is the best thing to do, to see whether such arguments dispense with deduction. I will try to show that they do not, partly by examining the words of those philosophers who say that they do. A few preliminary observations on the relation between *deciding that* and *deciding to* are necessary.

4. *Deciding that* and *deciding to*

Do we argue in defense of *the decision* that x is the best thing to do, or do we try to show that x is the best thing to do? This is a little like asking whether we defend that which we believe or our act of believing it. Ordinary language permits us to speak both ways. Do people defend or argue for *the statement* that God exists, or do they defend their believing in God? Actually the puzzle is not very serious. While for certain purposes it might be useful to stress the fact that even deductive argument should be regarded as a sequence of acceptances or believings rather than as a series of dead body-sentences or live soul-propositions, for other purposes it might not be. The important point is that we should speak uniformly of the elements of an argument once we have elected to construe arguments in a certain way, since a hybrid conception of argument which construes the premises in one way and the conclusion in another is at the root of a number of unnecessary confusions. *Deciding that* is closely related to *believing that,* so that if we construe a deductive argument as a defense of a *decision that,* each element or step of the argument should be construed as *a decision that.* But we may also speak of defending not the deciding but rather *that which* we decide, and then we may be inclined to regard an argument as a sequence of statements. The important thing is not to shift gear in the middle of an argument, for then we get the misleading impression that we're hopping from one sort of thing to a very different sort of thing and we can develop the mistaken view that some strange and new form of inference is at work.

Deciding *that* x is the best thing to do is closely related to coming to believe that x is the best thing to do, so that it will make
sense to say that one defends his belief that x is the best thing to do
whenever one defends his decision that x is the best thing to do.
Since we may speak of a man coming to believe truly that the cat
is on the mat, *and* of his belief as a true one, *and* of his making a
true statement when he gives voice to this true belief, an understanding philosopher should allow us to speak of a *true* decision
that the cat is on the mat without too much confusion being produced by its awkwardness. The reader should realize that I am
not advising this language as a practice but only trying to counter-
act a tendency to exploit the awkwardness of the phrase 'true decision' in a misleading philosophical way. The word 'judgment'
has a similar function in language. One may say that the cat is on
the mat, and one may speak of the true judgment that the cat is on
the mat. One may also regard a deductive argument as a sequence
of judgments. For this reason the following is confusing: " 'I decided that x was the right thing to do' is a descriptive statement,
true or false; but 'x was the right thing to do' is a practical or moral
judgment, right or wrong."[7] Granting that it is a "practical judgment" that is right or wrong, this does not mean that it cannot be
called true or false. It is said: "The judgments of the Lord are true
and righteous altogether." We have already quoted Russell's observation that propositions about practice are no more practical
than propositions about gases are gaseous. We must remember that
it is a judgment *about* action x and as such must not be confused
with the decision to do x (which is admittedly neither true or
false). Moreover, 'judgment', unlike 'decision', doesn't split up
into 'judgment that' and 'judgment to', so that only contexts
involving 'judgment that' make sense. The fact that it is a *right*
or a correct judgment and that this does not interfere with our
speaking of an associated true judgment is paralleled by the fact
we speak of believing rightly and also of a belief being true. What
is involved is a confusion between two uses of the word 'judgment'
that are also somewhat analogous to two uses of the word 'statement'. Judgment is sometimes construed as that which we make,
in which case we speak of it as true or false, but it is also construed

[7] *Ibid.,* p. 482, note 1.

as an action in which we engage, in which case we speak of judging rightly or correctly. Similarly with 'statement' and 'belief'. We may conclude that under ordinary circumstances nothing militates against regarding a decision that, a judgment that, a belief that, as true or false, and that this is a reply to another argument in favor of the view that ethical argument is what I have called inter-borough in nature. If its conclusion is a decision *that* or a judg-ment *that*, that conclusion *may* be spoken of as true or false. Be-cause of this we are tempted to view Hampshire as making a phil-osophical proposal to *alter* ordinary usage rather than giving a de-scription of it.

5. *The relevance of ordinary language*

So far we have not taken into account the view that our use of 'decided that' in ethics is different from that in science, just be-cause the former involves putting 'I've decided that' before sen-tences containing the words 'right', 'wrong', etc. We now wish to consider certain questionable arguments that urge *this* difference, particularly those based on observations of ordinary language. It should be remarked that this question is closely tied to the discus-sion of positivistic ethics in Chapter XI, where we concluded that the orthodox positivistic thesis on ethics is most consistent when framed as a proposal to withhold the terms 'true' and 'false' from ethical sentences or statements and not as a description of actual usage. In this section we will be dealing with another supposedly descriptive view of the matter.

It has been said that while we can *deny* that something is the best action under certain circumstances, such a denial is not nor-mally expressed by saying, 'It is false that this is the best action in these circumstances', and that " 'true' and 'false' are more naturally used with theoretical judgments and statements of fact". Moreover, it is said that "Although we can speak of believing that this is the right action we cannot speak of evidence that it is right. 'Evidence' is tied to statements which are true or false."[8] But how often do physicists put 'it is true that' before the formulae they accept and 'it is false that' before those they reject? How normally or naturally, therefore, are these phrases used by those who are preëminently

---

[8] *Ibid.*, p. 480; see also note 1 on that page.

concerned with theoretical questions? Therefore, if the philosophical theory that physical sentences are "descriptive" cannot be defended by saying that physicists normally use phrases like 'it is true that' and 'it is false that' (and I don't think it can be), neither can the philosophical theory that moral sentences are not descriptive make anything of the fact that we don't normally preface our moral conclusions with 'it is true that'. Indeed, as I shall argue shortly, we do sometimes preface ethical utterances with 'it is true that'. Moreover, the allegedly non-describing mathematicians use 'it is true that' and 'it is false that' with alarming frequency by comparison with the allegedly describing physicists. The safest conclusion on this score is that the actual usage of 'it is true that' is not a reliable guide for those who wish to make radical epistemological distinctions between mathematical, physical, and ethical utterances.

This brings us to the word 'evidence'. It has been virtually captured by empiricists, even though they sometimes speak of "empirical evidence" as though the qualifying adjective were not redundant. And yet the word 'evidence' is often used as synonymous with 'grounds for believing', so that when defenders of the view we are considering allow us to speak of having grounds for believing that x is the right action, they should also allow us to speak of having evidence that it is. If they hold, as some of them do, that we can speak of believing that an action is wrong, then we should be able to have true and false beliefs on these subjects. The alternative is, of course, that we *do and must* speak of moral beliefs as right or wrong, never true or false, and that we *do and* must speak of theoretical beliefs as true or false, never right or wrong. But this is absurd. We do speak of rightly believing that the cat is on the mat when he is on the mat; we speak of believing truly (not "truly believing") that the cat is on the mat; we *can* speak of believing truly that this is wrong even though we also speak of rightly believing that this is right. My feeling is that the philosophers we are considering probably hold the view that moral statements are not "descriptive", on the basis of considerations which have very little to do with ordinary usage of phrases like 'it is true that' and words like 'evidence'.

There is no basis in ordinary language for making a radical

distinction between 'It's wrong to steal the library's copy of the latest *Mind*' and 'The cat is on the mat' if we concentrate on the permissibility of prefixing phrases like 'I know that', 'I believe that', 'I judge that', and 'I feel that'. And while the matter is *somewhat* different in the case of 'it is true that', it is so only because this is a rarely used phrase and because its actual use might, with equal lack of cogency, be cited to defend the thesis that no physical statements are descriptive, as I have already suggested. This is a strong argument against the view under consideration, to the extent to which that view rests on the "normal" or "natural" use of the phrase 'it is false that'. If I should decide to speak unnaturally tomorrow morning, to say things like 'It is false that it's right to steal the library's copy of the latest *Mind*', proponents of the other view should want to say that even then I use the sentence 'It's right to steal the library's copy of the latest *Mind*' non-descriptively. And how would they show this? Surely not by concentrating on the unnatural part of my remark, but rather on the way in which I use the sentence 'It is right to steal the library's copy of the latest *Mind*' in direct discourse. Moreover, we can imagine someone saying, 'It's true that one ought not steal library books, but I did need that one'.

In general it is dangerous to base our sharp separations of traditional domains on what is or is not permissible in indirect discourse governing a given sentence or in ordinary metalinguistic discourse about that sentence. In this connection it is important to remember that the emotive theory does not rest its case on our habits in indirect discourse. It does not regard as particularly crucial the fact that people do say things like 'I believe that it's wrong to steal the library's copy of the latest *Mind*' or 'I know that it's wrong to steal the library's copy of *Mind*'. To the Moore-like question, "But surely you don't deny that when I say I understand the sentence 'It's wrong to steal the library's copy of the latest *Mind*', I'm saying exactly the same thing about this sentence as I say about the sentence 'The cat is on the mat' when I say I understand *it*?" the emotivist must reply that he *does* deny this. He must point out that too heavy a dependence on the presence or absence of such phrases as 'it is true that' and 'I know that' will mislead the philosopher who is interested in the logic of ethical sentences in direct discourse. The presumption is that a philosopher can criticize much *in*direct discourse as misleading, even to the point of saying (heroically) that you don't "really" understand moral sentences or (less heroically but heroically enough) that you understand them in a different sense of 'understand'. The theory that moral sentences are used to make statements receives considerable support from *ordinary* usage, and it takes a philosopher to show whether ordinary usage is misleading or illuminating on this point and to *recommend* avoidance of misleading ordinary language.

One suspects that those who classify some sentences as true-or-false and others as not, automatically view the word 'true' as if it were to be "analyzed" in accordance with the correspondence theory of truth, which is to say that they think that the application of 'true' to a sentence implies that we think it "corresponds with fact". Thinking this, they are willing to say that there are all sorts of facts to be corresponded with in the case of "scientific" statements but none in the case of "ethical statements". And yet it is plain that while ordinary language allows both, sound philosophical language should avoid both. What is most confusing is the tendency to say that "scientific" statements correspond to facts and to deny that "ethical" statements do, by appealing to ordinary language. Instead, it should be made clear that *ordinary* language allows us to speak of scientific fact *and* moral fact, and that it allows us to speak of both scientific and ethical statements as true-or-false. After pointing this out, the philosopher should call attention to the dangers of speaking of "facts" in both cases. Then, if he wishes, he may propose that we prohibit the application of the words 'true' and 'false' to so-called ethical sentences, while allowing its application in the case of scientific sentences. If he should do this, the nature of his intent would be clearer, and others would be in a position to argue for or against his proposal. My own inclination is to *reject* the proposal, out of the conviction that it can only be supported on the basis of an untenable empiricist theory of meaning or an invidious but unjustified hypostatization of "facts" to which scientific sentences allegedly correspond and to which ethical sentences allegedly don't correspond. More positively, I think that in *accepting* or affirming or believing ethical statements we do precisely what those who accept or affirm or believe scientific statements do, and that this is or may be signalized in both cases by use of the phrase 'it's true'. Moreover, I do not think that we can profitably single out "the meaning" or "method of establishing" an isolated sentence—ethical or scientific—in the manner required by those who see a distinction of kind between the method of establishing any given ethical statement and the method of establishing any given scientific statement. The reasons for this will emerge more clearly, I hope, in the remainder of this book.

Not only is the reference to ordinary usage not enough to support the view that sentences containing the word 'ought' and 'right' and 'best thing to do' are not used to make statements; it will not support the view that such sentences are not used to make "factual statements". The latter view resembles the view that arithmetical sentences are used to make statements which are not statements of "fact". But everyone knows that there is a normal and natural usage according to which we may say things like 'The fact is that this ought to be done'. Ordinary language allows this, surely. We say, 'The fact is that the cat is on the mat', 'The fact is that this is wrong', 'The fact is that all bodies attract each other', 'The fact is that nothing can achieve a velocity greater than that of light', 'The fact is that 43 multiplied by 3 is equal to 129'. From this point of view, so-called ethical statements are no less factual than what are called factual statements in a narrow sense by some philosophers, so that the distinction cannot be supported by relatively naïve reference to English usage. English, far from sanctioning the distinction between scientific statements and ethical statements, rather discourages it by its generous use of the idiom 'the fact is that . . .'

6. 'Is' and 'ought'

Some philosophers speak of a radical difference between 'is'-sentences and 'ought'-sentences in this connection, but that difference is not incompatible with the similarity I have been stressing. When we use the sentence 'The cat is on the mat' to make a statement, we do use it to make one which is quite different from that which we make when we use 'The cat ought to be on the mat', but this is wholly consistent with saying that both statements are factual on the usage mentioned. The point is that we can convert an 'ought'-sentence into an 'is'-sentence very quickly without changing the statement made. Many philosophers fail to see the difference between the relation which exists between

(1) This is done

and

(2) This ought to be done

and the relation which exists between (2) and

(3) This is something that ought to be done.

In general, 'This is P' is not equivalent with 'This ought to be P', and that is one important point about the relation between 'is'-sentences and 'ought'-sentences. But we cannot deny that (2) and (3) can be used to make the same statement. Every 'ought'-sentence is convertible into what I shall call an *associated* 'is'-sentence, but never into what I shall call its *corresponding* 'is'-sentence. Thus (2) is the 'ought'-sentence corresponding to the 'is'-sentence, (1); while (3) is associated with (2) and conversely. The relation is similar to the relation between 'is'-sentences and 'is not'-sentences. Philosophers who do not shy away from 'synonymous' will agree that no 'is'-sentence is synonymous with what might be called its corresponding 'is not'-sentence; but clearly by the principle of double negation there is always an associated 'is not'-sentence with which every 'is'-sentence is synonymous. For example, 'John is tall' is not synonymous with 'John is not tall', but it is synonymous with 'It is not the case that John is not tall'.

It should be remembered, however, that neither (a) the possibility of always translating every 'ought'-sentence into an associated 'is'-sentence, nor (b) the impossibility of translating any 'ought'-sentence into its corresponding 'is'-sentence, affects the doctrine of ethical naturalism. *Its* chief tenet is neither that we *can* translate every 'ought'-sentence in the way illustrated by the translation of (2) into (3), nor that we can translate every 'ought'-sentence into a corresponding 'is'-sentence. The first thesis is trivial, the second absurd. The chief tenet of naturalism is rather that we can translate every 'ought'-sentence into a so-called *naturalistic* 'is'-sentence, and this is stronger than a truism and weaker than an absurdity. That is why neither naturalists nor anti-naturalists need shrink with horror from the view that ethical sentences do express statements that are "factual" in a relatively neutral sense. Philosophers with certain ontological scruples can consistently shrink from this kind of language, but those who take their cue from a simple inspection of ordinary language cannot make the distinction they want to make. Our ability to speak of making ethical *statements* and of announcing ethical *facts* is simply the result of a decision to follow the lead of ordinary language without flinching. It leads from idioms like 'I say that this is right' to speaking of *the statement* that this is right just as quickly as the idiom 'I say that the cat is on the mat' leads us to speak of the statement that the cat is on the mat; and it leads from 'The fact is that this is right' to supposing that there are ethical facts with as much speed as 'The fact is that this particle repels that one' leads to postulating physical facts. Ordinary language has been influenced sufficiently by all of the traditional ontologies to have adopted modes of speech consistent with all of them. To rid ourselves of "ethical facts" and to retain others we must go beyond a *simple-minded* observation of the language we use.

7. *Prescribing and describing*

It is sometimes argued that we may make a sound dichotomy between sentences like 'The cat is on the mat' and 'It is wrong to steal the library's copy of the latest *Mind*' by attending to the difference between describing and prescribing, and that this difference is evident to any student of ordinary language. The issues here are quite similar to those that arise in Moore's philosophy, only he is concerned with the contrast between describing and evaluating, as we have seen. But ordinary usage of the words 'prescribe' and 'describe' is equally unsafe as a basis for a sound dichotomy between the sentence 'The cat is on the mat' and 'It is wrong to steal the library's copy of the latest *Mind*'. If one regards describing as something done by human beings (rather than by sentences) one can say that a person who says 'The cat is on the mat' is describing the cat as being on the mat. He is not prescribing anything. One can also say of a person who says 'It is wrong to steal the university's copy of the latest *Mind*' that he is describing the act of stealing the university's copy of the latest *Mind* as being wrong. We may also say of anyone who says that a certain act ought to be done that he is describing that act as one that ought to be done. But in this case we can also say that he is prescribing something. He *prescribes* the doing of x when he *describes* x as an act that ought to be done. Prescribing an act is not inconsistent with describing it as having a certain attribute, namely, that of being something that ought to be done. Far from suggesting a dichotomy between prescribing and describing, it is concentration on ordinary language occasionally supplemented by mildly official phrases like 'having an attribute' or 'being something that' that suggests the possibility of one sentence's being both prescriptive and descriptive at the same time. Therefore it is ordinary language which helps rather than hinders the philosopher who is moved to construe prescriptive statements as descriptive statements of a certain kind—namely, those which are used to describe acts as having the "nonnatural" attributes of being wrong or right, or as being those which ought to be done.

It has been said: "To pose the problem of ethics as the problem of 'ethical predicates' or 'non-natural characteristics,' is at the outset to suggest that moral judgments are to be interpreted as a peculiar kind of descriptive statement."[9] But this is not really posed *at the outset;* it is posed only after the philosopher has concentrated on the English phrases 'is on the mat' and 'is wrong' and has noticed similarities between them. To convince him that these are *very* different kinds of phrases by appealing to ordinary language is not easy. For one thing, one must face the fact that 'is wrong' is just as much a predicate of the English language as 'is on the mat'. No advocate of the view that philosophers ought to watch ordinary usage carefully can deny this. Nor can he maintain that the idiom according to which we *describe* acts as wrong when we say that they are wrong is "unnatural".

What we must do is to reject in a radical way the platonism that underlies the view that description, prescription, and evaluation are all species of ascription in the sense of ascribing a property. Once we have done this, we are left with prescribing, describing, and evaluating as modes of linguistic behavior, and the question becomes one of discovering whether the defense of the application of a predicate like 'ought to be done' or 'right' to an action involves a "logic" which is quite different from that which is involved in

[9] *Ibid.,* p. 472, note 1.

defending the application of the predicate 'ten feet tall' to physical objects. Unfortunately too many philosophers of ordinary language who are bent on the rejection of nonnatural qualities admit the existence of *natural* qualities, without seeing that *the very language* that encourages their own platonism is what encourages Moore's anti-naturalistic ethics. Therefore, if we are to get anywhere we must do more than cut off a branch of platonism— Moore's anti-naturalistic ethics—we must get to the root of the matter. And the root of the matter, as we have seen in an earlier chapter, is the view that there are attributes, entities whose presence in things justifies our ascribing them to those things. Once we have seen that, we are in a better position to consider the question whether there is a logic other than inductive or deductive logic that we use in the support of evaluative or prescriptive conclusions.

The wholly non-platonistic way of speaking recognizes a difference between prescribing and describing but regards it as a difference between the use of sentences that contain one kind of word as opposed to another. That is to say, we prescribe a course of action when we affirm a sentence which contains the name of that action followed by the phrase 'is right' or 'ought to be done'. Similarly, we describe that action when we affirm a sentence which begins with the name of that action followed by other kinds of expressions. Whether we can get some "criterion" of a linguistic kind that carves out the class of descriptive predicates in a more positive way I doubt very much; therefore the situation here is quite similar to that in the case of logical constants. It is important to realize, however, that there is only one "logic" that connects such sentences, whether they are all descriptions or a mixture of both descriptions and prescriptions in the sense of 'ought'-sentences. In both cases we accept sentences which are used to make statements, in both cases sentences to which people do preface phrases like 'I know', 'I believe', 'I say that', 'It's a fact that'. And in both cases deductive logic can carry us to conclusions.

8. *Against the view that ethics requires a special mode of argument*

Since the main support for the view that there is a third (neither inductive nor deductive) kind of peculiarly ethical argument rests on the view that the conclusion of ethical argument is as different from the premise as an action is from a statement (view (a) of Section 1), we have concentrated our criticism on it. But we have gone even further by criticizing philosophers who agree that we argue in defense of ethical *statements* (view (b)). We may pursue this by pointing out that at least one supporter of the view that ethical argument is *sui generis,* Hampshire, has said that presenting ethical arguments in behalf of the conclusion that actions are right consists in "quoting the different characteristics which are normally and generally taken to be sufficient grounds for deciding that they are the right actions",[10] and yet that: "From no consideration of facts, or accumulation of knowledge, can we ever deduce a moral judgment of the form 'this ought to be done' or 'this is the right action in these circumstances.' "[11] But far from supporting the view that ethical argument is *sui generis,* these very remarks show that deduction will suffice for the kind of argument that terminates in a so-called singular moral judgment like 'This ought to be done'.

In "quoting a characteristic" of actions, which is normally and generally taken to be sufficient ground for deciding that an action is right, can't we be referring to a characteristic whose linguistic expression is the subject of a universal or almost universal proposition whose predicate is 'right'? In other words, if we take an action's possessing characteristic C to be sufficient ground for deciding that the action is right, are we not implying something like 'All or most actions of kind C are right actions'? And if we say this, don't we *believe* what we say? And if we *believe* this, can't we go further on some occasions and say we *know* something like this? And if we know it as well as something that is expressed by a singular sentence 'This is C', why can't we sometimes at least *deduce* from the "knowledge" expressed in these sentences the knowledge expressed in 'This is right'? It may be protested that we don't "know", for example, that all actions which are C are right just because the word 'right' is a constituent. But on what grounds? Surely not on the grounds of ordinary usage, for many people say that they know no one ought to kill wantonly and that acts of treachery are wrong.

[10] *Ibid.,* p. 481.
[11] *Ibid.,* p. 472.

It may be said that an ethical argument in defense of the statement 'I ought to return the book to him' is given when I say, 'because you promised it to him', and that the clause following 'because' expresses a factual statement which completes the argument without entailing the ethical conclusion. But then by equally inconclusive reasoning, one may say that in explaining why the streets are wet one says simply, 'because it rained a few minutes ago', and thus may maintain that no scientific explanation ever presents a set of premises from which the statement or truth to be explained or defended can be deduced. Yet in both of the cases mentioned, it is plain that we can often supply a premise on demand which will convert the enthymeme into a valid deduction.

I realize, of course, that in the case of moral reasoning it is often difficult to supply the "principle" or general statement which will allow us to construct a strictly deductive argument, but it is also often difficult to do this when we try to defend our so-called factual beliefs. Very often we are asked to explain why a is Q, and reply 'because a is P'—even where we cannot justify the generalization 'All P is Q'. We often feel that there is *some* connection between a's being P and a's being Q without being able to specify the general law or laws connecting them, and one of the main tasks of empirical science is to increase our power to specify these laws, just as a growth of rationality in ethical argument is accompanied by a more explicit recognition of our ethical principles. Moreover, as we shall see later, it may be that in scientific explanation we take for granted a vast amount of knowledge which never figures explicitly in the explanation, just as we take for granted a great deal that is left inexplicit when we offer arguments in behalf of singular ethical conclusions. If this is true, we cannot say that ethical argument is *peculiar* because we do not have always a strict implication between our so-called premises and our ethical conclusions; the fact is that our scientific explanations are often, perhaps always, similarly incomplete.

9. *Conclusion*

In this chapter we have questioned and criticized the view that there is some third form of argument which is used or should be used in support of singular ethical conclusions. We have also seen that ordinary language, far from sanctioning a third form of inference, is on the side of those who oppose it, and we have suggested that it's no good legislating it into existence. With this we abandon the effort to install a trichotomy of methods corresponding to moral principles, scientific principles, and logical principles, and in the remaining chapters we shall try to show the triune nature of ethics, science, and logic.

PART IV

WHAT IS, WHAT MUST BE,
WHAT SHOULD BE

CHAPTER XIV

Ethics, Science, and Logic

1. *Moral principles and scientific laws*

In disputing the contention that a statement like 'This ought to be done' cannot be deduced from an "accumulation of knowledge", we needn't and don't dispute the contention that it can't be deduced from *factual* statements alone, when "factual statement" is construed so narrowly as to exclude moral principles. But this raises the question of whether and how one can distinguish between a so-called factual principle like 'All men are mortal' and a moral principle like 'One ought to keep one's promises'. Because ordinary language allows us to speak both of knowing and believing that one ought to keep one's promises and of the fact that one ought to keep one's promises, those who depend on our use of certain parts of ordinary language have not provided any clear or sharp epistemological distinction between moral principles and others. And, as already suggested, we can imagine someone saying, 'It's *true* that one ought to keep one's promises, but I do need the money very badly'. Once again, we are obliged to go beyond the more superficial aspects of ordinary language and to push more deeply into the logic of supporting ethical principles. We support singular ethical statements by deduction from singular factual statements and a body of ethical principles, but how do we support ethical principles?

If we say that we know that one ought to keep one's promises, we are properly asked how we know, not by philosophers who go around asking, 'How do we know anything?' but by simple people who want to know how we know this particular thing. In an effort to distinguish invidiously between different kinds of questions that can be raised in ethics, some philosophers have appealed to a distinction between several kinds of questions that may be raised about science, but often they fail to put their finger on the similarities and differences between ethical and scientific principles which cause the most serious puzzles. We may accept for the purpose of this discussion the account of scientific explanation as a process directed toward answering questions like 'Why does this stick in the water *look* bent when it doesn't feel bent?' But in that case we must see that the analogous question in ethics (for certain purposes) is a request for reasons for ethical decisions made in the face of specific problems. And we must realize that in both cases, that of scientific explanation and that of ethical argument, the response can often be a *de*ductive argument. Snell's Law, even though it contains no words like 'ought', functions in an explanation of a specific physical fact as a premise of a deductive argument, just as the general principle 'One ought to do whatever he promises to do' does in the kind of ethical argument for singular conclusions discussed in the last chapter.

There are a variety of questions about scientific explanation—some of them silly—which we may rightly distinguish from those asked by someone who seeks a scientific explanation of something. Some of these are usually asked not by professional scientists but rather by philosophers, and they are correctly distinguished from the limited scientific question 'why does the stick look bent when it feels straight?' Take, for example, the question 'Is light no more than very-very-high frequency waves?' This has been dismissed by some as quite different from the question about the stick looking bent (often by those who do not see how much it is like Moore's question about *good*). And the same thing has been done with the question 'Can *any* scientific explanation be correct?' But there is one similar-sounding question which is a legitimate scientific question, namely, 'Is *this* explanation correct?' once an explanation of the stick's looking bent has been attempted by a physicist. *This* question, when asked in some situations, suggests that the person who asks it is convinced that the formal *pattern* of the explanation is correct, that the physicist has made no mistakes in logic, but what the questioner wants to know is whether the physicist's universal premise is true or scientifically acceptable. He may want to know whether Snell's statement that the sine of the angle of incidence divided by the sine of the angle of refraction is constant for a given medium is acceptable, or he may question the truth of other assumptions used in the explanation. Now *this* question about Snell's Law is the illuminating parallel to asking whether it's true that one ought to keep one's promises, but too often some philosophers are inclined to treat it and its ethical counterpart as though they were like some of the woollier questions about science which are rightly dismissed as irrelevant to the scientific question of explanation. And yet when one asks it one is not necessarily a confused metaphysician demanding the justification of scientific method or anything of the kind. Similarly, the question 'But is *this* ethical principle acceptable?' should not be confused with 'But why be moral?' or 'Why do what is right?' but rather treated as the reasonable parallel to asking for a justification of Snell's Law.

2. *Rules*

Those who support the "third argument" sometimes say that the reasoning from 'You promised to return it' to 'You ought to return it' is governed by a rule which does not figure as a premise. But there is a similar temptation to say that the inference from 'Socrates is a man' to 'Socrates is mortal' or that the inference from 'The angle of incidence of this ray when going from air to water is 10°' to 'The angle of refraction of this ray is 40.5°' is really in accordance with a rule, as Mill and others have suggested. And then we must ask whether 'One ought to keep one's promises' is essentially rule-like, while 'All men are mortal' and Snell's law are not, or whether both are equally rule-like. If both are equally rule-like, it is obvious that we must work hard in order to show that the logic of justifying one kind of rule is fundamentally different from the logic of justifying another kind of rule. We have exactly the same situation when we try to hold that both physical laws and logical laws can be formulated as rules and that nevertheless there is a radical epistemological distinction between them. One might say that both physical laws and logical laws *might be* formulated as rules, even though logical laws are essentially rule-like while physical laws are not. But then we shall have a very difficult time explaining the difference between a rule which is essentially a rule and one which is accidentally one. At any rate, I don't know how to explain this. On the other hand, if one holds that they are both rules and yet fundamentally different in status, one must distinguish between the methods of justifying different kinds of rules. So no matter how the distinction is made, it's important to remember that we've abandoned the notion of rule as the basis for making the distinction. Everything's a rule now: the principle announcing the inferability of the conclusion of a syllogism from its premises, the principle announcing the inferability of 'The angle of refraction when going from air to water is 40.5°' from 'The angle of incidence of this ray is 10°', and the principle announcing the inferability of 'You ought to return it' from 'You promised to return it'. In short, the principles of logic, empirical science, and ethics.

Precisely because any one of these principles can be "made into" a rule, or in other words because we can at will formulate a counterpart of them that will be a rule in the sense of being a metalinguistic statement like ' 'a is a mortal' is inferable from 'a is a man' ' instead of an "object-language" statement like 'All men are mortal', we cannot use the notion of rule of inference very effectively in this context. If we were willing to place more confidence in the notion of analyticity, we might be able to say that logical principles are analytic, as some do, and in that way at least distinguish between logic on the one hand and empirical science and ethics on the other. But we have rightly denied ourselves this easy way out. Moreover, this course would not help in distinguishing between Snell's Law and the Golden Rule even if it were to distinguish the law of excluded middle from both of them, especially if we abandon the emotive theory of ethical judgment.

3. Ethics, science, and logic

Our earlier treatment of the notion of analyticity and the a priori suggested that one of the great stumbling blocks in the way of philosophical understanding is the tendency to suppose that the process of accepting a sentence amounts merely to examining a certain kind of extra-linguistic entity and seeing whether it has a certain property or whether several properties are related in a certain way. In the theory of the a priori, this tendency is illustrated by the view that we must look only at meanings in order to test truth; in the theory of the a posteriori, it is illustrated by the view that we examine certain "natural objects" and decide whether they have certain natural properties; in the theory of moral judgments it is illustrated by the view that we must look at some natural objects to see whether they have nonnatural properties.

Such views are not only handicapped by the obscurity and uselessness of the elements they postulate but also untrue to the actual procedure of logic, empirical science, and ethics. What they neglect is something that is best understood when we see logic, empirical science, and ethics operating simultaneously in ethical argument. For there, as we have already suggested, at least one premise is a moral principle that links an "empirical predicate" with an "ethical predicate", other premises are purely empirical assertions, and the conclusion is reached by means of a principle of formal logic which may also be construed as a premise of the argument. Our conclusion is one in which we assert that an action is right or the best thing to do under the circumstances. But now what if the conclusion is unacceptable? What if the whole machinery of logic, ethics, and empirical science that has been applied to our problem produces a conclusion that we find unacceptable simply because we do not feel that that course of action is right or we do feel that it is hideously wrong? Clearly, from a deductive point of view we are at liberty to do several things: to disregard our feelings and impulses, to reject the moral principle, to reject the factual statement, to reject the logical principle; and some have gone so far as to reject the entire structure of rational argument under such circumstances, as Ivan Karamazov rejects truth itself when he says: "If the suffering of children serves to complete the sum of suffering necessary for the acquisition of truth, I affirm from now onwards that truth is not worth such a price."

The view of Pierre Duhem that scientific explanation and prediction puts to the test a whole body of beliefs, rather than the one which is ostensibly under test alone, may be generalized so that it becomes evident that not only other scientific principles but also the logic and mathematics we use in our explanatory and predictive reasoning are implicated. But this view, most recently advocated by Quine, is usually limited to the case where (1) a system of scientific discourse is related to (2) sensory experience. When we study the logic of ethical argument, however, we must broaden our linguistic structure so that it includes ethical statements, and broaden the other element in the situation beyond sensory experience to include moral feelings of approval, revulsion, loathing, etc., toward actions. Then we may say that just as Duhem's view, when pushed to the extreme, makes it difficult to maintain a radical separation between the analytic and the synthetic and the method of establishing logical as opposed to empirical truth, so the view we have advocated will break down the remaining dualism between logic-*cum*-empirical science and ethics. Logical principles can, of course, be distinguished from others because they contain only logical constants and variables essentially; moral principles can be distinguished through the appearance of the word 'ought' and others; and different branches of empirical science will also be syntactically distinguishable from each other. But a radical *epistemological* difference of kind can not be drawn. According to this view, every individual comes to his moral problems with a complex of moral and scientific beliefs that are under test or scrutiny, a scientific theory and moral code that lead him by logic to say what will be and what ought to be. And just as so-called empirical principles will, for the most part, have a closer relation to experience than those of logic and mathematics, so ethical principles will be more intimately connected with feeling.

There is no doubt that the principles of logic are less frequently challenged than are those of ethics, and I suspect that those of ethics are less frequently challenged within a given culture than are those of physics, though this might be doubted by some. It is not surprising, therefore, that both the principles of logic and those of ethics are said to be established by peculiar activities like "seeing" the connections between meanings or intuiting the presence of a nonnatural quality. What the proposed view achieves is a way of avoiding this invention of entities and of queer relations between them that are detected in queer ways. We dispense not only with the need for platonic meanings but also with the need for nonnatural qualities. We recognize the connections between logic, ethics, and physics by seeing how they function together.

This is confirmed not only by the fact that when we test our moral principles we often reject them if they are out of kilter with our moral feelings but also by the existence of casuistry in the pejorative sense, by the fact that we often strain to fit our facts into the framework of accepted morality or stretch our moral principles to fit facts. On the other hand, when our logic and our scientific beliefs are allowed to remain unchallenged, we sometimes reject our moral principles if they lead to conclusions that are out of kilter with our direct moral responses. The pattern of surrendering a moral principle is very similar to the surrender of an isolated physical principle when everything else is held constant. One exception after another eats away at the principle, and the same commitment to logical consistency forces its rejection as forces us to reject physical theories that go against observation. We come to forge our own positive ethical principles in a similar way; they are the principles which together with our other beliefs systematically organize our elementary moral convictions. I repeat that whether you construe them as "rules" in the "metalanguage" or as premises within the "object-language" of ethics has little bearing on the actual method of rejecting and accepting moral principles. Nevertheless, as we shall see later, a decision to make one principle a "rule" may record our determination to maintain it at all costs.

The resulting picture is that of the scientist bringing a system of logical and scientific theory to experience and that of the moralist bringing a combination of logic, scientific theory, and moral principle to bear on his moral problems. By traditional standards it involves a breakdown of the epistemological differences between the logical, the physical, and the ethical. By positivistic standards it involves a breakdown of the semantic walls between the analytic, the synthetic, and the emotive.

I do not mean, of course, that every human being who engages in reflective thinking actually is conscious of putting this enormous system or framework to the test whenever he says that the sun is shining. I mean rather that thinking under certain circumstances, notably when a person is faced with a problem or a crisis, often follows the pattern drawn. The fact that the ordinary man and the scientist can, from a logical point of view, remove inconsistency by revising beliefs other than that one which is ostensibly under test suggests that the philosopher should enlarge his portrait of reflective thinking. Stated more accurately, a philosopher can propose a procedure which the rational man would do well to adopt in a time of crisis. If, when his belief is challenged by experience or moral feeling, a man should persist in rejecting only the belief which is *ostensibly* under fire, a philosopher can point out (1) that this man is adopting a course of action which is very different from that which he might adopt, and (2) that he is adopting a course of action which is different from that which has been adopted by highly successful thinkers whose aims he shares. In general, the philosopher calls his attention to the fact that the ordinary man makes a number of different kinds of assumptions in the course of his reasoning and that any one of them *might* be challenged in moments of crisis. It is this susceptibility to challenge that all principles, whether logical, moral, or empirical, share, and it is this that we should not forget when we come to talk about their supposedly profound epistemological differences. When we view any of them at work, they do not seem to have their single jobs that we can describe merely by reference to the discipline from which they come and without reference to the jobs of the others, particularly when we concentrate on the relation between such principles and our feelings and experiences. We *need* not trace a false prediction to a failure of "scientific" law, for we can trace it to a failure of logic; we *need* not trace moral horror to a mistake in ethics. And, in general, we cannot say *where* the fault *must* lie. It can lie in us, in the stars, or in the principle of the excluded middle.

4. *The "old" ethics and the "new"*

Because of its concentration on the analogy between justification in ethics and explanation or prediction in science, recent work in ethics has been viewed as radically different in purpose from the work of Moore and others. And yet this contrast has been exaggerated by those who think of the search for definition and the study of argument as radically different. Thus, speaking of what he calls "the traditional method," S. E. Toulmin says: "Its principal aim is not so much to discover what reasons and arguments should be accepted in support of ethical decisions, as to pin down—to characterize—ethical concepts by means of some kind of definition."[1] But this contrasts the search for a definition and the search

[1] *An Examination of the Place of Reason in Ethics* (Cambridge University Press, 1950), p. 5.

for reasons and arguments much too sharply. The word 'definition' is certainly not one about which philosophers have spoken with a great deal of consensus, but I think we can say that presenting a definition of 'right' is a special case of establishing what "reasons and arguments" should be accepted in support of ethical "decisions". For clearly, if we conclude that 'right' is to be defined as 'conducive to pleasure' or anything like that, we say in effect that the following is a good argument: 'This act is conducive to pleasure, therefore it is right.' In the same way, when we say that 'man' is to be defined as 'rational animal', we say that the argument 'Socrates is a rational animal, therefore Socrates is a man' is a good argument.

Viewed in the light of what has been said, there are two main differences between the traditional search for a definition and more recent concerns in ethics: one of them is connected with the distinction between analytic and synthetic, the other with the distinction between a conditional or 'if'–statement and a biconditional or 'if and only if'–statement. We have already seen that Moore thought of definition or of philosophical analysis as involving at least a search for biconditionals or equivalences that are analytic in ordinary language. But if we drop the requirement of analyticity, then the main logical difference between the definition that moral philosophers were supposed to seek according to Moore's view and the rules of ethical argument on which more recent moral philosophers focus lies in the fact that the goal of the definition-minded moral philosopher would be a biconditional—a round trip ticket from an "empirical predicate" like 'maximizes pleasure' to an ethical predicate like 'right'—while those sought by more recent moralists are only one-way tickets, like ' 'It is right' is inferable from 'It is a case of truth-telling' '. This is a much less important difference, as is easily seen by comparing the following two passages, the first from Moore and the second from the very stimulating article by Stuart Hampshire which I have already discussed at considerable length in the previous chapter.

Moore asks:

"What, after all, is it that we mean to say of an action when we say that it is right or ought to be done? And what is it that we mean to say of a state of things when we say that it is good or bad? Can we discover any general characteristic, which belongs in common to absolutely *all* right actions, no matter how different they may be in other respects? and which does not belong to any actions except those which are right? And can we similarly discover any characteristic which belongs in common to absolutely all 'good' things, and which does not belong to anything except what is a good? *Or again, can we discover any single reason, applicable to all right actions equally, which is, in every case, the reason why an action is right, when it is right? And can we, similarly, discover any reason which is the reason why a thing is good, when it is good, and which also gives us the reason why any one thing is better than another, when it is better? Or is there, perhaps, no such single reason in either case?* [my italics]"[2]

Hampshire says:

"One can only clarify the use of the principal moral (or aesthetic) terms—'good,' 'right,' 'ought,' etc.—by describing specimens of conduct to which they are applied, that is, by quoting the different characteristics of actions which are normally and generally taken to be sufficient grounds for deciding that they are the right actions. The type of analysis which consists in defining, or finding synonyms for the moral terms of a particular language cannot illuminate the nature of moral decisions or practical problems; it is no more than local dictionary-making, or the elimination of redundant terms, which is useful only as a preliminary to the study of typical moral arguments. An informative treatise on ethics—or on the ethics of a particular society or person—would contain an accumulation of examples selected to illustrate the kind of decisions which are said to be right in various circumstances, and the reasons given and the arguments used in concluding that they are right."[3]

It should be evident from this pair of passages and an excusable mixture of metaphors that some younger moral philosophers seek one-way tickets to righteousness from many different places, while Moore sought an analytic round-trip ticket to it from one

---

[2] Moore, *Ethics* (New York: Oxford University Press, 1949 edition), pp. 7–8.
[3] Hampshire, "Fallacies in Moral Philosophy," *Mind*, 58:481.

place. Viewed in this way, the abandonment of the search for a definition *whose definiendum and definiens are synonymous* in ordinary language is a far more important component of the revulsion against philosophy as analysis in the manner of Moore, than is the abandonment of the search for definitions. The point comes out rather strikingly in another pair of passages. When Moore asks, "What, after all, is it that we mean to say of an action when we say that it is right or ought to be done?" he looks for an analytic statement as the conclusion of his labors, as Hampshire does not when *he* asks for the meaning of a term. "If I am asked what I mean by saying of someone that he is intelligent," Hampshire says, "I explain my use of the word by describing specimens of the type of behavior to which I apply the word; I give some specimens of the types of statements about his behavior which would be taken as sufficient grounds for asserting or denying that he is intelligent."[4] Had Hampshire not included the phrase "or denying" in this passage, his view of philosophical activity in connection with descriptive terms like 'intelligent' would have had the same "one-way" character as his view of moral philosophizing. But once he introduces this phrase, he reveals, perhaps unwittingly, that a philosopher need not be limited to producing *sufficient* conditions but may also produce *necessary* conditions, since if the possession of a certain characteristic P is sufficient for *denying* that a person is intelligent, the logical complement of that characteristic, not-P, is a necessary condition for affirming that he is intelligent. And if not-P happened to be sufficient for affirming intelligence, as it might be, it would be a necessary *and* sufficient condition for being intelligent. Thus even on the view of the newer moralists there is no a priori reason for saying that a philosopher *can't* discover a necessary and sufficient condition for an action's being right. Therefore the *main* difficulty with the attempt to produce definitions is the difficulty of producing conditions which are necessary and sufficient, and is seen in pure form when once we are freed from the responsibility of registering connections between platonic meanings. Moreover, it is the same in all cases of trying to produce a necessary and sufficient condition, whether the terms in question be ethical or not. In the case of 'right' we reject defini-

4 *Idem.*

tional utilitarianism simply because some actions which we call right don't maximize pleasure. In short, it is an extensional failure that stands in our way even after we have surrendered an intensional view of philosophical definition.

5. *The real trouble lies in the notion of meaning*

A philosopher who abandons intensional analysis may blame its failures on the obscurity of 'synonymy' or of platonic meanings, as we have done in earlier chapters; or he may deny that there are pairs of distinct synonymous expressions, as Nelson Goodman has done.[5] But if he does any one of these things, he really *abandons* the effort to give the meaning or connotation of one expression by means of another as a hopeless task. For this reason philosophers should avoid the misleading habit of construing the alternative conception of philosophizing as the presentation of the *meaning* or teaching the *meaning,* lest their readers underestimate the difference between the newer conception of philosophy which they espouse and that of Moore or of the philosophical tradition behind him. The new approach is, I think, very close to the one we have adopted in insisting that we test *systems* of belief even when we are ostensibly testing an isolated hypothesis or moral principle, but persistent use of the word 'meaning' in characterizing this point of view is, I think, misleading and foreign to the theory which is being advocated.

If it is held that the question 'What do you mean by the predicate *E*?' is a question which can only be answered by showing *the use* of *E*, and if showing the use involves showing specimens to which *E* applies as well as presenting lots of sentences in which *E* figures, along with others which are used to support or attack those in which *E* figures, along with others which may be supported or attacked by those in which *E* figures, what is one doing but presenting an answer which if it were completed would present the whole of the language-system or scientific theory or moral code in which the expression *E* figures as a part? We may therefore doubt the wisdom of calling this a process in which we are presenting *the meaning* of *E*, for that is so reminiscent of the kind of view which

---

[5] "On Likeness of Meaning" in Linsky, *Semantics and the Philosophy of Language.*

it is supposed to replace that it can only cause confusion to continue to use the word 'meaning' in connection with the task of philosophy. One reason is that other philosophers who have spoken of the analysis of meaning have thought of the meaning of an expression as something that might be given in one fell swoop, by means of an expression which had a peculiar connection with the expression under consideration. Therefore, it seems quite misleading to say that the question 'What do you mean by saying that he is intelligent?' is always interpreted either by philosophers or by laymen as the same question as 'What are your reasons for saying or why do you say that he is intelligent?' This wrongly suggests that we *never* interpret it as the same question as 'What is it that you mean to say of him when you say that he is intelligent?' The fact is that ordinary language allows both questions, and it's better to recognize this fact and say that the second question is often misleading and obscure (when construed intensionally) than it is to identify them. It is far better to give up the language of intensional semantics than to burden a fundamentally different outlook with the associations of 'meaning'.

Once we abandon the notion of meaning conceived as hypostatic intension and the notion of nonnatural quality, we abandon a very influential and very traditional way of distinguishing between logic, physics, and ethics. We may continue to recognize them as disciplines whose sentences make use of very different vocabularies, but it is only when we view them in action, in the process of collectively helping us say what will be and what should be, that we can see interesting similarities and differences in individual cases. Some statements are on the front line, directly exposed to experience, and others are well to the rear and likely to fall, if ever, only after a very penetrating thrust. Some of them are more exposed to the viscissitudes of moral feeling. But all of them are subject to revision, all of them *capable* of being rejected in the event of a conflict with reports of experience or feeling or any other beliefs we hold sufficiently firmly. Once we view ethics, science, and logic in this way we recognize their separateness and their federal union. We do not *insist* on reducing any two of them to a third, but neither do we think of them as functioning autonomously.

CHAPTER XV

The Right to Believe

1. *Recapitulation*

It is time to begin connecting some of the conclusions of the early parts of this book with those arrived at in the consideration of ethical questions, for it will be recalled that we turned to ethics not simply out of concern with its problems but also in the conviction that a consideration of its problems might illuminate the questions on existence and the a priori with which we began our study. In the part on existence we came to the conclusion that so-called ontological statements are not radically different in kind from other existential statements; that they could form part of the body of science in a way that does not justify the claim that they are all meaningless or the claim that they are all analytic; that a set of premises from which existential statements can be deduced must contain or presuppose at least one existential statement, and that these premises might or might not be of the kind designated as "philosophical" or "ontological" by some. Moreover, it was concluded that the difference between a postulated existential statement and one that isn't postulated is the most illuminating philosophical distinction in this context. And postulation, it was said, is not a very mysterious process, but a linguistic activity which is performed by writing the sentence taken as a postulate under the word 'postulate', or perhaps merely putting the sentence at the very beginning of our study, at the top of the page, so to speak. The act of postulation, it was then said, can be distinguished from the justification of that act.

All of these conclusions on existential statements are relatively general compared to one other: the refusal to accept platonism as it was conceived in those early chapters. Platonism was construed as a doctrine to the effect that there are meanings or attributes, and it was criticized for being a doctrine which did not do the job its proponents supposed it could do, namely illuminate the notion of understanding or knowing a priori. We did not *prove* that there are no meanings but merely argued that we could dispense with this postulate.

Rejecting the view of the a priori according to which all and only a priori sentences are analytic in the sense of being true by virtue of the (platonic) meanings of their terms, we turned to more positivistic views of the a priori. We came to the conclusion that several attempts to produce a non-platonic characterization of it were ineffectual when applied to sentences in ordinary language, and that the conventionalistic view that an analytic sentence is one which is called analytic in an artificial language, or called true by the semantical rules, accomplishes something very different from what some of its proponents think it accomplishes. We came to the conclusion that at best 'analytic' might be viewed as we view 'postulate', for just as being a postulate simply amounts to being called a postulate, so being analytic might amount to being called analytic; once again we concluded that we must distinguish between the act, in this case analytic-calling, and its justification.

The notions of being a definitional equivalence, being a defined term, and being an undefined term were viewed similarly, as was the notion of being an empirically meaningful term in the positivistic sense. Indeed, in the last case the development of the positivistic view of the subject points even more obviously to some such conclusion. To be meaningful, it would appear, is to be called meaningful, and therefore the empiricist theory of meaning is in no sense an analysis of the concept of meaningfulness as applied to terms in ordinary discourse.

By so construing the predicates 'postulate', 'analytic', 'definition', 'undefined', and 'meaningful' as used by logical legislators, we have another reason for rejecting a variety of platonism, for in each of these cases we reject the view that there is some property of linguistic expressions on which we can report and which forces us to take them as postulates, definition-sentences, undefined expressions, or meaningful expressions. But we are obliged to defend our linguistic legislation, and so our attention was directed to the defense of statements like 'This is rightly taken as a postulate',

'This is rightly left undefined', 'This is rightly called meaningful'. We turned, therefore, to ethics for illumination.

There we discovered that ethics itself had gone through a development analogous to that which we found in ontology and epistemology, beginning with Moore's simple, nonnatural qualities and continuing through the positivistic efforts to distinguish between cognitive and emotive meaning. But then we discovered the first glimmering of light in a theory of ethical argument which does not seek *synonyms* of 'ought to be done' or 'right', but which attempts to elucidate in a more general way the structure of rational argument that concludes in normative statements. This proves illuminating in a consideration of the notions *rightly made a postulate, rightly called analytic, rightly taken as undefined,* and it jibes with our conclusions about the structure of scientific belief.

2. *The general significance of ethical reasoning*

Let us now turn to the way in which this view of ethical and scientific reasoning combines with previous reflections, to clarify the problems with which we began this study. First of all, it shows that a conclusion like '*S* is rightly made analytic' cannot be substantiated by saying that the sentence has a nonnatural quality which is expressed by the phrase 'rightly made analytic'. The same is true of the other judgments in which we justify our selection of certain terms as undefined, certain terms as empirically meaningful; and, more generally, it shows that judgments like 'Sentence *S* ought to be accepted' cannot be justified by appealing to a nonnatural quality. Secondly, it cooperates with our own doubts about meaning and synonymy to explain why we are unable to find some "descriptive" synonym of 'ought to be accepted' or 'ought to be made analytic'. Thirdly, even if we give up the search for a descriptive *synonym* of 'rightly accepted', or 'rightly made analytic', or 'rightly left undefined', and confine ourselves to producing necessary and sufficient conditions, we are likely to be as disappointed as students of ethics are when *they* seek necessary and sufficient conditions for being a right action. The best we seem to be able to produce are one-way tickets—if we can produce those— from certain characteristics of sentences to the conclusion that they ought to be accepted, i.e., labeled 'accepted', that they ought to be taken as postulates, i.e., labeled 'postulates', that they ought to be made analytic, i.e., labeled 'analytic', that some rather than other equivalence-sentences ought to be made definitional, i.e., labeled 'definitional'. Part of epistemology then becomes a body of quasi-moral one-way tickets which connect predicates of sentences like 'certain' with those like 'ought to be made analytic', or 'ought to be converted into a definitional equivalence', principles that have obvious analogies with the principles that make up a moral code in the ordinary sense. Who can produce the *sufficient and necessary* condition for 'ought to be made a definition' that will help us say that we ought to make the equivalence (a) 'man = rational animal' rather than (b) 'man = featherless biped' as our *definitional* equivalence, once we surrender the comforting but untenable platonistic view that (a) is analytic or antecedently true by virtue of the meanings of its component terms while (b) is not? In support of our judgment that we ought to make it the definition goes our certainty of its truth, our conviction that it does not controvert other things we believe, that its acceptance into the body of knowledge will contribute to the organization of our experience and hence to our power to predict most effectively. And the fact that we make it a definition serves notice of our reluctance to surrender it in a scientific crisis.

Once we view the process of 'analytic'-making in this way we may well ask ourselves: "Why engage in this ritual? And is it as necessary as the act of postulation or as useful as the act of defining?" We may ask a similar question about the ritual involved in calling certain terms empirically meaningful, remembering, of course, that they are linguistic rituals of a philosophy which has been associated with logic and not rituals of logic and mathematics conceived as sciences. In answer to this I say that 'analytic'-making is not a useful activity, in the hope that the rest of the book has conveyed my reasons. I should add, of course, that the useless process of 'analytic'-making must not be confused with the very useful process of making certain expressions definitions. It would be very nice to end our discussion of 'analytic' on an irenical note and to say that the partisans of analyticity have never maintained that an analytic sentence is anything but a sentence which is "true by definition" in the exact sense in question, so that an analytic sentence in a given language would merely be an identity-sentence corresponding to one beside which 'Df.' had been written in a performatory way. But obviously this has not been the point of view of those who speak of analyticity in *natural* languages, and it has not been the point of view of those who regard the axioms (as opposed to the definitional equivalences) of formal logic as analytic. We may safely say that the most serious partisans of analyticity demand more satisfaction than any conciliatory gesture like the above can afford them.

3. *Agreements and differences with pragmatism*

The reader will have already seen many connections between the view advocated and pragmatism, but it is just as well to distinguish the chief respect in which it resembles pragmatism and the respect in which it doesn't. The most important link between the doctrine advocated in this book and that usually associated with pragmatism is the emphasis upon the word 'ought' as an integral component of the expressions 'ought to be made analytic', 'ought to be left undefined', 'ought to be called meaningful', 'ought to be accepted', 'ought to be believed'. Here the influence of Dewey and James should be obvious. Dewey has insisted that the central notion of logic as he conceives it is that of *warranted assertibility*,[1] while James, as we have already seen, made the notion *ought to be believed* the key notion of his pragmatic theory of truth. But instead of encouraging us in thinking that these notions are likely to receive *definitions* in the sense in which even James sought a definition of 'ought to be believed', my own views do just the opposite, and in this respect they mark a departure from pragmatism. The contrast is best seen by recalling two facts: first that James's pragmatism has deep affiliations with what might be called definitional utilitarianism, and second that the sort of view we have been defending in ethics involves a break with definitional utilitarianism.

Pragmatism, James tells us, "agrees with nominalism . . . in always appealing to particulars; with utilitarianism in emphasizing practical aspects; with positivism in its disdain for verbal solutions, useless questions and metaphysical abstractions".[2] We have already

---

[1] *Logic: The Theory of Inquiry* (New York: Henry Holt, 1938), p. 9.
[2] William James, *Pragmatism* (New York: Longmans, Green, 1907), pp. 53–54. See also my *Age of Analysis* (Boston: Houghton Mifflin, 1955), chs. 9 and 10.

expressed our sympathy with nominalism while criticizing the platonic postulation of universals conceived as attributes or as meanings of predicates, but platonists also postulate *propositions* conceived as the meanings of sentences, and this part of their doctrine was especially antithetical to the tenor of James's philosophy.

Certain platonists distinguish between the sentence 'Socrates is a man' and the proposition that Socrates is a man, the point being that this sentence bears a relation to this proposition identical with a relation that the predicate 'man' is supposed to bear to the attribute of being a man. According to this view a sentence is said to be true only in an elliptical way. It is true just in case the proposition it expresses is true. But what does it mean to say that a proposition is true? Here there is considerable variation within the tradition I have in mind: one view emerges according to which a proposition is true just in case it "corresponds" with a *fact*, another according to which the sentence that expresses it denotes what Frege called the truth-value *Truth*. But both propositions and truth-values are abstract, and the tenor of James's nominalism was to find this multiplication of entities unnecessary. (I say "the tenor" purposely, for there is no doubt that he said other things that appear to be inconsistent with this, and Charles Peirce, whom he called the founder of pragmatism, was a platonist by our standards.)

This brings us to James and positivism. It should be remembered, of course, that, writing in 1907, he was not thinking of *logical* positivism but rather of the positivism of Auguste Comte and Mach. Nevertheless his congeniality with these ancestors of logical positivism foreshadowed the cordial relations between some of his own American disciples and some logical positivists of a later generation. From James's point of view, a correspondence theory of truth was merely an example of the kind of metaphysics that Comte had attacked for postulating occult entities that do not explain anything. James held, and rightly I think, that a scientist who is faced with the problem of deciding between two theories cannot be advised to accept that which "corresponds to the facts" in a way that will be helpful.

This brings us to the very important link between James and the utilitarianism of John Stuart Mill who, it should be recalled, was not hostile to platonic realism even though he was quite sympathetic to Comte. (The point is that Mill was willing to adopt a platonistic semantics because he did not see that it was inconsistent with his own comteian aversion to occult entities.) The important *link* between James and Mill is forged when James comes to present his own theory of truth. It is also the point at which his view, in its concern with a *definition* of 'ought to be believed', diverges from that which is advocated in this book. What James did was to generalize Mill's utilitarianism so that it was not only applicable to 'right' or 'ought to be done' but also to 'ought to be believed'. This makes it easier to understand why James dedicated *Pragmatism* "To the memory of John Stuart Mill, from whom I first learned the pragmatic openness of mind and whom my fancy likes to picture as our leader were he alive today", a dedication that is made more understandable when we read the following famous passage in the book: " 'The true,' to put it very briefly, is only the expedient in the way of our thinking, just as 'the right' is only the expedient in the way of our behaving."[3]

The gist of James's pragmatic theory of truth may be put in the following bit of reasoning:

(a) The true is that which we ought to believe;
(b) That which we ought to believe is that which it is
      expedient for us to believe;

therefore,

(c) The true is that which is expedient for us to believe.

It is the counterpart of a utilitarian argument with 'true' put for 'right' and 'believe' for 'do'.

Those who attack James's pragmatism are likely to focus on several points in the argument. Its formal logic is impeccable, so the premises have borne the brunt of the attack. Some have said that even if (a) and (b) are true identities, they are not analytic. Some have said that the premises are false. Some have said that the phrase 'expedient for us' is either hopelessly vague or so clear that it makes evident the falsity of statement (b). Moreover, some might have pointed out that far from becoming a leader of the pragmatists, John Stuart Mill would have been the first to question

----

[3] *Pragmatism*, p. 222.

(a), since he had said in the second chapter of his essay *On Liberty*: "If we would know whether or not it is desirable that a proposition should be believed, is it possible to exclude the consideration of whether or not it is true?"

Let us begin with this last criticism. Mill's implication that truth must be established prior to deciding whether to accept a statement involves him in an argument that might also be applied to the utilitarian theory of rightness. For couldn't it be asked (rhetorically), "If we would know whether or not a certain action should be done, is it possible to exclude the consideration of whether or not it is right?" And wouldn't that prevent our defining a right action as one that ought to be done, and then defining what ought to be done as that the doing of which maximizes pleasure? Those who imagine that we first find out whether something is true and then decide whether we ought to believe it think of truth as correspondence to "ready-made" platonic facts; they adopt a spectator's view of the matter, rather than a view of the man who is doing science, i.e., making truths and falsehoods in the sense of deciding what sentences should be assigned what truth-values, i.e. accepted as true. Here we may call attention to our earlier analogy in the case of law. We the people should call something a statute only if it *is* a statute, but its being a statute is dependent on the creative activity of a legislator who makes it a statute and must then produce reasons for doing so. The legislator can no more appeal to an inherent statutory quality than a creative scientist can appeal to a correspondence with platonic facts. The parallel in the case of ethics is that between the creative moralist and the follower. The follower calls a kind of action right only if someone else has handed down a moral rule to him, but that someone else must defend his moral rule on another battleground.

Step (a) in James's argument is defensible and best construed with the help of more recent linguistic philosophy. The true is that of which we are justified in saying 'It's true' or 'I accept it', where 'I accept it' and 'It's true' are both performatory in Austin's sense, as P. F. Strawson has argued.[4] But what we must justify is a whole set of these performances, a set of acceptances, with no platonic "facts" out there to fall back on for support.

Of all the criticisms of James, the charge that statement (b)

4 "Truth," *Analysis* (1949), 9:85–97.

is false or hopelessly vague is most serious and really raises the fundamental objection to pragmatism as he conceived it as well as to pragmatism as more recently defended. The charge that (a) and (b) are not analytic does not faze us if it is granted that they are true. After having defended (a) we must face the charges against (b): 'That which we ought to believe is that which it is expedient for us to believe.'

4. Neo-pragmatism

In considering this question it is necessary to return to considerations that were broached earlier in our treatment of some recent reflections on ontology which have given rise to a neo-pragmatic tendency, a tendency that has specific bearing on the questions of existence and general bearing on the whole pragmatic outlook. They bring to focus the chief questions considered in this book.

One of the main points of the earlier chapters was that we have no clear semantic or epistemological device for distinguishing different kinds of existential statements prior to our construction of a scientific system. Once we have started to build a scientific system, we *make* distinctions between those we accept or mark 'true' and we also *make* distinctions between those that are postulates and those that are not. But we have rejected the view, defended by Carnap, that some questions about existential statements concern the framework, while others are internal to that framework in a way that calls for a different kind of answer. To build a science, we have argued, is to accept certain existential statements—some of them likely to be called ontological, like 'There are classes', and others likely to be called scientific, like 'There are electrons'. But building a science is not a matter of building a house whose walls inevitably correspond to the traditional statements of metaphysics and whose movable furnishings correspond to statements usually assigned to science. If a philosophically and logically minded scientist asks whether he should quantify in a certain way, that is tantamount to asking whether he ought to say there are certain entities of very general kinds—classes, say, or physical objects. And once he has decided to quantify over them, once he has satisfied himself that it is wise or justifiable to *say* that there are physical objects and he then goes on to consider an existential question that is less general, like 'Are there gorgons?' he is faced with a problem that is separated from the first only by degree of generality. But he sometimes reaches a point at which he surveys the totality of his decisions, and he may at that point decide to rescind a previous acceptance of an ontological statement for reasons that are not radically different from those that would lead him to rescind a non-ontological statement.

The point may be made in another way. There are philosophers who maintain that a logico-philosophical prolegomenon to science consists in making decisions about whether we ought to quantify in a certain way, or decisions about whether we should call certain sentences analytic, or decisions about whether we should call certain expressions meaningful. These, they say, are external questions, and answering them depends on what they call pragmatic considerations. They imply that these questions are different in principle from those that we raise about any given "scientific statement" within the system itself, like 'Is the statement 'There are electrons' true?' This second type of question they regard as answerable by reference to "fact" in a way that distinguishes it sharply from the first, which they take as "pragmatic". But I am questioning this dichotomy and arguing that in both cases a *decision* is involved. In the case of a decision to quantify in a certain way, we decide whether to call 'There are classes' true, and in the case of a statement "inside the framework" we also decide whether to call it true. In the case of a decision to adopt the empiricist theory of meaning, we decide whether to say that certain predicates are *meaningful*; in the case of a decision to make certain sentences analytic, we decide whether to call them *analytic*. However, the difference between the first two decisions to apply 'true' and the other decisions to apply 'meaningful' and 'analytic' is mainly a difference about what *predicates* to assign to what expressions, and it involves no radical methodological or epistemological difference between the ways in which we justify these assignments.

While I have held so far that in both cases a *decision* is involved and to this extent have opposed a carnapian dichotomy, I have not concluded as Quine does that both kinds of questions are always *pragmatic*.[5] I have not said that the decision to accept a statement which is not a sensory report is always pragmatically

---

[5] From *A Logical Point of View*, pp. 45–46.

justified. All I have maintained so far is that all of these questions call for practical *decisions* and that we may ask of these decisions "Ought they be made?" To be what I shall call a *definitional pragmatist* is to be a philosopher who immediately transcribes the question 'Ought I make this decision?' into the question 'Is it expedient to make this decision?' and this pragmatic variant of definitional utilitarianism is unsatisfactory for reasons like those which have been dealt with in ethics proper. Therefore I should reject James's statement (b) 'That which we ought to believe is that which it is expedient to believe'. Let me explain.

5. *Beyond pragmatism*

Carnap distinguishes between the justification of accepting a framework and the justification of statements made within a framework already established, and in this sense is a dualist. Quine, on the other hand, rejects this dualism. And yet even Quine seems to preserve a dichotomy between the linguistic framework which is accepted as a whole and the sensory reports which are accepted on the basis of a relatively direct and seemingly nonpragmatic basis for ascribing truth to them, for he tells us that the major basis for concluding that we ought to accept a total system or framework is the fact that it predicts future experience.[6] But how do we know that it does, unless it is related in some way to sensory reports of that future experience which are judged to be true in some nonpragmatic way when the future experience does occur? Such a question must be answered whether we view the sensory report as 'It looks exactly as if I am seeing a tower' or as the half-objective, half-sensory 'The Eiffel Tower looks green now'. When we are told by Quine that total science meets experience at the periphery, it seems reasonable, while we extend the metaphor, to think of some linguistic fragments of science—sentences—as being the feelers that make contact with experience in some nonpragmatic way.

The situation, as I see it, is something like this. Most philosophers who are concerned with the problem I am considering regard inquiry as a process in which we come to accept statements or linguistic frameworks, and they are willing to say that the typical outcome of our reflection on such matters is a statement to

[6] *Idem.*

the effect that some are accept*able* and others not. But then they go on to draw a fundamental line between those parts of the linguistic structures whose acceptability is supported by so-called pragmatic considerations and those whose acceptability is supported in some other way. *They differ among themselves only about the place at which to draw the line.* In approximate order of abstractness or "logical distance" from sensory experience, we have the following typical judgments of acceptability and judgments of how we ought to label certain statements:

(a) *Ontologies and theories of meaning:* e.g., 'We ought to accept (reject) quantification over attributes' (platonism versus nominalism); 'We ought to accept the empiricist criterion of meaning' (empiricism).

(b) *Laws of formal logic:* e.g., 'We ought to accept the principle of the syllogism.'

(c) *Decisions to make certain statements analytic:* e.g., 'We ought to call 'All vixens are foxes' analytic'.

(d) *So-called synthetic, general statements of fact:* e.g., 'We ought to call 'All vixens are cunning' true'.

(e) *So-called synthetic, singular statements of fact:* e.g., 'We ought to call 'This desk weighs more than two pounds' true.'

(f) *Sensory reports:* e.g., 'I ought to accept 'This page looks white to me now' '; 'I ought to accept 'It looks exactly as if I'm seeing a tower'.'

Now there are some philosophers who wish to draw the line between (c) and (d), holding as they do that we defend the *ought*-judgments (a), (b), and (c) pragmatically. One asks them *why* one ought to make these decisions to accept or to label, and they reply in words like those which Carnap has used in connection with accepting a mode of quantification: "Because doing so is expedient, fruitful, conducive to the aim for which the language is intended." On the other hand, the *ought*-judgments below the line between (c) and (d) are treated differently by some of these same philosophers. Roughly speaking, the decisions urged in (d), (e), and (f) are said to be justified respectively by "the fact" that all vixens are cunning and that you can tell by studying them, by the fact that this desk does weigh more than two pounds and that you can tell by weighing it, and by the fact that this page *does* look white to me now. Now it is precisely because such a defense of the decisions urged in (d) and (e) is likely to elicit the question "How do you know?" whereas the corresponding defense of (f) is less likely to elicit such a question, that some philosophers have preferred to dig the great ditch between (e) and (f). One is tempted to say that this is where Quine digs it, if only because he does speak of "recalcitrant experiences", by which I understand experiences which controvert sensory reports that I feel obliged to accept—for example, the page's looking blue to me at a time when the rest of my scientific theory leads me to say that it will look white.

What we must appreciate in this situation is the fact that although sometimes Carnap and Quine appear to use the same pragmatic criterion of acceptability (even though Quine wants to push its application further), there is reason to believe that they understand the pragmatic criterion differently. This may explain why it is that when Quine comes to discuss questions like those involved in (a) he comes to conclusions that are very different from those of Carnap. Carnap appeals to the pragmatic criterion *in defense* of quantification over class, property, and proposition, while Quine has been equally firm in using it in order to proscribe some of these methods of quantification. This *suggests* (though, of course, it doesn't prove) that the dispute is not merely the result of a disagreement about the application of a clearly and jointly understood criterion of acceptability; it suggests that the criterion itself is ambiguous, indeed ambiguous in a way that has divided pragmatists in the past. Quine's pragmatism lays heavy emphasis on prediction, while this is not altogether true in the case of Carnap. Carnap appears to espouse a pragmatic criterion like that which James occasionally has in mind when he (James) speaks of the consequences of *accepting* a given statement as opposed to the logical consequences of the statement itself, while Quine, insofar as he speaks of prediction, appears to have a more logical version of pragmatism in mind, a version that is more frequently associated with the name of Peirce.

The result is a problem which has worried pragmatists for a half-century. If it is a matter of accepting a framework or a way of quantifying, it is clear that Carnap cannot speak of predictability as the basis of his pragmatic decision, because his *chief* point is that frameworks don't have predictive consequences in the way that empirical statements *within* the framework do. At this point, however, Quine's view that the linguistic framework must be conceived as containing its methods of quantification or its "categorial" or "ontological" existential statements comes into play as a saving device. *His* main point is, in his metaphor, that all of the stockholders face "the tribunal of experience" as a "corporate body". Therefore, I suggest that his pragmatism is quite different from Carnap's precisely because of his concentration on prediction and his holistic view of science as something that contains logic and "ontology". But if we adopt the notion of prediction as the basis of our pragmatism, we must remember that there is a difference between a mechanism which *causes* us to make accurate predictions and a scientific system that leads to those predictions by logical steps. T. H. Huxley once said, "If some great Power would agree to make me always think what is true and do what is right, on condition of being turned into a sort of clock and wound up every morning before I got out of bed, I should instantly close with the offer."[7] But living scientists and living persons don't operate like the clock that Huxley wanted to be. Even if we should close with the offer, some young Clerk-Maxwell would ask "Yes; but I want you to tell me the *particular* go of it!"[8] and in seeking it he would come upon the difference between being wound up to predict correctly and predicting correctly in the way that we call scientific or rational. In ethics, it is the difference between the man who simply does the right thing and Aristotle's man who does it for the right reason, etc., etc., or Kant's man, of course.

It is this sort of consideration that leads many pragmatists to introduce considerations other than successful prediction, just as Mill introduced considerations other than quantity of pleasure in his utilitarianism. James spoke of the deference we must pay to "the older stock of truths" and pointed out that "an *outrée* explanation, violating all our preconceptions, would never pass for a true account of novelty. We should scratch around industriously

---

[7] Quoted in Noel Annan, *Leslie Stephen* (Cambridge: Harvard University Press, 1952), pp. 145–146.

[8] Quoted in James, *Pragmatism*, p. 197.

till we found something less excentric." Quine has repeated this and also emphasized the factor of simplicity in choosing a scientific system. But a philosopher must inject what Nelson Goodman has described as the counterpart of conscience in the philosophical or logical reconstruction of science.[9] It is a notion which is just as difficult to define as that of simplicity, but it is nonetheless a factor in what may be called the quasi-ethics of belief. And once we do acknowledge it as a factor, we can hardly describe ourselves as pragmatists in any usual sense, for we now recognize philosophy as a discipline that aims at something else besides successful prediction.

Even though the task of clarifying scientific beliefs is removed only by degree from what the scientist does, it is precisely the scientist's preoccupation with prediction that makes it essential for the philosopher to stress the importance of *relating* scientific belief to whatever it is that he regards as clear, true, or acceptable. And while some philosophers are willing to restrict themselves to discovering the actual behavior of men, this enterprise, as we saw in the last chapter, will result in finding out only what the actually accepted totality of statements is. So surely there is further room for a consideration of what totality of statements is rightly accepted. It is here that the scientific passion to predict correctly and to construct a simple theory may be supplemented by the preeminently philosophical interest in making contact with quasi-conscientiously fixed points, so long as the philosopher realizes that this is only one of the virtues to be considered in the choice of a scientific system or a moral code. A philosopher is not simply a recording secretary who registers the actual use of scientific and ethical terms. A philosopher can also perform a critical and creative function; he can examine the unexamined lives of science and morality.

[9] Nelson Goodman, *Fact, Fiction, and Forecast* (Cambridge: Harvard University Press, 1955), p. 38.

CHAPTER XVI

Beyond Positivism and Pragmatism

1. *Philosophy is partly normative*

As soon as one regards philosophy as partly the critique of science and routine morality, one recognizes that it is to that extent a "normative" discipline. Therefore pragmatism or empiricism—it makes no difference how you label the concern with successful prediction in science and smooth decision in morals—emphasizes only one factor in the justification of a scientific system or a way of life. And this may be seen in another way. Whether we adopt a logical pragmatism according to which some parts of our system are *logically* related to the linguistic record of our experiences, or a more *causal* pragmatism according to which science is like a powder or a pill that will *make* us expert at predicting our experiences, some of the reports of these experiences will be tested nonpragmatically at that moment. They will be temporary absolutes, so to speak, accepted nonpragmatically as the anchors of the scientist's system. Even a pragmatically conceived system of science and moral philosophy will appeal to such sentences, and so this raises the following related questions: (a) Is there any principle for selecting this class of terminal sentences of which at least some sensory reports are members? and (b) What is its composition?

Philosophers and ordinary human beings always begin their thinking by accepting a set of sentences, statements, or beliefs that are terminal in the sense of being pinned down at that moment, statements on which we are prepared to stake a great deal at that moment without considering their "consequences", logical or psychological. These statements are not only accepted by us, but we feel that we are justified in accepting them. Our total stock of accepted statements at any given moment consists of pinned-down statements and others that are accepted partly because they stand in certain relations to the pinned down. This distinction may be viewed as the meta-moral and meta-scientific counterpart of the kantian distinction between the categorically and hypothetically imperative within ethics in the narrow sense, provided that we avoid Kant's absolutism. The pinned-down statement is one whose acceptability is asserted in the categorical statement 'This ought to be accepted', while the rest of the acceptable statements are acceptable because it is expedient to accept them, meaning in part that they stand in certain relations to those that are categorically acceptable. Consequently, for reasons that are parallel to those adduced in ethics proper, it will not only be difficult to produce a "criterion" for the categorically acceptable, but even difficult to present sufficient conditions that yield absolute meta-moral and meta-scientific principles.

Various traditional philosophies have accepted this distinction though they have not always formulated it in this way. They have usually gone further and have tried to set up universal theses according to which whole classes of statements characterized syntactically or by the "discipline" from which they come are included among the categorically acceptable, while some empiricists have insisted that only sensory reports are categorically acceptable. Quine sometimes writes as though he held that all statements within "total science" and above the level of so-called sensory reports are hypothetically acceptable. My own view is that no such "istic" generalization known to me is tenable. Therefore I am unable to defend an *ism*, if defending an *ism* consists in defending such a generalization. I believe that the class of categorically acceptable statements is at any given moment heterogeneous with respect to traditional classifications of statements, as is the hypothetically acceptable. For this reason I find it difficult to say that all or only so-called sensory reports are terminal; I find it difficult to defend common sense in a wholesale manner; I find it difficult to say that all so-called logical statements are pinned down; I find it difficult to say that they are all creatures of convenience. In the same vein I find it difficult to regard all so-called ontological statements as hypothetically acceptable, and therefore I cannot leave all of ontology at the mercy of pragmatic considerations. Like some of one's moral beliefs, one's basic philosophical commitments are not easily surrendered in exchange for pragmatic successes—even of the purest kind.

Pragmatism, even when it is conceived as the doctrine that treats only sensory sentences as terminal and then adds the factors of simplicity and respect for the older truths in a conciliatory way, does not go far enough. We must distinguish between our un-pinned and our pinned-down sentences, but I see no reason for thinking that the pinned-down must be or can be characterized in a general way. They may be logical, commonsensical, physical, chemical, mathematical, or, for that matter, any kind of statement. In this respect the pinned-down is a random sample of the totality of our beliefs. I hope that Whitehead meant something like this when he said:

"Deductive logic has not the coercive supremacy which is con-ventionally conceded to it. When applied to concrete instances, it is a tentative procedure, finally to be judged by the self-evidence of its issues. This doctrine places philosophy on a pragmatic basis. But the meaning of 'pragmatism' must be given its widest exten-sion. In much modern thought, it has been limited by arbitrary specialist assumptions."[1]

2. Ethics and science

May some of the pinned-down statements be ethical? We have already said something about this in Chapter XIV, where it was pointed out that scientific, logical, and moral beliefs figure in the reflection of a person who is deciding what ought to be done, so that he may, from an abstract point of view, reject any one of his previ-ously accepted beliefs in solving his problem. Any previously ac-cepted statement of ethics, logic, mathematics, physics, biology, psy-chology, sociology, history, or geography may figure in his defense of a singular judgment that 'This is the right thing to do', in a way that would permit him to reject some one of them should he reject the conclusion. The logical aftermath of moral crisis may resemble the aftermath of unsuccessful scientific prediction. In the scientific case I expect that the thermometer will be at the 80° mark, but it doesn't look as though it's there; in the moral case I conclude that

[1] *Modes of Thought* (New York: Macmillan, 1938), p. 144.

I ought to do a certain thing, but the thought of doing it sends shivers down my back. Let us suppose that in one case we've tried our best to eliminate parallax, washed our eyes, and looked hard; in the other we've taken counsel and a good night's rest. The next look produces the same failure to reach the 80° mark; the next thought of the recommended course of action produces the same shivers. We are therefore driven to reëxamine the superstructure that implies the prediction and dictates the course of action. Is there any a priori reason to suppose that changes which will accommodate our "recalcitrant" experiences and emotions should be made in the scientific rather than the moral parts of our structure of belief? Is there any reason to suppose that the bending or breaking of the unified structure of moral and scientific conviction must take place in one area rather than another? These questions require us to distinguish the two cases.

Where we are faced with a moral conclusion that horrifies us and we are impelled to revise our previously accepted moral and factual beliefs, we have no principle that tells us in advance where we must make adjustments, but we are likely to say that if no *other* evidence goes against the scientific statements we have assumed, the changing had best be done in the moral sphere. Moreover, when we make a scientific prediction that flies in the face of our experience, we are likely to alter our scientific rather than our moral beliefs, because it is rare that a moral belief will figure logically in an attempt at scientific prediction. If there are no moral beliefs among the premises of the argument that lead to the rejected conclusion, no moral belief need be changed.

All of this requires us to consider the following statement of William James: "If a certain formula for expressing the nature of the world violates my moral demand, I shall feel as free to throw it overboard, or at least to doubt it, as if it disappointed my demand for uniformity of sequence, for example: the one demand being, so far as I can see, quite as subjective and emotional as the other is."[2] The distinguishing feature of James's point of view is the fact that he is willing to count among the "moral demands" a certain emotional attitude toward the belief itself. That is, he regards it as

[2] "The Dilemma of Determinism," *The Will to Believe* (New York: Longmans, 1898), p. 147.

counting against a metaphysical theory that it should imply statements which we should hate to believe; so that if determinism
should imply the absence of a freedom that we should hate to think
ourselves without, we may feel logically free to throw determinism
overboard. The fact that the principle of uniformity of sequence or
causality was James's illustration in "The Will to Believe" is in-
cidental; it might just as well have been a more conventionally
scientific and less metaphysical principle, as his other writings
made clear.

The problem which we must face is made more acute by the
position previously taken in this book. That is to say, if one refuses
to defend uniformity of sequence as analytic or as synthetic a
priori, and if one appeals to pragmatic considerations in its defense because one cannot honestly maintain that it (or a principle
of logic, if that is a more comfortable illustration) copies reality in
any clear sense, how does one avoid the conclusion of James? Only,
I think, by making clear that one's pragmatism is logical. In other
words, a logically pragmatic defense of a principle like uniformity
of sequence views it as a principle which, together with other principles, hangs together logically and simply with statements that
conform with experience and others we accept categorically; it is
not a principle whose virtues are to be tested merely by examining
the moral emotions of those who accept it. This is why the principle
has been more effectively questioned in our time by those who work
in quantum mechanics than by William James. Moreover, while we
might be forced to reconsider certain scientific beliefs as a result
of reaching a moral conclusion that we recoil from, the *kinds* of
moral conclusions that drive us to revise our factual views usually
do not reflect moral attitudes toward the beliefs themselves so much
as moral attitudes toward the objects of those beliefs. If our moral
principles and our scientific premises lead to the conclusion that
we ought to drop a hydrogen bomb at a certain time, and if the
prospect of such an action horrifies us, we *may* be led to reconsider
our so-called factual beliefs, as I have said. Here we are evincing a
moral attitude toward an object of our belief—an action—which
impels us to reconsider our belief about it. It's not as if we hated
to believe the principle of uniformity of sequence or excluded
middle and were *therefore* led to revise or reject them. What we

hate is an action whose rightness seems to be implied by our beliefs—both moral and scientific. It is this moral hatred or revulsion
which can lead us to change or reëxamine the "scientific" premises
among those leading to the conclusion that the hated action is
right. There is no defensible principle of reflective thinking which
dictates that our revisions must *always be* in the moral sphere. And
there is no "criterion" according to which one conclusion should
prevail simply because it is physical or metaphysical while the
other is ethical.

3. *No positivism, no pragmatism*

The previous remarks indicate my answers to the questions
raised earlier: Is there any principle for selecting the class of terminal sentences? What is its composition? I know of no principle
for selecting it and therefore I cannot specify its composition. I
cannot produce a necessary and sufficient condition for being a
pinned-down statement nor for those that I or anyone else ought
to pin down. Hence my remarks in the earliest pages of this book:
"There is in philosophy no positivism, no pragmatism, no empiricism." I cannot justify a definition of the rightness of an action, so
the right to believe something or the right to take certain beliefs
as anchors of science and morals cannot be established by appealing to some "definition" of the essence of rightness. The ship of
science and morals is not moored by any easily specified set of beliefs or sentences. There are pinned-down statements in science and
morals, and there are quasi-ethical principles of epistemology
which connect factors like the power to predict experience, the
capacity to guide action, the capacity to organize our moral feelings, the degree to which the older truths are respected, and the
simplicity of our system with the notion of warranted acceptance.
The names of these factors may be likened to the descriptive terms
that appear in moral principles, so that normative epistemology
becomes a body of principles that are quasi-moral in nature. If
pragmatism is just this, I am a pragmatist, but I fear that it is characteristic of all *isms* to emphasize some one factor in the quasi-
ethics of acceptance to the exclusion of others. Pragmatism is more
pluralistic in metaphysics than it is in epistemology. The notion
that one is still a pragmatist—nay even a better pragmatist some

might say—even after one has added considerations like respect for the old truths, simplicity, and clarity to that of capacity to predict sensory experience, is too much like the notion that one is still a utilitarian even after one had added *quality* of pleasure to quantity as a factor in the determination of rightness of action.

4. *The meaning of 'science' and 'ethics': more semantic dust*

To suppose that these principles of epistemology and morals may be discovered by examining the meaning of 'science' or the meaning of 'ethics' is to make one more hopeless effort to build a philosophical church on semantic dust. There is a tendency in contemporary ethical theory to make a distinction similar to Carnap's distinction between internal and external questions. Certain ethical questions are said to occur inside a moral code, and it is held that *they* are answered by appeal to rules that form part of the accepted code itself. But when we ask for a justification of these rules, we are said to be raising a question about the moral code as a whole that can be answered by reflecting on the meaning of the word 'ethics'. The distinction is strikingly like one we have met in the case of ontology. There, it will be recalled, the counterparts of traditional metaphysical questions were transferred to a higher level, transformed into questions about whether to speak in a certain way, while ordinary existential statements were pictured as answerable within the framework in a less pragmatic way. But just as I rejected this effort to distinguish between ontological and scientific existential statements, so I reject its ethical counterpart which tries to relegate traditional philosophical questions to meta-ethics in a way that seals them off from the questions of the moral agent.

One of the most articulate representatives of this point of view has distinguished radically between an argument like 'I ought to give him the book because I promised it' in defense of a specific action and an argument in favor of the social practice of keeping promises. In the latter case, where we consider the morality of social practices, we are supposed to be operating in meta-ethics, and here we are supposed to find our answer by examining the use of the word 'ethics' or the function of ethics. "The answer to be given will (remembering the function of ethics) be reached by estimating the probable consequences (i) of retaining the present

practices, and (ii) of adopting the suggested alternative." Furthermore, it is maintained that in our defense of a social practice we
do not appeal to the meaning of 'good practice' or 'the right practice', for S. E. Toulmin says:

"Of course 'This practice would involve the least conflict of
interests attainable under the circumstances' does not *mean* the
same as 'This would be the right practice'; nor does 'This way of
life would be more harmoniously satisfying' *mean* the same as 'This
would be better'. But in each case, the first statement is *a good
reason* for the second: the 'ethically neutral' fact is *a good reason*
for the 'gerundive' moral judgment. If the adoption of the practice would genuinely reduce conflicts of interest, it is a practice
worthy of adoption, and if the way of life would genuinely lead to
a deeper and more consistent happiness, it is one *worthy of pur-
suit.* And this seems so natural and intelligible, when one bears
in mind the function of ethical judgments, that, if anyone asks me
why they are 'good reasons', I can only reply by asking in return
'What better kinds of reason could you want?' "[3]

It is central to this point of view to distinguish the inference
from 'I promised to give it to him' to 'I ought to give it to him'
and the inference from 'This practice reduces conflicts of interest'
to 'This practice is worthy of adoption'; but plainly, as R. M. Hare
has pointed out,[4] *both* may be construed as inferences from the
"factual" to the "normative" which omit a major premise that is
itself a normative principle, and it does seem unusually strange to
say that such a principle can be established by examining the
meaning of 'ethics' or "the job of ethics". Viewed in the light of
our own previous conclusions, reflecting on the question 'Ought
I to accept the statement 'I ought to return the book to him'?' can
bring us to a consideration of the whole moral code as quickly as
reflection on the question 'Ought I accept the principle 'One ought
to keep one's promises'?' so that we cannot single out moral practices or principles as fundamentally different from singular conclusions in their mode of justification. In this respect we see an
analogy in science, for the justification of the statement that this

---

[3] *An Examination of the Place of Reason in Ethics,* p. 224.
[4] In a review of Toulmin, *Philosophical Quarterly* (1951), 1:372–375.

light ray bends so many degrees upon entering water (counterpart of 'I ought to give it to him') is not so different from the justification of Snell's Law that we must repair to the meta-level, to the meaning of 'science', or to "the job of science" in order to justify the latter while we stay on the first floor in justifying the former.

5. The a priori and the a posteriori: a concession withdrawn

If one accepts the view for which I have been arguing, one rejects as superfluous the postulation of platonic entities, the platonistic distinction between the analytic and the synthetic, the anti-naturalistic view of Moore, the "orthodox" positivistic view of the analytic and the meaningful, the various positivistic views of ethical statements, the positivistic contrast between "ontology" and science. But if one treats knowledge and morals as a "seamless web", how does one distinguish between accepting things a priori and accepting them a posteriori?

Accepting statements a priori is a matter of pinning them down, whether they be statements of logic, mathematics, physics, biology, history, or daily life. Naturally the class of statements so pinned will not coincide with the conventional extension of 'a priori', but that conventional extension is often the product of a philosophy we reject. The term 'a priori' is a philosophical term that philosophers introduce in order to mark out a class of statements which hold a privileged position in the system of our beliefs, and I use the term as coextensive with my own term 'terminal sentence', or a sentence that we accept without considering the impact of its acceptance on any other sentence in that system of knowledge. In some cases we signalize their terminal status by making them definitions, but the initial legislative act of making them definitions is carried out by means of a performatory sentence for which we should not expect equivalents or "analyses".

Earlier we argued that the difficulties of the term 'analytic' should not be saddled on the notion of the a priori, and at some points we suggested that some admirers of 'analytic' might very well couch their thesis in a quasi-moral way, after the fashion of 'All a priori statements should be called analytic', thereby suggesting that the phrase 'a priori statement' might be descriptive (as the word 'lying' is the descriptive predicate in 'Lying is wrong').

But now that we have spurned the rituals of analyticity we may ask ourselves what attitude we should take toward the *a priori*. It is to be remembered that we began by supposing that there were some sentences that were a priori in some clear sense, and that the task which certain philosophers accepted for themselves was to show that all such sentences were analytic or, at any rate, to make them analytic. But now, in the light of what has been said in this chapter, we see that our initial expository neutrality toward the notion of the a priori itself must be qualified. The closest we can come to converging with the traditional view of the notion is to say that an a priori statement is one that we believe quite firmly and one that we therefore *resolve* to make immune to overthrow at a given moment. It is, in short, a sentence of which we say, 'This is pinned down'. Austin has called attention to the performatory nature of 'I know', pointing out its similarities with 'I promise'. And when we remember that calling *S* an a priori statement is another way of uttering 'I accept' followed by *S*, followed by 'without attention to experience', we see the element of performance in calling a sentence a priori. In the light of this we must go even further than we have already gone. We have already suggested that the epistemological "fact" of knowing something a priori might be what justifies our calling a sentence analytic, but now we go even further and treat the initial application of 'a priori' in a performatory way. In this way the root epistemological phenomenon is that of firm belief. Believing it firmly, I call it a priori or I take it as pinned down (performatory). Enough ritual for our purposes.

We do not think systematically without such stable points, but they may very well shift as time goes on. To call attention to this distinction between the terminal and the non-terminal is not to say 'Once terminal always terminal', but the myth that we fix our stable points by peering at meanings, qualities, attributes, or propositions must be surrendered. And if we do this we see that reflection is a process of resolving tensions and conflicts and that there is profound truth in the pragmatic view, provided that we become even more pluralistic in our conception of a terminal belief. To the question 'Is there a criterion whose application can assure us that we've resolved these tensions effectively?' I can only answer, 'You will know when you've reached Nirvana'.

CHAPTER XVII

How Do We Go From Where?

1. *Clearing the ground*

One of the most touching passages in the literature of philosophy is the "Epistle to the Reader" with which Locke begins his *Essay,* and in which he portrays himself in such modest, janitorial terms:

"The commonwealth of learning is not at this time without master-builders, whose mighty designs, in advancing the sciences, will leave lasting monuments to the admiration of posterity; but every one must not hope to be a Boyle or Sydenham: and in an age that produces such masters as the great Huygenius and the incomparable Mr. Newton, with some others of that strain, it is ambition enough to be employed as an under-labourer in clearing the ground a little, and removing some of the rubbish that lies in the way of knowledge."

Unfortunately this hygienic job is never done, and the philosopher must take up his broom periodically, to clear the way not only for scientists but also for himself, for he too should advance and he too can build. Sometimes, as in Locke's case, the sanitation can be carried on with crusading enthusiasm, with a sense of deep antipathy to a philosophy which one opposes on every major issue, and which one would like to see extirpated. But at other times criticism can be conducted in the spirit of Erasmus rather than Luther, by one who admires a philosophical framework so much that he wishes to cleanse it of its shortcomings rather than demolish it. Much of the negative part of this book is intended in the second spirit, since I believe that the analytic, the empiricist, and the pragmatic movements of which I have sometimes spoken critically have been the most important and most enlightening tendencies in twentieth-century philosophy.

The early platonism of Moore and Russell, the distinction between analytic and synthetic statements, the attempt to formulate a criterion of cognitive meaning, the emotive theory of ethics, the pragmatic philosophy of science—all of them were at one time liberating forces in the philosophy of the twentieth century. They helped divert philosophical attention from a number of pseudo-problems; they increased respect for logic and exactness in philosophy; they encouraged a laudable degree of self-consciousness among philosophers which led to a healthy reëxamination of philosophical methods and philosophical aims. But, as one might have predicted in the light of the previous history of philosophy, ideas that were once liberating and which helped puncture the inflationary schemes of traditional philosophy were soon collected and composed into a tradition. A scholastic phase of the analytic movement emerged, in which cliché and shibboleth threatened to replace insight and excitement. The terms 'analytic', 'meaningless', 'emotive', and 'naturalistic fallacy'—to mention only some—became empty slogans instead of revolutionary tools; the quest for meaning replaced the quest for certainty; orthodoxy followed revolt. Logic, physics, and ethics were assigned special and unique methods of justification; ancient metaphysical generalizations about everything being fire or water were erased and replaced by equally indefensible universal theses, according to which all logical statements are like this, and all physical statements like that, and all ethical statements very different from both.

Much of this misplaced generality came from imitating the greatest intellectual achievement of the analytic tradition in philosophy—and, indeed, one of the greatest achievements of the century in any field: the reduction of mathematics to logic carried out in the monumental (there is no other word) *Principia Mathematica* of Russell and Whitehead. Like so many great mathematical and scientific achievements in modern times, *Principia Mathematica* became an imposing model for the philosophy of its age. Just as Descartes tried to generalize what he supposed was the method of analytic geometry, and as Hume tried to apply his version of Newton's method to moral subjects, so Russell and his positivistic followers tried to emulate the techniques of a great logical system. Russell and Whitehead, building on a great tradition which had culminated before them in the work of Frege, showed that all mathematical constants might be defined in terms of logical constants and that classical mathematics might be deduced from logic. Immediately a lesson was drawn for other parts of philosophy. The apparent universality of the logistic thesis suggested something similar to philosophers who were entranced with the idea of establishing universal claims in other branches of the subject, even while they repudiated general metaphysical speculation from Thales to Hegel. General metaphysics was replaced by general metalinguistics, and philosophers took to saying that *all* metaphysical statements are meaningless, that *all* logical and mathematical statements are analytic, that *all* empirical statements about material objects are reducible to statements about sense-data, that *no* ethical statement is translatable into an empirical statement. Whereas their metaphysical predecessors, whom they regarded as benighted and befuddled, made startling generalizations about all of existence, analytically minded philosophers (and those who were pragmatically minded too) defended apparently sober but equally dubious claims about linguistic expressions or their meanings.

One of my main purposes in this book is to discourage this spurious universalism, the postulation of non-entities that explain nothing, and the easy use of terms like 'analytic' which seem equally expendable. The latter two aims have received ample expression in the previous pages; in what follows immediately, I shall indicate something of my discontent with universalism. Once that is done, it will be easier to see what philosophical energy can be made available to master builders by diverting it from otiose ontology, misleading metalinguistics, and misplaced generality. We shall also see how the positive functions of philosophy are related to each other.

2. *The finite character of the logistic thesis*

Although it became the model for so much general philosophizing in the twentieth century, the logistic thesis—in the hands of those who have expressed it even more felicitously than Russell and Whitehead—is not really a universal law in the sense in which the generalizations of physics are. Upon close examination the definitional part of it, by which I mean the part that does not have to do with setting down the axioms and carrying out the deductions, turns out to be a finitely long list of statements which assert the definability of mathematical expressions in terms of logical expressions. It is not surprising, then, that no one tries to establish it by reflection on the "meanings" of the comparatively unimportant terms 'logical' and 'mathematical', not even the most analytically minded. In this respect the logistic thesis is fundamentally different from that other famous universal thesis of the analytic tradition, the thesis of Moore that no ethical property is identical with any natural property. It is not surprising that Russell should have been associated with an affirmative doctrine connecting disciplines, and that Moore should have called attention in a negative thesis to a difference between ethics and empirical science. Their theses are not only different in logical quality, but they reveal other contrasts which are extremely illuminating. Russell's thesis is not lawlike, while Moore's is supposed to be; Russell's thesis involves an element of performance (defining) and an evaluation of that performance, while Moore's is thought to describe a realm of attributes. These differences have profound significance for the development of recent philosophy.

As we have seen, some of the universal theses advanced by analytic philosophers assert that all verbal expressions of one kind are related in a certain way to expressions of another kind. Because of their universal form these philosophical generalizations resemble the laws of physics and chemistry, and this can mislead us. It is characteristic of a law of science, like the law of universal gravitation or the law of freely falling bodies, that it is not equivalent to a logical conjunction of a finite number of singular statements. The statement that all bodies attract each other is not logically equivalent to a statement of the form 'The moon and the earth attract each other, the earth and the sun attract each other, and Newton's apple and the earth attract each other', which merely sums up the relations of attraction between finitely many bodies. Those universal statements which are laws can support a contrary-to-fact conditional statement, by contrast to universal statements which are not laws, like 'Everything in my right coat pocket as I write this chapter is a dime'. We can say of the pencil that has just fallen from my desk and which does not fall 16 t^2 feet in t seconds that *if it had fallen in a vacuum*, it *would* have fallen 16 t^2 feet in t seconds. But we would not say of a half dollar not in my pocket that if it were in my pocket it would be a dime. On the contrary, we would say that if the half dollar were in my pocket, my original statement about the contents of my pocket would be false.[1]

If one applies this same test to a statement like 'All mathematical expressions are definable in terms of logical expressions', one sees at once that it resembles 'Everything in my pocket as I write this chapter is a dime' in a crucial respect, and that in that same respect it does not resemble the law of falling bodies. For example, we would not say that if the term 'red' as ordinarily understood were a mathematical term, 'red' would be definable in terms of logical expressions. On the contrary, we would say that if 'red' were a mathematical term, the logistic thesis would be indefensible, since 'red' is not definable in terms of logical constants. We can conclude from this that the definitional part of the logistic thesis is not a law but a disguised conjunction of a finite number of assertions of definability. It is established by showing that all members of a certain list of mathematical expressions, specified by enumeration, are definable in terms of, say, 'every', 'neither-nor', and 'is a member of'.[2]

This result jibes with another result of recent reflection on terms like 'logical expression' or 'logical constant', namely, that we are not able to produce a criterion for being a logical constant. The most we seem to be able to do is to enumerate a set of expressions like those mentioned earlier which we *call* logical constants. We then say that other terms, *called mathematical,* are definable in terms of them. But clearly our inability to characterize the logical constants in some nonenumerative way is no serious objection to the logistic thesis. That thesis is finite in character and need not be thought of as connecting "realms" of knowledge which must be characterized by disciplinary adjectives like 'logical' and 'mathematical'.

By contrast, many other universal theses which connect or

---

[1] See Goodman, *Fact, Fiction, and Forecast*, ch. 1, "The Problem of Counterfactual Conditionals."

[2] See Quine, *Mathematical Logic* (rev. ed.; Cambridge: Harvard University Press, 1951).

separate different "realms" are quite different from the logistic thesis, just because they are not easily construed as joining one finite set of terms with another. Moore's anti-naturalism is just such a thesis, and the fact that it is not formulable in finite terms is of profound significance.

3. The universal character of Moore's anti-naturalism

According to one formulation of Moore's view, no natural predicate is synonymous with any ethical predicate, and in its more platonic version it asserts that no natural attribute is identical with any ethical attribute. Alternatively, without altering the issue under consideration here, we might construe it as a less general, but nevertheless general, statement to the effect that 'good' is not synonymous with any natural predicate, or as a statement about the corresponding attributes. If the word 'natural' were as expendable here as the word 'logical' in the case of the logistic thesis, there would be a finite number of natural predicates—say A, B, and C—about which one would assert (1) 'good' is not synonymous with A, (2) 'good' is not synonymous with B, and (3) 'good' is not synonymous with C. But we know of no such list, and we feel that even if three such predicates were available, such a conjunction of three statements would not convey what was in Moore's mind when he announced his universal and allegedly lawlike thesis.

In trying to formulate Moore's thesis we must avoid trivializing it. For example, we must not define a natural predicate as one which is not synonymous with 'good', 'bad', 'right', 'wrong', or compounds containing them, on pain of converting Moore's claim into a truism. That is to say, Moore surely means to say something more than what is conveyed by ' 'Good' is not synonymous with any predicate which is not synonymous with 'good', 'bad', 'right', 'wrong', or compounds containing these'. Those who are not afraid to use the word 'analytic' would not only call *this* thesis analytic, but trivial. And yet, are the opponents of ethical naturalism likely to improve their situation by construing their thesis so that it becomes non-trivial and analytic? I shouldn't have thought so. The point is that these grand theses about the relations between different kinds of linguistic expression or different kinds of attributes cannot usually be regarded as analytic at all. For if they were analytic, their truth would be established, as it is said, by reference to the meanings of their *component* terms, like 'ethical', 'natural', 'logical', and 'mathematical', and not by reference to the terms to which these components apply, like 'good', 'pleasant', 'or', and '2' respectively. If analytic, they would resemble 'All bachelors are males'. And while partisans of analyticity are prepared to say that we can establish this statement without looking at bachelors, they surely would not say the corresponding thing about 'All mathematical expressions are definable in terms of logical expressions'. According to their view, the former statement may be established without establishing statements like 'Kant is a bachelor and Kant is male', but the latter cannot be established without establishing statements like ' '2' is definable as 'the class of all two-membered classes' '.

The point is, then, that the thesis of anti-naturalists is not construed as a conjunction of finitely many singular statements of nonsynonymy, and it is not construed as a universal analytic statement, and therefore it seems necessary to regard it as a universal, lawlike, nonanalytic statement whose key term, 'natural', is admittedly obscure. To see why this is necessary, we must turn to the second respect in which Moore's thesis differs from Russell's logistic thesis, the fact that the former makes essential use of the notions of synonymy or identity of meaning in describing the relation between ethical and natural predicates.[3]

4. *The link between universalism and intensionalism*

Although there are many loose formulations of the logistic thesis in which something else is suggested, the program as carried out is wholly extensional in character. Saying defensibly that one expression is definable in a certain way requires no more than showing that the replacement of the definiens for the definiendum will preserve truth-value.[4] Truths will remain truths and falsehoods falsehoods. In this respect it differs radically from Moore's

[3] The main theme of the preceding three sections is developed in my article "A Finitistic Approach to Philosophical Theses," *Philosophical Review* (1951), 60: 299–316.

[4] But see Goodman's contention that some philosophical definitions require less, in *The Structure of Appearance*, Ch. 1.

program, as we have seen in an earlier chapter. Moore thought
of himself as analyzing concepts, attributes, or meanings, that is to
say, intensions or connotations of words. Once he had discovered
the relation of identity between these meanings, he thought he
could then assert the synonymy of the predicates connoting them.
But the identity of meanings or attributes is the fundamental fact
for Moore, as we have already seen. In defending the claim that
a given attribute was not identical with another one, his procedure had to be quite different from what it might have been if he
were asserting merely that a given class was not identical with another one. Unlike difference of classes, which is the extensional
counterpart of difference of attributes, the latter is a mysterious
notion. And in order to eliminate some of the mystery in using it,
Moore is forced, as we shall see, to introduce another mysterious
notion: that of a nonnatural attribute.

Had Moore limited himself to a purely extensional thesis involving two finite sets of *classes* (as opposed to attributes), his task
would have been, in principle, easier. He would have had to show
only that the ethical classes $E_1, E_2, \ldots E_n$ are not identical in mem-
bership with any of the natural classes $N_1, N_2, \ldots N_n$; for example,
that the class of good things is not identical with the class of pleasant things. And this he might have done by producing a counter-
example, in the way that we show that the class of good things is
not identical with the class of round things. But refuting assertions
of class-identity was not enough for Moore's purposes. He thought
that philosophical definition consisted in asserting the identity of
attributes, and therefore that the refutation of philosophical definitions required the refutation of such assertions. Naturally, where
the classes could be shown to be different, as in the case of good
things and round things, the corresponding attributes would be
shown different by an a fortiori argument. But Moore wanted to
show that goodness would be different from, say, pleasantness, even
if the class of good things were identical with the class of pleasant
things. But how does one prove this sort of thing, especially in the
absence of any clear definition of difference of attributes? By showing that goodness is one "kind" of attribute and pleasantness another "kind", and that no attribute of the first kind is identical
with one of the second kind. That is how the absence of anything

like a clear criterion for the identity of attributes creates the need for universal theses and Moore's classification of attributes. The notions of being an ethical characteristic and being a natural characteristic (at least the latter) are indispensable in Moore's case because he needs some general principle which will allow him to say that goodness is not identical with pleasantness *just* because one is not natural and the other is natural. That is why his universal negative thesis cannot be treated, as the definitional part of the logistic thesis can be treated, as a finite set of statements. That is why the words 'ethical' and 'natural' are essential in Moore's case, while the words 'logical' and 'mathematical' are not in Russell's. Moore's intensionalism drives him to a universalism which he cannot defend with confidence because of the obscurity of the term 'natural'. It should be added that the situation is not improved when the thesis is converted into a statement about linguistic expressions. The problem of synonymy is as acute as the problem of identity of meanings, and the problem of natural predicate is just as acute as the problem of natural attribute.

How can something be salvaged in the situation? By seizing once again on the clue which Moore gives us when he says that a natural attribute is the sort of attribute we ascribe to a thing in the course of *describing* it. Here we come to the element of profound truth in Moore's moral philosophy—the fact that describing is a kind of linguistic activity which is different from the activity we engage in when we sometimes use the word 'good'. As soon as we approach the problem in this way, as soon as we give up attributes altogether and concentrate on what Austin calls speech-acts, on linguistic activity, we can avoid nonnatural qualities and concentrate profitably on these different activities in great detail. Indeed, we can even come to the conclusion that there are contexts in which one and the same word is used to describe something *and* to evaluate it. Or we can conclude, as I did earlier in this book, that the activities of describing and prescribing are sometimes so intertwined as to make it necessary to consider units of language which are more than sentences; in other words, to think of what can only be described as a system of sentences, some of which are used mainly prescriptively and others mainly descriptively.

'Describing', 'commending', 'prescribing', and even 'perform-ing' (as applied to what we do when we utter performatory phrases in Austin's sense) all become second-order philosophical words which are themselves words in ordinary language. But they are very different from the predicates which appear in the universal theses of philosophers who concentrate on the attribute or the dead expression out of context. That is why such universal theses are not likely to be advanced by philosophers who take this newer point of view seriously. For example, it seems unlikely that anyone should be so bold as to say that wherever we use a word in describ-ing we don't use it for prescribing; it seems unlikely that we should want to say that whenever we engage in describing we don't per-form in Austin's sense. We should hesitate to go so far as to say that all such generalizations are false, but most of them seem to be indefensible. It follows that one descriptive task of the philosopher in this area is to concentrate on specific expressions or systems of expressions in an effort to see their use in specific context. Where the use is single, he can report that; where it is a combination of such uses he can report that too. Sometimes his report will be of purely linguistic interest, but sometimes it may help remove philo-sophical puzzlement. This is Wittgenstein's great insight in philos-ophy, and I think it is fair to say that it is more obviously in the line of Moore than it is in the line of Russell. Mysterious inten-sionalism and indefensible universalism give way to a description of the many different uses of specific bits of language with an eye to the removal of philosophical perplexity.

5. Description, performance, and evaluation in philosophy

The ordinary man isn't the only one who describes, performs, and evaluates. The philosopher does too. This is brought out by reflecting on the third respect in which the logistic thesis is dis-tinguished from others of the century. A logician who participates in this program does at least two things: he defines and he makes a judgment on his definition. In other words, he performs and he evaluates his performance. He not only says in a performatory way 'I define 'If p then q' as short for 'Either not-p or q' ', but he also wishes to say that it is well to do this. Earlier I suggested that the 'able' ending in 'definable' brings out the evaluative element in this situation, but the point I am making now is not dependent on that earlier comment. Even if one were to reject that construal of 'definable', one would have to admit that the construction of logical systems is not the only thing in which a logical philosopher is interested. He must make out a philosophical case for that construction; he must justify his defining and his postulating, as we have seen in previous chapters.

In this way we see how the tradition of the analytic movement merges with that of pragmatism. Moore was interested in describing the relations between meanings and his work was followed by a preoccupation with the uses of language, as in the later Wittgenstein. Russell's constructionalism encouraged the work of philosophers like Carnap and more recently that of Goodman in his *Structure of Appearance*. The contribution of the pragmatic tradition is the notion that assertion, definition, and postulation are modes of performing, and the view that such performance is to be evaluated in a certain way. The ultimate aim of this book is the reunion of philosophy, which will be achieved only by recognizing that describing, doing, and evaluating are all of them important and connected parts of the enterprise.

Like the honest, intelligent legislator, a philosopher must be familiar with custom, he must be willing to change it, and prepared to defend what he does. Having concentrated in great measure on removing some of the obstacles in their way, I hope that the master describers, the master builders, and the master moralists in philosophy will be able to work with fewer hindrances and with a greater understanding of each other. More than that, I hope that these occupational barriers will disappear and that we shall once more realize that philosophy can be as varied and full as life itself.

Acknowledgments

Grateful acknowledgment is made to the following for permission to quote from the works indicated:

Cambridge University Press: G. E. Moore, *Principia Ethica* and S. E. Toulmin, *An Examination of the Place of Reason in Ethics.*

Oxford University Press: Bertrand Russell, *The Problems of Philosophy* and G. E. Moore, *Ethics.*

The Macmillan Company: Bertrand Russell, *Introduction to Mathematical Philosophy* (1919).

Harcourt, Brace and Company: G. E. Moore, *Philosophical Studies.*

The Dial Press, Inc.: *John Dewey: Philosopher of Science and Freedom* (1950) ed. Sidney Hook.

Professor Gilbert Ryle: "Fallacies in Moral Philosophy", by Stuart Hampshire, *Mind,* Vol. 58 (1949).

Professor Leopold Infeld: Albert Einstein and Leopold Infeld, *The Evolution of Physics,* published by Simon and Schuster.

Passages from *Language, Truth, and Logic* by A. J. Ayer are reprinted through permission by Dover Publications, Inc., New York 10, New York ($1.25).

Index of Proper Names

General Index

'About' 32, 114ff, **122ff**
Abstract entity, *see* Attributes, Class, Dispositions, Facts, Intension, Meanings, Number, Universals
Acceptability 24; categorical 280ff
Acquaintance 43ff, 124
Analysis 10, 27, 169ff, 259ff, 296ff. *See also* Definition, Identity, Meanings, Synonymy
Analyticity 6, 12ff, 16, 57; and a priori 13, 20, 35ff, 105, 132, 137ff; and categories 87ff; and definition 20, 126, 128, **267; and logic 127ff; and mathematics 125ff; and meaning 104ff, 133ff, 202ff;** and naturalistic fallacy 179ff, 193; and ordinary language 156ff; and performatory phrases 154, 160ff, 167ff, 267ff; and self-contradiction 129ff, 144ff; and synonymy 128ff, 132ff, 136ff, 143ff, 148, 150, 163, 170. *See also* Identity, Meanings
A posteriori, *see* A priori
A priori: and analytic 13, 20, 35ff, 105, 132, 137ff; and a posteriori 34ff, 287; and attributes 113ff; and experience 6, 12; and general logical laws 129ff; and mathematics 79ff; and meaning 113ff; and modality 114ff; and performatory phrases 288; and positivism 135; and terminal sentences 287ff; defined 6; Russell's early view of 10; subject matter of 6ff, 113ff. *See also* Analyticity, Synthetic a Priori
Approval 290, 222ff
Arithmetic, *see* Mathematics
Artificial language 156ff. *See also* Rules
Attitude: disagreement in 200, 209, 215ff
Attributes: and analysis 171ff; and a priori 113ff; as meanings 6ff, 28ff; compared with classes 29ff, 174ff, 296; complex 183ff; epistemological argument for 34ff; existence of 4ff, 31ff, 63,

71; identity of 136ff, 296; intrinsic 189ff; natural vs. nonnatural 7ff, 11, 176, 186ff, 192, 195ff, 199; simple 169, 171ff, 177ff, 192ff. *See also* Meanings, Universals
Axiom, *see* Infinity, Postulate

Begging the question 49ff
Being, *see* Existence
Belief 230, 234ff, 245, 255ff, 262; and attitude 200, 209, 215ff
Biconditional 201, 203ff, 259. *See also* Coextensiveness, Extensional
Bound, *see* Variable

Calculus of propositions 127, 131
Categorical acceptability 280ff
Category 73ff, 87ff; and postulation 95ff, 100ff
Certainty 53
Choice 232ff. *See also* Decision
Class: and attribute 29ff, 174ff, 296; as denotation 30ff; as heap 183; class-identity 179ff, 296
Coextensiveness 145. *See also* Biconditional, Extensional
Cognitive meaning 12, 97, 200, 207ff
Complex, *see* Attribute
Conceptual, *see* Framework
Connotation 28ff, 211ff. *See also* Attributes, Meanings
Conscience 20, 278
Constant 83, 94, 127ff, 132, 293
Contingency 118
Contradiction: Law of 130; self-contradiction and analyticity 129ff
Conventionalism 150ff
Correspondence, *see* Truth

Decision 231ff, 259, 272ff, 279
Definition: and analyticity 20, 126, 128, 267; and ethics 171ff, 177ff, 258ff; and performatory utterances 161ff, 193ff;